Bodies of Water

Environmental Cultures Series

Series Editors:

Greg Garrard, University of British Columbia, Canada
Richard Kerridge, Bath Spa University, UK

Editorial Board:

Franca Bellarsi, Université Libre de Bruxelles, Belgium
Mandy Bloomfield, Plymouth University, UK
Lily Chen, Shanghai Normal University, China
Christa Grewe-Volpp, University of Mannheim, Germany
Stephanie LeMenager, University of Oregon, USA
Timothy Morton, Rice University, USA
Pablo Mukherjee, University of Warwick, UK

Bloomsbury's *Environmental Cultures* series makes available to students and scholars at all levels the latest cutting-edge research on the diverse ways in which culture has responded to the age of environmental crisis. Publishing ambitious and innovative literary ecocriticism that crosses disciplines, national boundaries, and media, books in the series explore and test the challenges of ecocriticism to conventional forms of cultural study.

Titles available:
Cities and Wetlands, Rod Giblett
Ecocriticism and Italy, Serenella Iovino
Literature as Cultural Ecology, Hubert Zapf
Nerd Ecology, Anthony Lioi

Forthcoming titles:
Colonialism, Culture, Whales, Graham Huggan
Climate Crisis and the 21st-Century British Novel, Astrid Bracke
The New Nature Writing, Jos Smith
The New Poetics of Climate Change, Matthew Griffiths
This Contentious Storm: An Ecocritical and Performance History of King Lear, Jennifer Hamilton

FOR
MY FELLOW
MOVER
+
GROOVER
JM XX
R

Bodies of Water

Posthuman Feminist Phenomenology

Astrida Neimanis

BLOOMSBURY ACADEMIC
LONDON • NEW YORK • OXFORD • NEW DELHI • SYDNEY

BLOOMSBURY ACADEMIC
Bloomsbury Publishing Plc
50 Bedford Square, London, WC1B 3DP, UK
1385 Broadway, New York, NY 10018, USA

BLOOMSBURY, BLOOMSBURY ACADEMIC and the Diana logo
are trademarks of Bloomsbury Publishing Plc

First published 2017
Paperback edition first published 2019

Cover design: Paul Burgess / Burge Agency
Cover image: © Maria Whiteman

A catalogue record for this book is available from the British Library.

A catalog record for this book is available from the Library of Congress.

ISBN: HB: 978-1-4742-7538-5
PB: 978-1-3501-1255-1
ePDF: 978-1-4742-7540-8
ePub: 978-1-4742-7539-2

Series: Environmental Cultures

Typeset by Integra Software Services Pvt. Ltd.

To find out more about our authors and books visit
www.bloomsbury.com and sign up for our newsletters.

Contents

Acknowledgements   vii

Introduction: Figuring Bodies of Water   1
     Bodies of water (a genealogy of a figuration)   4
     Posthuman feminism for the Anthropocene   9
     Living with the problem   15
     Water is what we make it   19
     The possibility of posthuman phenomenology   22

1   Embodying Water: Feminist Phenomenology for Posthuman Worlds   27
     A posthuman politics of location   27
     Milky ways: Tracing posthuman feminisms   31
     How to think (about) a body of water: Posthuman phenomenology
         between Merleau-Ponty and Deleuze   40
     How to think (as) a body of water: Access, amplify, describe!   49
     Posthuman ties in a too-human world   63

2   Posthuman Gestationality: Luce Irigaray and Water's Queer
   Repetitions   65
     Hydrological cycles   65
     Elemental bodies: Irigaray as posthuman phenomenologist?   69
     Love letters to watery others: *Marine Lover of Friedrich Nietzsche*   78
     Gestationality as (sexuate) difference and repetition   86
     The onto-logic of amniotics (queering water's repetitions)   94
     Bodies of water beyond humanism   104

3   Fishy Beginnings   109
     Other evolutions   112
     Dissolving origin stories   116
     Carrier bags and Hypersea   121

Wet sex   126

Waters remembered (moving below the surface)   131

Unknowability as planetarity (or, becoming the water
    that we cannot become)   139

Aspiration, that oceanic feeling   147

4   Imagining Water in the Anthropocene   153

Prologue/*Kwe*   153

Swimming into the Anthropocene   156

Learning from anticolonial waters   168

Water is life? Commodity, charity and other repetitions   175

Material imaginaries and other aqueous questions   182

Notes   186
References   207
Index   223

Acknowledgements

Bodies of Water has been writing itself for over a decade. Many humans and more-than-humans have helped it surface.

This book is dedicated to the memory of Barbara Godard and Samuel Mallin. Barbara Godard was my most significant teacher and mentor in this project's earliest stages, and simply awe-inspiring during the time of its completion and defence as a doctoral dissertation. Barbara died in 2010. Sam Mallin taught me almost everything worth knowing about phenomenology. While we did not always agree, Sam was one of my best teachers, reminding me that we think as bodies, and not only about them. Sam died in 2013. While this book is quite different from anything Sam or Barbara might have written, it is nonetheless a citation of their generous pedagogies, their irreplaceable encouragement, and their singular approaches to academic labours.

I am grateful to Mielle Chandler as one of the earliest readers of some of these chapters and for her formative suggestions. I am also indebted to Mielle for many of the extra-textual influences that are central to this project's unfolding: what it means to exist ethically as a thinker in a corporatized academy; what it means to be a parent and an academic; what deep collegiality and intellectual generosity can look like; why feminism is never immaterial. My thanks also to Catriona Sandilands, who gently nudged this project in various key directions, and who remains a pathbreaker in feminist environmental humanities! During my PhD years, the world of EPTC/TCEP (The Society for Existential and Phenomenological Theory and Culture) was also a formative training ground; my thanks especially to David Koukal, as well as to Chloe Taylor, whom I met through EPTC and who has supported the workshopping of some of these ideas at various subsequent fora since that time. I am also grateful to Christine Daigle and Helen Fielding for their multiple forms of support.

Over this book's long gestation, my working relationship and friendship with Cecilia Chen and Janine MacLeod deeply invigorated my relationship to this material. Our three-headed-hydra efforts in coordinating and editing

Thinking with Water (MQUP 2013) not only gave me the opportunity to think alongside Cecilia and Janine's exceptional scholarship in relation to water, but also provided an important apprenticeship in the sweaty work of collaboration and intellectual generosity. During the making of *Thinking with Water*, I was fortunate to benefit from the mentorship of Peter van Wyck. I would also like to thank all of the other contributors to *Thinking with Water* who sharpened and expanded my aqueous understandings exponentially. I am particularly grateful to Stacy Alaimo for her ongoing support of my work, and to Dorothy Christian and Rita Wong for their practical teachings in the art of solidarity, and for their subsequent invitation to take part in the *Downstream* project; I am truly honoured to keep company with its other contributors.

I spent parts of 2011 and 2012 at the Gender Institute of the LSE in London. My gratitude to the wonderful staff and faculty at the GI and Emma Spruce as well. Working in the UK also facilitated my engagement in a number of key European-based networks. Cecilia Åsberg first invited me to be a Visiting Scholar with the Posthumanities Hub at Tema Genus at Linköping University in 2011. Being a Visiting Scholar with the Hub transformed my scholarship, and Cissi Åsberg's support of me and my work over the past five years has surprised and humbled me. Our collaborations continue, and I am delighted that this book is also a contribution to the projects emerging out of *The Seed Box: A MISTRA/Formas Environmental Humanities Collaboratory*. Thank you also to Renee Valiquette for her unswerving willingness to discuss, debate, dissect, and dream, in the context of both her work and mine. The most important kinds of support rarely come in properly hierarchized institutional packages.

I am grateful for all of the comments and critiques I have received in relation to presentations of this material at various places: meetings of EPTC at the Congress of Social Sciences and Humanities in Saskatoon (2007) and Vancouver (2008); the 'Nature Matters' conference organized by Cate Sandilands in Toronto (2007); the *Body. Art. Philosophy.* symposium organized in honour of Sam Mallin in Toronto (2010); the 'Rethinking the Non-Human' symposium in Edmonton (2010); the 'Sensible Flesh' seminar series at Kings College in London (2011); the *downstream* symposium organized by Rita Wong and Dorothy Christian in Vancouver (2012); the New Materialisms international conference in Linköping (2012); the 'Life Matters' conference and the invited roundtable workshop on critical life studies organized by Jami Weinstein and Frida Beckman in Linköping (2014); the *Gender, Science, Wonder* symposium organized at the ANU in Canberra (2016). In addition to these events where I was able to workshop and consolidate large chunks of this material, many other public fora have given me the opportunity to try out some of the smaller ideas found in these pages. The possibility to speak with and listen to other warm bodies at meetings and events are the lifeblood of my work, and the organization and facilitation of these events are too often thankless and invisible labours. So thank you to all the participants and organizers! Additionally, I am indebted to the Nida Art Colony and members of the 2014 Inter-format Symposium, where I was invited to think through the work of water in new ways (and a special thank you to the Liminal Dome).

Some of the material in this book appears in partial and different forms in the following places: Neimanis, A. (2009), 'We Are All Bodies of Water', in J. Knechtel (ed.), *Alphabet City: Water*, MIT Press; Neimanis, A. (2009), 'Bodies of Water, Human Rights and the Hydrocommons', *Topia: Canadian Journal of Cultural Studies*, 21: 161–182; Neimanis, A. (2011), 'We Are All Bodies of Water', in Beatriz Hausner (ed.) and Deborah Barnett (Designer), *Fine Art Print*, Someone: Water: Toronto; Neimanis, A. (2012), 'Hydrofeminism: Or, On Becoming a Body of Water', in Henriette Gunkel, Chrysanthi Nigianni, and Fanny Söderbäck (eds), *Undutiful Daughters: Mobilizing Future Concepts, Bodies and Subjectivities in Feminist Thought and Practice*, New York: Palgrave Macmillan; Neimanis, A. (2013), 'Feminist Subjectivity, Watered', *Feminist Review*, No. 103: 23–41; Neimanis, A. and M. Chandler (2013), 'Water and Gestationality: What Flows Beneath Ethics', in A. Neimanis, C. Chen, and J. MacLeod (eds), *Thinking with Water*, McGill-Queen's University Press; Neimanis, A. (2014), 'Natural Others? Nature, Culture and Knowledge', in Mary Evans et al. (eds), SAGE *Handbook on Feminist Theory*, Sage; Neimanis, A. (2016), 'Thinking with Matter, Rethinking Irigaray: Bodies of Water for a Planetary Feminism', in Chloe Taylor and Hasana Sharp (eds), *Feminist Philosophies of Life*, McGill-Queen's University Press; Neimanis, A. (2016), 'Water & Knowledge', in R. Wong and D. Christian (eds), *Downstream*, Wilfred Laurier University Press; Neimanis, A. (forthcoming 2017), 'Posthuman Phenomenologies for Planetary Bodies of Water', in Cecilia Åsberg and Rosi Braidotti (eds), *Feminist Companion to the Posthumanities*, Springer. Thank you to the editors and publishers of those publications again for giving me the opportunity to think through these ideas, and help me sharpen them.

I revised and freshly wrote a considerable number of these pages buoyed by strange Antipodean seas. I moved to Sydney, Australia, in 2015 to take up a job in the Gender and Cultural Studies Department of The University of Sydney. This place has provided a wonderful wealth of intellectual energies to finish this project and I am truly lucky to be surrounded by such engaging colleagues, interlocutors, and friends. My appreciation to Lee Wallace, Annamarie Jagose, Fiona Probyn-Rapsey, Pru Black, Ruth Barcan, and Elspeth Probyn for going out of their way to make sure I had a soft landing; to Vicki Kirby and Catherine Waldby for their support of my work and for welcoming me to an extended scholarly community down here; to Thom van Dooren, Eben Kirksey, and Stephen Muecke at UNSW's Environmental Humanities program for providing me with a second intellectual home in this city; as well as to other members of the UNSW *Environmental Humanities Saloon* for reading a draft and commenting on one of the chapters here. My other specific thanks go to Jennifer Mae Hamilton, Lindsay Kelley, Elspeth Probyn, as well as members of the 'Bodies' reading group organized by Barbara Caine at the University of Sydney, who have all read different chapters of this text and provided me with thoughtful and encouraging feedback. Jennifer and Lindsay have been irreplaceable interlocutors as I spent a lot of the last year thinking aloud about the propositions I finally settle on in these pages. The lively conversations of the Composting Feminisms and Environmental Humanities Reading Group, co-organized with Jennifer Mae Hamilton, have kept my intellectual engine running strong. Thank you also in particular to Jaya Keaney for her help in preparing the final manuscript.

At Bloomsbury Academic, I am grateful to Greg Garrard for welcoming this work as a part of the *Environmental Cultures* series, and thanks as well to David Avital and Mark Richardson for the always responsive editorial guidance and support, and to James Tupper and team on the production end. You have all been a pleasure to work with.

I would also like to warmly thank Maria Whiteman for the artwork that forms the basis of the book's cover design. Fittingly, I met Maria on a beach in Australia but only afterwards realized that we had met before, on the edge of Lake Ontario, about a decade earlier and several oceans and half a world away. In many ways, my relation to this cover image thus echoes the tangle of bodies, times, and waters that gathers us up in a global hydrocommons and which is the centre of this book. Maria's work in the 'Elemental Ecology' series evokes the palimpsestic ways in which human and more-than-human watery bodies overlap, and acknowledges the embodied knowledges that facilitate our contact with one another.

Thank you to my parents, Ieva and Janis, my sisters Aleksija, Laima, and Aelita, and my other family and friends for their many gifts. Finally, an immeasurable bucket of gratitude to Kim, for having the courage to imagine that we might inhabit a world of hailstorms, a morning star, and the deep part of the ocean, together. One needs a reliable compass on such journeys. And to Krusa Livija, Hugo, and Dzelme: you are my unfathomable watery heart.

Introduction:
Figuring Bodies of Water

Water is what we make of it.

> −Jamie Linton (2010: 3)

We are in this together.

> −Rosi Braidotti (2006a: 16)

The problem was that we did not know whom we meant when we said 'we'.
> −Adrienne Rich (1986: 217)

Blood, bile, intracellular fluid; a small ocean swallowed, a wild wetland in our gut; rivulets forsaken making their way from our insides to out, from watery womb to watery world:

we are bodies of water.

As such, we are not on the one hand *embodied* (with all of the cultural and metaphysical investments of this concept) while on the other hand primarily *comprising water* (with all of the attendant biological, chemical, and ecological implications). We are both of these things, inextricably and at once – made mostly of wet matter, but also aswim in the discursive flocculations of embodiment as an idea. We live at the site of exponential material meaning where embodiment meets water. Given the various interconnected and anthropogenically exacerbated water crises that our planet currently faces – from drought and freshwater shortage to wild weather, floods, and chronic contamination – this meaningful mattering of our bodies is also an urgent question of worldly survival. In this book I reimagine embodiment from the perspective of our bodies' wet constitution, as inseparable from these pressing ecological questions.

To rethink embodiment as watery stirs up considerable trouble for dominant Western and humanist understandings of embodiment, where bodies are figured as discrete and coherent individual subjects, and as fundamentally autonomous. Evidence of this dominant paradigm underpins many if not all of our social, political, economic, and legal frameworks in the Western world. Despite small glimmers of innovation, regimes of human rights, citizenship, and property for the most part all depend upon individualized, stable, and sovereign bodies – those 'Enlightenment figures of coherent and masterful subjectivity' (Haraway 2004 [1992]: 48) – as both a norm and a goal. But as bodies of water we leak and seethe, our borders always vulnerable to rupture and renegotiation. With a drop of cliché, I could remind you that our human bodies are at least two-thirds water, but more interesting than these ontological maths is what this water does – where it comes from, where it goes, and what it means along the way. Our wet matters are in constant process of intake, transformation, and exchange – drinking, peeing, sweating, sponging, weeping. Discrete individualism is a rather dry, if convenient, myth.

For us humans, the flow and flush of waters sustain our own bodies, but also connect them to other bodies, to other worlds beyond our human selves. Indeed, bodies of water undo the idea that bodies are necessarily or only human. The bodies from which we siphon and into which we pour ourselves are certainly other human bodies (a kissable lover, a blood transfused stranger, a nursing infant), but they are just as likely a sea, a cistern, an underground reservoir of once-was-rain. Our watery relations within (or more accurately: *as*) a more-than-human hydrocommons thus present a challenge to anthropocentrism, and the privileging of the human as the sole or primary site of embodiment. Referring to the always hybrid assemblage of matters that constitutes watery embodiment, we might say that we have never been (only) human (Braidotti 2013: 1; Haraway 1985, 2008). This is not to forsake our inescapable humanness, but to suggest that the human is always also more-than-human. Our wateriness verifies this, both materially and conceptually.

Moreover, as Virginia Woolf (2000: 124) reminds us, 'there are tides in the body'. Or in the words of Syilx Okanagan poet Jeanette Armstrong (2006), 'water is siwlkw' and *siwlkw* is 'coursing / to become the body' – 'waiting', 'over

eons/ sustaining this fragment of now'. Water extends embodiment in time –
body, to body, to body. Water in this sense is facilitative and directed towards
the becoming of other bodies. Our own embodiment, as already noted, is never
really autonomous. Nor is it autochthonous, nor autopoietic: we require other
bodies of other waters (that in turn require other bodies and other waters) to
bathe us into being. Watery bodies are gestational milieus for another – and for
others often not at all like us (Chandler and Neimanis 2013). Our watery bodies'
challenge to individualism is thus also a challenge to phallologocentrism, the
masculinist logic of sharp-edged self-sufficiency. Phallogocentrism supports
a forgetting of the bodies that have gestated our own, and facilitated their
becoming, as some feminist philosophers have long argued (see Irigaray 1991,
1992; Cixous and Clement 1986). But crucially, this watery gestationality
is also decidedly posthuman, where human reprosexual wombs are but one
expression of a more general aqueous facilitative capacity: pond life, sea monkey,
primordial soup, amphibious egg, the moist soil that holds and grows the seed.
As *themselves* milieus for other bodies and other lives that they will become
as they relinquish their own, our bodies enter complex relations of gift, theft,
and debt with all other watery life. We are literally implicated in other animal,
vegetable, and planetary bodies that materially course through us, replenish us,
and draw upon our own bodies as their wells: human bodies ingest reservoir
bodies, while reservoir bodies are slaked by rain bodies, rain bodies absorb
ocean bodies, ocean bodies aspirate fish bodies, fish bodies are consumed by
whale bodies – which then sink to the seafloor to rot and be swallowed up again
by the ocean's dark belly. This is a different kind of 'hydrological cycle'.

   Watery embodiment thus presents a challenge to three related humanist
understandings of corporeality: discrete individualism, anthropocentrism,
and phallogocentrism. We also note that these three 'isms' are all deeply
entangled, mutually enforcing the claims of each other. The work of bodies of
water is thus in part to remind us of this still-pervasive ontological Old Boys'
Club. To imagine ourselves as bodies of water is to stage a clubhouse break-
and-enter, a direct-action protest that floods up from the basement.

   Such a refiguring of our (always more-than-human) embodiment is thus
the primary aim of this book. Beginning with our bodies' mostly watery
constitution, these chapters present an understanding of embodiment as both
a politics of location, where one's specific situatedness is acknowledged, and

as simultaneously partaking in a hydrocommons of wet relations. I call this a posthuman politics of location. This version of embodiment draws on feminist theories of subjectivity, but parses them through contemporary feminist and posthuman understandings of agential realism, transcorporeality, and queer temporalities. I unfold these ideas through phenomenological descriptions of the various ontologics of watery bodiedness. Posthuman gestationality – that is, the facilitative logic of our bodily water for gestating new lives and new forms of life, never fully knowable – is, again, fundamental to these logics. This gestationality challenges the primacy of human heteronormative reprosexuality as the cornerstone for proliferating life, yet without washing away a feminist commitment to thinking the difference of maternal, feminine, and otherwise gendered and sexed bodies. Posthuman gestationality is expanded by exploring evolutionary science and related stories of embodied indebtedness, where past and future bodies swim through our own. In a rejection of a binary logic of either/or, posthuman gestationality stresses that as bodies of water we are *both* different *and* in common; water calls on us to give an account of our own (very human) politics of location, even as this situatedness will always swim beyond our masterful grasp, finding confluence with other bodies and times. In the end, my wager is that bodies of water as specifically gestational can help us think against current understandings of water as an exchangeable and instrumentalizable resource – what geographer Jamie Linton has called 'modern water' and 'global water', and what I expand in Chapter 4 as 'Anthropocene water'. To figure ourselves as bodies of water not only rejects a human separation from Nature 'out there'; it also torques many of our accepted cartographies of space, time, and species, and implicates a specifically watery movement of difference and repetition (Deleuze 2004). Always aswim in these explorations is a call to consider our ethical responsibility towards the many other bodies of water we are becoming all the time.

Bodies of water (a genealogy of a figuration)

The promise of feminist theory, suggests Elizabeth Grosz (2012: 14), is its ability to generate concepts that allow us 'to surround ourselves with the possibilities for being otherwise'. I am strongly drawn to the idea of the concept as something that makes radical change possible, and enables our own becoming-other (15). Indeed, this torquing of our imaginaries so that matter can matter differently is what I hope 'bodies of water' as a concept might do. But in Grosz's reading (following Deleuze and Guattari) concepts are 'the production of immaterial forces that line materiality with incorporeals, potentials, latencies' (14). They are (Deleuzian) 'virtualities of matter' (14) and 'excess over matter' (15), where 'materiality does not contain this incorporeal' (15). Instead of sticking with the Deleuzian concept (see also Deleuze and Guattari 1994), I therefore prefer the posthuman feminist understanding of concepts as 'figurations'. I suggest we might understand figurations as *embodied concepts*. Donna Haraway (2007: 4–5) calls them 'material-semiotic' knots, referring to their conceptual power, but also to their worldliness. Similarly, Rosi Braidotti (2011: 10) refers to figurations as 'living maps' that acknowledge 'concretely situated historical positions' (90). Figurations are keys for imagining and living otherwise, but unlike a concept unfettered by the world we actually live in or as, figurations are importantly grounded in our material reality (I have never been entirely convinced by theory that frames anything as wholly 'immaterial' – more on this in Chapter 1). I like the idea that our best concepts are already here, semi-formed and literally at our fingertips, awaiting activation. Never conceptual fantasy or metaphor, these imaginative 'interventions' (Braidotti 2011: 14) describe what we already are, but *amplified*.

Moreover, as Braidotti underlines, figurations are not arbitrary, but arise in response to a particular contemporary question or problem. Clearly, our planetary waters and water systems are wounded in many ways. Worsening droughts and floods, aquifer depletion, groundwater contamination and salination, ocean acidification, as well as commodification and privatization schemes that too narrowly seek to direct water's flows, all speak to this. My contemporary figuration of bodies of water is a direct response to these issues. Our bodies are also of air, rock, earth – even plastic at a growing rate – but figuring ourselves specifically as bodies of water emphasizes a particular set of planetary assemblages that asks for our response *right now*. Figurations can also be a mode of feminist protest: a 'literal expression' of those parts of us that the 'phallogocentric regime' has 'declared off-limits' and 'does not want us to become' (Braidotti 2006: 170) – and bodies of water, in my imagining of them, underline this feminist impetus. And finally, in Haraway's (1992: 86) words, 'feminist theory proceeds by figuration at just those moments when its own historical narratives are in crisis'. In this sense, bodies of water also take up the challenge of a feminism potentially circumscribed by its attention to humans, as I outline below. Bodies of water are about 'resetting the stage for possible pasts and futures' (Haraway 1992: 86) – here, in terms of environmental waters, feminist theory, and our corporeal implication in both.

Figuring embodiment as watery, then, is a deliberate extension of feminist theories of embodiment into distinctly posthuman waters. This work finds me keeping intellectual company with many notable feminist theorists who are rethinking bodily matters beyond a humanist imagination – Stacy Alaimo, Karen Barad, Rosi Braidotti, Mel Y. Chen, Elizabeth Grosz, Donna Haraway, Myra Hird, Jasbir Puar, Elizabeth A. Wilson, Kathryn Yusoff, Cecilia Åsberg … the list is much longer, but this might do for a start. It is within this emerging conversational feminist space that my work finds its closest and most comfortable affinities. But all stories have several ways of being told, and tracking the trickle of these bodies of water back to their source is neither linear nor simple. Figuring bodies of water, for me, did not start in a place called 'posthuman feminism' but rather made its way there. (Or, you could say that like so many awkwardly fitting beings, I found there some conceptual company that responded well to the beating heart of my project.) I'll say more about posthuman feminism later. *Bodies of Water* actually began (as much as anything ever simply 'begins') in three places simultaneously. In theoretical terms, one of these was embodied phenomenology, learned primarily through Maurice Merleau-Ponty. The second was the rhizomatics of Gilles Deleuze and Felix Guattari, whose work initially spurred me to consider what a posthuman or rhizomatic phenomenology might look like. The space that combusted between Merleau-Ponty and Deleuze and Guattari – that is between phenomenology and posthumanism – in terms of a methodological orientation for this book, is plumbed in Chapter 1, and I return to the significance of posthuman phenomenology as a way of conceiving this project later.

But French *écriture féminine* – the third starting point – is for me the most significant, and seduced me long before phenomenology and rhizomatics fluttered for me their fine pages. Despite appearing in English translation in the last decades of the twentieth century, namely at the height of Western feminist theory's concerns of 'biological essentialism', these French feminist philosophers refused the terms of this debate from the outset. Literally writing a new kind of embodiment into being, thinkers such as Luce Irigaray and Hélène Cixous instead affirmed the materiality of embodiment in its fleshiest, most material sense, at the same time insisting that these bodies were still unknown, still becoming. The bodies of *écriture féminine* were certainly susceptible to cultural discipline and containment – these bodies were lived materialities under the regime of phallogocentrism, after all – but as these philosophers averred, this same materiality offered a way of experiencing the sexual difference of bodies differently. (Choosing a temporal orientation for this story is difficult – the past tense isn't quite right, as these writers and their texts still very much animate discussions within feminism and beyond. Yet it seems nonetheless important to signal the precociousness of their theory, somewhat out of step with the time in which it was written and translated, yet prefiguring some of our most significant contemporary feminist theoretical 'breakthroughs'.) Water and fluid embodiment is a particular anchor here. In these works, the wateriness of bodies is always more than metaphorical, and watery matter is recognized as a literal wellspring for new ontological and ethical paradigms. Luce Irigaray's work on water and sexual difference is a particular touchstone for my work here. This is not only because of her book-length treatment of water bodies in *Marine Lover of Friedrich Nietzsche*, but also because of her direct engagement with phenomenology, alongside a mounting re-evaluation of her role in prefiguring what some now call material feminisms and/or new materialism.

This is not to say that Irigaray provides, fully formed, the theory of bodies I am looking for. Her work has been critiqued on the grounds of an implicit heteronormativity, and her limited interest in more-than-human bodies (despite heightened attention to these questions in her recent writings) cannot sustain an ecological ethics or politics on its own. Both of these are issues that I return to in Chapter 2. But in tracing the arc of my project, this French feminist philosophy is a vital spark that ignites much of the theoretical development that follows. Precisely because of its attention to materiality, embodiment, imaginaries, and corporeal relational ethics *that begins to extend beyond the individual human,* this work must be acknowledged as an important precursor to posthuman thinking in general, despite seldom being acknowledged as such outside of more circumscribed feminist conversations. Part of my objective in this book is to sketch out the relationship between French feminist *écriture féminine* – and the work of Irigaray on bodies of water in particular – and an ecologically oriented posthuman feminism to follow. In doing so, I am keen to draw on these key feminist insights into intercorporeality and sexual difference, but also push them into queerer waters. Here, human, cis-gendered, female reproductive bodies become but one source of life proliferation, in a posthuman world of facilitative bodily seas.

The question of origins is still a prickly one (something our bodies of water illuminate, as I discuss in Chapter 3 in relation to evolution stories). Just like bodies of water, stories are rarely autochthonous; they usually begin in many places at once, with many unspoken debts. I am also compelled to recognize the ways in which other kinds of feminist thinking seep into the development of this book's principal proposition. Not least, I do this because there is a pressing need to acknowledge feminist, anticolonial, and queer thinking more generally as facilitating much of our 'new' ecological thinking, and 'new' materialisms particularly (see Ahmed 2008; Sullivan 2012). For four decades, ecofeminism in particular (e.g. Gaard 1993; Kheel 1993; Warren 1997) has been encouraging us to recognize the connections between the derogation of certain kinds of human bodies, and a mistreatment of environmental bodies, including other animals; queer feminisms (e.g. Ahmed 2006; Chen 2012; Gaard 1997; Sandilands 2001; Seymour 2013) have asked us to pay attention to those bodies – *both human and more-than-human* – which challenge teleological norms and straight stories of proliferation and fecundity; anticolonial feminisms have asked us to resist human exceptionalism in our valuations of worlds that sustain us – which connects strongly to feminist approaches to environmental justice that argue that when it comes to intercorporeal vulnerabilities, some skins are more porous than others (e.g. Andrea Smith 1997; LaDuke 1999). Some versions of feminist technoscience studies have encouraged more critical and creative views of the matters that corporeally make us and connect us (see Åsberg 2013). Black feminisms, and other women of colour feminisms, above all, have taught us about difference – as a prerequisite for justice, and as a source of empowerment and strength (see Anzaldua 1987; hooks 2000; Lorde 1984). Meanwhile, while not necessarily concerned with the more-than-human, corporeal feminist strains within continental philosophy (sometimes overlapping with the above) have significantly questioned the idea of bodies as autonomous and as stopping at 'one's own' skin (see Gatens 1996; Grosz 1994; Kirby 1997; Probyn 2000; Shildrick 1997). I'll come back to some of these inheritances in later chapters, but it is crucial to note from the outset that feminist theory *very broadly speaking* has long challenged the autonomous phallogocentric notion of embodiment. Whether through the material implications of pregnancy, lactation, and placental relations, or through non-reprosexual theories of care, inherent technologization, political solidarity, and social reproduction, an ecologically oriented posthuman theory of bodies draws from a deep well of inheritance.

A feminist politics of citation (Wekker 2007) is about recognizing debts, but more importantly about allowing certain bodies to continue flourishing – not unlike the logic of bodies of water themselves. Just as my own body is a citation, a repetition, of many myriad bodies of water that proceed me and bathe me into being, so to are my writings and intellectual labours drawn from the wells of many others that have created the conditions of possibility for this work. So, if the above is beginning to sound like an unruly acknowledgements page, I apologize. But in a book that argues for the relationality necessary for living well with all measure of embodied others, it seems important to press the point that no one ever thinks alone, and that gratitude is worth deliberately, even meticulously, cultivating. 'Bodies of water' as a figuration might have emerged from these other kinds of feminism (Greta Gaard's 'Explosion' [2003] and Jeanette Armstrong's 'Water is silwkw' [2006] show, for example, that such figurations are already there within ecofeminism and anticolonial thinking). But because mine is also an explicit intervention in phallogocentric history of philosophies of bodies – both challenging and drawing from the thinkers whose work I inherit as a Western feminist theorist – I situate my work deliberately within posthuman feminism.

Posthuman feminism for the Anthropocene

Posthuman feminism can be understood on the one hand as a response to other contemporary ideas and theories of posthumanism. In popular discourse, the 'posthuman' often indexes a belief in modern technological progress, where technoscience might save us from our bodily vulnerabilities – 'even from death' (Åsberg 2013: n.p.). This kind of posthumanism morphs into a transhumanism that seeks an escape from worldly embodiment and its presumed limitations (the best packaging of this idea is surely the trademarked name 'Humanity+'. For an earlier version of a feminist critique, see Midgely 1992). In Åsberg's (2013: n.p.) view, such circulations of the term uncritically celebrate 'Enlightenment ideals of anthropocentric humanism' and 'translate into a form of super-humanism [...] working to *complete* the mind-body split'. Feminist posthumanisms, as both Åsberg, Braidotti, and others argue, explicitly counter this popular version of posthumanism that desires *dis*embodiment and the overcoming of worldly bodily difference. Alongside this rejection of technophilia, feminist posthumanisms also provide a counterpart for technophobic posthuman theories, that is, those that seek to safely cordon human bodies off from 'a bioengineered assault on our fundamentally pure, sacrosanct human nature and our essential dignity', as Åsberg describes Fukuyama's (2002) dystopian vision in *Our Posthuman Future*. Feminist posthumanisms refuse such a self-evident split between a 'natural' and 'cultural' human bodiedness; Donna Haraway's (1985) celebrated figure of the cyborg reminds us that bodies have been technological (and racialized, and gendered, and hybrid assemblages of naturalcultural worlds) all along.

But taking Haraway as a case in point, we should note that feminist posthumanisms have not only been reactive; they also have a deep genealogy of their own. In many ways, as Åsberg (2013: n.p.) argues, 'feminist critiques of androcentrism already put feminist theory firmly in the posthuman line of thought' – suggesting that feminism has always been posthuman, *even avant la lettre*. In Braidotti's (2013: 24–26) assessment, feminist critiques of abstract masculinity, triumphant whiteness, and a colonial drive to mastery and European universalism were all criticisms of the humanistic ideal and its unitary subject – which cannot be said about all contemporary forms of the posthuman 'turn'. In Zakiyyah Jackson's (2015) important critique, she warns that some of these 'appeals to move "beyond the human" may actually reintroduce the Eurocentric transcendentalism this movement purports to disrupt, particularly with regard to the historical and ongoing distributive

ordering of race' (215). These appeals for a posthumanism are ʔ
a racism, which may even, Jackson suggests, overdetermine the
problem is compounded by gestures towards the 'post' or the 'beyond' that
ignore or assimilate critiques of humanism by black people (216).[1] The kind of
feminist posthumanism that interests me is one that strives to connect to the
many subjects of feminism that were never granted access to the designation
of 'human' in the first place. These feminist posthumanisms emerge from,
include, and learn from black and anticolonial (as well as queer and crip)
feminist critiques. This politics of citation moves ahead and circles back.

Finally, as Åsberg, Braidotti, Haraway, and Jackson all stress in their own
ways, a feminist posthumanism is a deeply ethical orientation. The kinds of
ontologies it inaugurates – connected, indebted, dispersed, relational – are
not only about correcting a phallogocentric understanding of bodies, but also
about developing imaginaries that might allow us to relate differently. Relating
differently as bodies both different and in common seems a particularly pressing
question, as scientific evidence mounts that we have indeed entered the post-
Holocene geological age of the Anthropocene. First suggested by biologist
Eugene Stoermer in the 1980s, but popularized by Nobel prize-winning
chemist Paul Crutzen at the beginning of the millennium, the Anthropocene
refers to the proposition that human beings have become a significant factor
in the Earth's geological, lithospheric, and biological systems. From climate
change to biodiversity loss, to even altering the Earth's rotation with the filling
of the Three Gorges Dam, a growing consensus suggests that humans are
leaving a planetary mark that will be clearly legible in the planetary archive
of the future – and that this territorialisation may be very bad news for many
earthly inhabitants, ourselves included.

While the Anthropocene raises many important questions about our
callous interference with the planet, the concept itself is also troubling. If the
Anthropocene arises from a kind of human exceptionalist approach to life,
how can we address this with a term that puts humans right back in the centre
(see Crist 2013)? What kinds of license for further marking of the Earth –
in geoengineering, for example – might Anthropocene talk inaugurate (see
Steffen et al. 2011; Minteer 2012)? The undertone of 'Anthropocenomania'
seems at times to be less a plea for curbing the Human, and more an insistence
that we *do* matter, and always will. These are ethical questions that feminist

posthumanism is well suited to engage, particularly as these issues concern anthropocentrism and a continued binaristic phallogocentrism of Man versus Nature. As for bodies of water specifically, one key critique of Anthropocene discourse concerns what Lesley Head (2014) calls the 'species-error'. What erasures of *intra-species difference* are at work here, if we humans are apparently all in the same boat? Critiques of these anthropocentric, androcentric, and white hegemonic premises are gathering steam (see Chakrabarty 2012; Crist 2013; Head 2014; Malm and Hornborg 2014; Mitchell 2015). A feminist figuration of bodies of water, I argue, offers a way of confronting these differences, but it also extends the key critique of an Anthropocene talk that pits Man against Nature 'out there'. *Bodies of water* insists that if we do live as bodies 'in common,' this commonality needs to extend beyond the human, into a more expansive sense of 'we'.

Yet, despite the seeming usefulness of posthuman feminist approaches to thinking through contemporary human relations to more-than-human worlds, it may be fair to say that this area of scholarship is not exactly taking the world by storm. Resistance to feminist modes of thinking within masculinist-dominated posthuman thought and new materialisms is not much of a surprise, given a long tradition of erasure of feminist voices from philosophy canon-building. Even as we acknowledge notable exceptions, the status quo in this emergent field is still 'white men' (as an institution replete with mechanisms for ensuring its own reproduction, if not necessarily attached to white male bodies, as Sara Ahmed argues (2014)). The very recent critical work on the Anthropocene is a telling case in point of such institutional reproduction. When in 2014, UK journalist Kate Raeworth offered us the *#Manthropocene* Twitter hashtag, she was specifically referring to the relative absence of women, save five, from the thirty-six member Anthropocene Working Group – a subset of a branch of the International Commission on Stratigraphy charged with deciding whether or not the Anthropocene should be designated a 'bona fide' geological era. As Raeworth (2014: n.p.) puts it, 'leading scientists may have the intellect to recognize that our planetary era is dominated by human activity, but they still seem oblivious to the fact that their own intellectual deliberations are bizarrely dominated by white northern male voices'. Raeworth's argument is primarily an 'outcome-based' one, where the inclusion of diverse, more representative voices will lead to the application of a broader range of experience and better collective insight to the task at hand – giving us ultimately a better result.

The point here is not to rehearse old debates about the correlation – and lack thereof – between female bodies at the table, and the inclusion of feminist perspectives; of course, one doesn't guarantee the other. This red herring could happily swim away, if we were actually able to point to sustained recognition of long-standing feminist critiques of humanism within these debates, regardless of the author's gender. Until then, counting kinds of bodies around the table is another way of putting a question on the table: what does telling the story of humans in relation to more-than-humans in one way, rather than another (here – either acknowledging feminist contributions or invisibilizing them) mean for how these stories will unfold? While Raeworth notes similarly abysmal diversity among Nobel sciences and economics laureates, we too might raise an eyebrow at the tables of contents and bibliographies that accompany recent interdisciplinary critical theory scholarship on the subject. For example, a full text search of the first four issues of the *Anthropocene Review* – a new explicitly transdisciplinary journal whose 'overall aim is to communicate clearly and across a wide range of disciplines and interests, the causes, history, nature, and implications of a world in which human activities are integral to the functioning of the Earth System'– yields one hit for 'feminism' – a reference by Lesley Head to Val Plumwood's 1993 monograph *Feminism and the Mastery of Nature*. My specific concern is not about recognition per se (although we know the politics of recognition also has very material consequences), but about openings and closures for future stories – stories according to which some of us will thrive, and others will not. I suppose that too could be called an 'outcome-based' argument.

This book is an oblique response to these omissions, and at one level, it can be read as a sustained argument for why feminist work is so crucial within posthuman thought, particularly as this dovetails with environmental humanities in relation to the Anthropocene. For one, if the dominant posthuman scholarship is anything to go by (here, I am thinking as well of Object-Oriented Ontology that has engendered some infamous debates on the subject of its tense relation to feminism[2]), I share the very legitimate concern of others that a lack of acknowledgement of feminist contributions to these issues transmutates into a lack of attention to intra-human difference, and a concomitant levelling of matter, things, and objects altogether. This is feminist theory's important contribution: while 'we' might be more like other animals than our Enlightenment forefathers would like us to think; while 'we' might be part of, rather than separate from, the mud at our feet and the rain whipping our faces; and while 'we' might have become 'a geological force capable of affecting all life on this planet' in the Anthropocene (Braidotti 2013: 5), in the words of Adrienne Rich (1986: 217), 'the problem was we did not know whom we meant when we said we'. This is the academic face of the 'species-error' noted earlier: although much has been made in this general scholarship of the idea of human exceptionalism within Anthropocene studies and environmental humanities more generally, much more needs to be made of the fact that 'we' is probably the most fraught word in the English language.

Yet, we can hardly *not* use the word 'we' – you've been tripping over it constantly since you began reading this! How can I denounce it, then, just as I pull it swiftly back into circulation? 'Yes, *we*', writes Robyn Wiegman (2012: 13). 'That towering inferno of universalism. That monstrous display of self-infatuation. That masterstroke of white-woman-speech'. Like Wiegman, I too hear 'voices warn[ing] me away from the danger' – my own among them. But like Wiegman, I too persist: 'if the protocols of critical speech have taught us to avoid the risk, it is just as true to say that identity knowledges rarely take political or critical aim without some measure of hope that *we* will struggle into existence – partial and contingent to be sure, but resonant and agential' (13). As Wiegman notes, the alternative – a safe refuge in the 'small cave of the I' – is not an option for her, for the *I* is hardly a safer bet (being just as conditioned by scripts of power and belonging). In the context of bodies of water, that cave of self-secureness, moreover, dissolves in the dissident facticity of transcorporeal flows. Bodies of water, from a feminist perspective, insist that I find a way of challenging the myth of the 'we' within a *nonetheless mutually implicating* ontology. I explore these questions at length in relation to a posthuman politics of location in Chapter 1. For now, Wiegman says it best: 'in the taut space between the *we* that must be disciplined and the *we* that is desired ... my strategy [...] is to inhabit the error, not to avoid it' (13).

Particularly in the Anthropocene, with its growing indices of stratification, we need to unpick and confront the slide into homogenization – of women, of humans, of objects in general. The waters that we comprise are never neutral;

their flows are directed by intensities of power and empowerment. Currents of water are also currents of toxicity, queerness, coloniality, sexual difference, global capitalism, imagination, desire, and multispecies community. Water's transits are neither necessarily benevolent, nor are they necessarily dangerous. They are rather material maps of our multivalent forms of marginality and belonging. The idea of the Anthropocene, in its most useful sense, places some demands upon humans to account for past actions and recalibrate present ones; *Bodies of Water* offers some imaginative tools for rising to this challenge. Yet, while an ethical self-help quick-fix may seem appealing, I orient my work more in line with Haraway's (2007: 15) claim that 'outcomes' are never guaranteed: 'there is no teleological warrant here, no assured happy or unhappy ending, sociologically, ecologically, or scientifically. There is only the chance of getting on together with some grace'. In other words, this book does not seek a romantic vision of watery repair, nor does it imagine ecojustice through a naive invocation that 'we are all the same water' – even if our joint implication within a hydrocommons is one of its key themes. Living ecologically demands more attention to difference, and any theory on the relationality of bodies of water must readily answer this demand. Again, as bodies of water, 'we' are all in this together (Braidotti 2002), but 'we' are not all the same, nor are we all 'in this' in the same way.

Living with the problem

Dominant theories of posthumanism and the Anthropocene underplay the important contributions of feminism to these issues. At the same time, feminist work on non-human worlds has also been met with a certain resistance within feminism itself. This tension can be phrased in a number of ways: what does a concern with environments or non-humans have to do with feminism's (even feminisms's) 'core mission'? Why think about non-humans and the environment when there is so much *human* suffering? Isn't the non-human a bit of a *distraction*? And not least: if this is indeed a *feminist* theory, isn't there something important still to say about human *women*?[3]

Resistance is easy to feel, but not always easy to 'empirically' substantiate (why didn't she get that grant? Why was that candidate chosen over that other one? Is a corridor comment after a conference paper a citable critique?).[4] But since finger-pointing and defensiveness never get us very far, it is more useful to think about the basis for the resistance to posthuman orientations within some feminist academic circles, and what might be at stake in these tensions. For example, if posthuman embodiment encourages us to challenge the idea of a discrete and autonomous body, we might recall how various kinds of feminisms have also (wittingly, unwittingly, or even strategically) supported a version of the dominant neoliberal paradigm of normative embodiment – discrete, zipped-up, free. From reproductive rights to anti-violence campaigns, for many feminist social justice movements, claiming autonomous control over one's 'own body' has been a hard-fought battle: 'get your laws off my body', 'our bodies, ourselves', 'my body, my choice'.[5] So, in turning to the posthuman, what might we forfeit by troubling this idea of a body as 'mine'? In decentring the human, what other centres – of action, of responsibility, of gravity – might we lose?

These are serious questions. Political theorist Anne Phillips offers a thoughtful critique of feminist posthumanism. Wary about where all this 'decentring the human' might lead, she eloquently states: 'If we are troubled by hierarchies, we should warm to the critique of anthropocentrism. If we are additionally troubled by failures to act, we may worry about what gets lost in this' (Phillips 2015: 130). While sympathetic to critiques of 'species-narcissism', Phillips (drawing on the work of Iris Marion Young and Hannah Arendt) is concerned that a posthuman orientation risks weakening our specific human responsibility to act politically, and to urgently address structural inequalities as identified by feminist critique.

Yet we've already noted that feminist philosophy has long argued that our bodies depend on one another for their literal survival – not only through entanglements of gestation, childbirth, and lactation, but also through networks of care, and material and affective patternings of bodies, subjects, communities, and worlds, that encompass far more than the female reprosexual womb. So, while Rosi Braidotti (2013: 3) announces posthumanism as a response to a new paradigm brought about by the 'effects of scientific and technological advances', we also need to stress that new advances in technoscience only underline a distributed vulnerability and collaborative ontology that were there all along. Phillips's main concern is not so much the relationality of bodies as it is what happens to equality once we decentre the human – the risk that we will just be too overwhelmed by all of that distributed agency, all that 'vibrant matter', in Jane Bennett's terms, to *do* anything, anymore. Indeed, she points out that distributed agency is already there in the feminist politics on the *human* – in Iris Marion Young's work, for example. But, as Phillips (2015: 129) puts it, 'in Young's account, it remains humans who are the agents, humans who need to assume their responsibility for the systems in which they are enmeshed'. But it is unclear to me why this enmeshment would stop at the species boundary. In fact, I read Young here as calling for precisely the kind of posthuman responsibility that I hope *Bodies of Water* might encourage. I agree that taking responsibility in the context of what Alaimo (2010: 20–21) calls the 'swirling landscape of uncertainty' engendered by a world of often 'incalculable' material agency can be overwhelming, and we may indeed lose our centre. But posthuman ethics may depend upon pushing against the borders of comfort. I'm not sure if any real gains for social and ecological justice, in the broadest of senses, have ever been achieved any other way. The challenge is to assume responsibility, even as we stay with the trouble.

Imagining ourselves as bodies of water, I argue, provides a vector for at least partially mapping these responsibilities. When we pee antihistamines into waterways, the 'distributed agency' of those drugs on hydroecologies, on riparian flora and fauna, and on weather systems, drips from our bodies, too. When we get bored of fossil fuel talk and become complacent with ineffectual government policies, we too let out our hot breath onto the thawing tundra that grounds Arctic communities. I do not mean this as an appeal to a neoliberal individualism where the onus would shift away from structures and onto supposedly free, autonomous individuals – quite the opposite. (Nor, I should note, is that the kind of responsibility that Phillips calls for.) A posthuman feminist ethics commits to understanding our multivalent implications in these questions, as a place to begin.

In other words, even as a priority within some dominant strains of feminist theory has been to argue for bodily autonomy (particularly as it was withheld from specific kinds of bodies – female, black, gay, disabled, colonized), feminist thinkers have also been at the vanguard of challenging the humanist and masculinist notion of bodies as coherent wholes – and importantly, sometimes in the same breath. Luckily, feminist theory is known for having 'only paradoxes to offer' (Scott 1997), and the question of embodiment is no exception. Thus, the paradox of bodies – bodies that we are willing to defend to the death, even as we know they are falling apart at the seams – is not, as Elizabeth Grosz would say, a problem to be solved. Most big problems, Grosz (2012: 14) reminds us, 'like the problem of gravity, of living with others, or that of mortality, have no solutions'; instead we need to seek 'ways of living with problems'. In other words, the challenge is not to solve the feminist paradox of bodies, but rather to experiment in how to live this paradox, and live it well. My conviction is that negotiating paradox is one of feminist theory's best plays, and my proposition in this book is that the figuration of bodies of water might be one means for such experimentation.

This is all to say: the posthuman feminism of *this* book is not a rejection of social justice–oriented feminisms that continue to struggle, in quite human terms and in very human contexts, for the ability of human bodies to be allowed to be. Given the proliferation of versions of posthumanism that tend towards an erasure of the specificity of human difference, and that are quick to entrench the species error in response to (or really, in the *ongoing instalment of*) an Anthropocene discourse, it is no wonder a feminist scepticism towards a posthuman turn abides. Indeed, it is but an updated version of the question that Donna Haraway asked a quarter century ago around the 'death of the subject', so heralded within 'nonfeminist poststructuralist' theory at the time. Isn't it funny, Haraway (2004 [1992]: 57) muses, that 'the breakup of "coherent" or masterful subjectivity' emerges 'just at the moment when raced/sexed/colonized speakers begin "for the first time", (…) to represent themselves'? As Jackson (2013) reminds us, this irony also echoes the arguments of black scholars such as Lewis Gordon, who explains why certain subjects might be unwilling to give up the 'humanist prize', after being excluded from humanity for so long.[6] In the Anthropocene, when the stakes are nothing less than clean water to drink, a home above sea-level, and relative safety in the eye of a perpetual storm, these elisions are not just an ironic question, but an urgent demand.

Bearing these sleights of hand in mind, I am not quite on board with Grosz's suggestion that the future of feminist theory – through the work of concepts, or even figurations – is to move beyond what she calls feminism's obsession with the politics of representation towards something quite 'new'. In order to accomplish this moving beyond, Grosz suggests, we need to displace questions (even critiques) of identity politics, the primacy of epistemology, the human subject, and current understandings of oppression within feminist thought. Grosz is right: we need to think about difference, ontology, the inhuman, and new understandings of oppression. But what do we suggest by staging this as a flight *from* some kind of passé feminism, or its overcoming? I prefer to understand anything 'new' as a rearticulation of and with (in the sense of 'fitting together') feminist work already wagered, and still ongoing. This is not to dismiss crucial disagreements about the efficacy of a posthuman politics, nor to claim that there is *nothing* new going on with current feminist posthumanism, but rather to remember that we are the condition of each other's possibility (another lesson of water, as we'll see). In this very specific sense, I *do* think we are all in this together.

Water is what we make it

The primary aim, then, of *Bodies of Water* is to reimagine embodiment along feminist and posthuman trajectories – but it is just as much about *reimagining water*. Put otherwise, changing how we think about bodies means changing how we think about water.

As geographer Jamie Linton (2010: 14) convincingly demonstrates, the idea of water as something that 'can be and should be considered apart from [its] social and ecological relations' is a relatively new phenomenon. Water was first expressed as the chemical formula H_2O only as recently as the eighteenth century, and recognized as a substance that animates the hydrological cycle with the rise of the hydrological sciences in the nineteenth – at which point we became able to conceive of it as abstracted from bodies and environments. Linton calls this 'modern water' – indexing both a historical view but also the Enlightenment scientistic positivism that this understanding of water espouses. In Linton's genealogy, modern water is 'the dominant, or natural, way of knowing or relating to water, originating in Western Europe and North America, and operating on a global scale by the later part of the twentieth century' (14). On this view, water is deterritorialized, rendered 'placeless' (18). 'All water is made known as an abstract, isomorphic, measurable quantity', all reducible to that fundamental unit 'H$_2$O' (14). And, as Linton (drawing on the work of David Harvey) reminds us, like all hegemonic discourses, the 'naturalness' of modern water as abstraction reproduces itself through the same ideas, institutions, and mechanisms that it installs in the first place (9).

The key aim of Linton's book-length genealogy is to help us understand the reasons for the current water crisis. 'Water' constitutes one of the so-called Anthropocene's most urgent, visceral, and ethically fraught sites of political praxis and theoretical inquiry. Our reshaping of this planet is occurring not least through the rechoreography and rematerialization of its waters: ancient aquifers are being rapidly depleted; rivers that once ran fast are now exhausted before they reach the sea; dams, canals, and diversions undermine many vital waterways. Large-scale extraction such as in the Tar Sands of Alberta, Canada pollutes more water, volume-wise, than the quantity of energy resources removed from the earth. Oceans are acidifying, and the composition of life they sustain seems to be shifting at breakneck speed. Simultaneously, markets in water rights and bulk exports commodify and further deterritorialize this substance and attempt to profit from scarcity and pollution. Linton's important point, however, is that the water crisis is also a social crisis. He does not mean that people will suffer – although many are clearly suffering – but that this crisis is largely precipitated by a social imaginary of what water is. In Linton's words, 'water bears the traces of its social relations, conditions, and potential' (7). Or, in Karen Barad's (2007) terminology of mutually emergent intra-actions, we could say that the water crisis is *worlded* from the entanglement of material water scarcity and pollution *with* our idea of water.[7] From hydroengineering to global water management regimes, Linton demonstrates how our watery imaginaries directly impact how we treat water – how we think it should serve us (limitlessly), and what we think we can make it do (anything we need).

Pointing to these water crises underlines the pressing ecopolitical context of my argument. As I noted above, reimagining our embodied relation to water seems particularly important now, as the man-made currents of the Anthropocene pull us increasingly further away from any 'safe operating space for humanity' (Rockstrom et al. 2009). Linton's argument also helps me understand why my own project of thinking bodies as watery, and water as embodied, is perhaps more challenging than it might seem on the surface. Bodies of water as figuration goes against the imaginary of 'modern water', consolidated now for centuries, that sees water as something 'out there'. The task of this book, then, is to intervene in, and disturb, this hegemonic worldview. That said, I'm not suggesting that 'modern water' can be – or even should be – entirely undone. Thinking water as a vast generality has indeed engendered some worrying consequences, as Linton outlines, but it also opens up to new kinds of thinking that can be empowering, and useful, in our current situation – for example in thinking about water as a universal human right. It also opens to one of the principal questions of this book – namely, of how to think our commonality as water bodies alongside, rather than against, a more specific politics of location. In any case, paying closer attention to how we imagine water, and attempting to forge alternatives to our dominant imaginaries, is not just a thought experiment. It is a means for cultivating better ways of living with water *now*.

So I agree with Linton: 'water is what we make it'. In the first place, 'water' is our idea, our imaginary, our naming of matter in a way that corresponds to our worldviews. In this sense, our 'making' of water as an imaginary is necessarily forged in the entanglement of our values with the very material matter at hand. It follows that our 'making' of water also includes all of the problematic ways we currently *re*make it and *un*make it – as dirty, depleted, deterritorialized, for example. From the polluted tailings ponds of the Alberta Tar Sands to the extremities of the Californian drought, these waterscapes are certainly material, but they would not be worlded without a certain aqueous imaginary that delimits what we think water should be, and should do. But water is also 'what we make it' quite literally. Since we human and more-than-human animators of life are all bodies of water, we give material form, shape, and meaning to that which exists in the abstract in only a very circumscribed way. As a part of our lifeworld, water must take up an expression in some body, and human embodiment is one of these particular expressions. Water is thus also specifically what *we* make it, in the sense that it is not simply something 'out there' – environment, resource, commodity, backdrop – but also the stuff of human bodies, and never separate from our own incontestable materiality. Crucially, in understanding the ways in which we give shape to water, we can't slip into a naïve constructivism, as though this wet stuff were somehow conjured by human minds. Water – whatever we call it – calls to us too, from a realm of materiality that is also, simultaneously, more-than-human and beyond any kind of intentional grasp. As I argue in Chapter 3, dissolution of knowability, or containability, or mastery, is part of water's ontologic. And, inasmuch as it is what we make it, water is always making us too.

The possibility of posthuman phenomenology

Just as corporeal figurations are never 'immaterial', rethinking water demands a position that is never 'just' metaphoric. We might, for example, note a 'fluid turn' in social, political, and cultural theory in the last decade or so, where fluidity serves as a trope for poststructuralist and anti-atomistic thinking *par excellence*. (The plethora of recent calls-for-papers whose main theme is thus designated could be a case-in-point.[8]) Yet, from Zygmunt Bauman's turn-of-the-millennium books on our 'liquid' situation (*Liquid Love, Liquid Life, Liquid Times, Liquid Fear* ...) to James L. Smith's recent chapter on the 'Fluid' in a new publication on *Inhuman Nature* (2014), we see that liquid and fluid are not necessarily synonymous with *water* as a worldly substance. Here, these terms might refer rather to a certain physics whose purpose it is to inform a certain metaphysics.

The 'mechanics of fluids' (as Irigaray calls them in her 1985 essay of the same name), and the ways in which they impact our possibilities for thinking, is certainly a question that pervades these pages. But I distinguish my work from these other theoretical currents on fluidity in two important ways. First, water is not only fluid. Its behaviours and logics are multivalent. In this book I thus also attend to watery logics (or 'mechanics') of milieu, dissolution, and differentiation, among others. If my aim is to think *with* water, and even learn *from* water, then keen attention to its chemistry and physics quickly reveals a phenomenality beyond fluidity. This brings me to my second point: in this book I am not interested in fluidity or any other watery logic *only in the abstract*. When we focus on actual waters, rather than water-in-the-abstract, the reduction of water to fluidity is really just a good old-fashioned stereotype (i.e. based on some aspect of a material reality, but far more complex when you pay closer attention). If this book is to make a worthwhile contribution to rethinking our relations to the waters with which we live and upon which we depend, then it seems important that we pay attention to the specific ways in which water travels, and the specific kinds of bodies that certain waters comprise, transform, and dissolve. As Janine MacLeod (2013) has argued, this is part of our ethical obligation to the increasingly vulnerable waters that give metaphors of fluidity their traction in the first place.

One way to be attentive to the complexity and specificity of water(s) is through close 'naturalcultural' and multispecies ethnographies,⁹ or other kinds of interdisciplinary 'case studies'. Excellent examples of this include Veronica Strang's (2013) work on the Murray-Darling river in Australia, Rita Wong and Dorothy Christian's (2013) embodied and embedded research on Vancouver's 'invisible' waters, Margaret Wooster's (2009) richly layered natural history of the Great Lakes watersheds in New York State and Quebec, Canada, and the collection of artists who collaboratively reimagine Western Australia's Lake Clifton in the 'Adaptation' project (SymbioticA 2012), among many, many others. My methodological approach in this book, however, is somewhat different. I propose a posthuman phenomenology.

Phenomenology has sometimes been read as antithetical to, or at least a poor fit with, posthuman or new materialist understandings of matter (a position I unpack in more detail in Chapter 1). I argue, however, that this presumed dissonance rests on a certain ontological view of body-subjects as both practitioners and objects of phenomenological inquiry. As I've suggested, posthuman feminism provides understandings of bodies as operating simultaneously across different interpermeating registers, from the biological or chemical to the technological, social, political, and ethical. Bodies – including bodies of water – live both above and below the level of the human individual as classically conceived in liberal humanism, and as scaled to a human spatiotemporal sensibility. Alongside posthuman feminist theory, the work of Deleuze and Guattari has been a key contemporary force for rethinking what we mean by 'bodies'. While our bodies (the body of the phenomenological practitioner, in this case) are clearly human, *we are also* more-than-human bodies in ways that question the boundedness, autonomy, and coherence of the humanist subject (Deleuze and Guattari 1987; see also Protevi 2001: 3–4). According to Edmund Husserl's (2001: 68) famous dictum, phenomenology goes 'back to the thing itself' in order to account for things as they appear *in experience*. My wager, however, is that our experience as bodies is not only at the subjectivized human level. These convictions provide the condition of possibility of a posthuman phenomenology.

In *Bodies of Water*, my explanation of this possibility is inflected by a Deleuzian reconsideration of bodies, but importantly, it begins with the phenomenology of Maurice Merleau-Ponty. His work offers a detailed theory of embodiment, in which he argues that the body is not something we 'have', but is rather something we inescapably *are*. For Merleau-Ponty, going 'back to the things themselves' is necessarily an embodied undertaking – but significantly for my project, Merleau-Ponty's extraordinary understanding of embodiment arguably already moves in a posthuman orientation. Merleau-Ponty draws us towards 'an image of nonhuman nature' and reminds us that 'nature outside of us must be unveiled to us by the Nature that we are … We are part of some Nature, and reciprocally, it is from ourselves that living beings and even space speak to us' (Merleau-Ponty 2003: 206). William Connolly (2011: 45) has suggested that such insights invite us to disclose and investigate 'preliminary affinities' between human and non-human natures, leading to the 'organiz[ation of] experimental investigations to uncover dimensions of human and nonhuman nature previously outside the range of that experience'. The practice I propose and develop in *Bodies of Water* is one such 'experimental investigation'. I draw deliberately on such lessons learned from Merleau-Ponty as I attempt to both describe and enact a phenomenological practice of deep description and knowledge-creation through an amplification of multimodal and posthuman embodiment. How is water in and of my body? When I drink a glass of water, where does it go? How does it animate me? Where does it come from? How does water ask me to move, what sensations does it evoke, what affect does it engender, in me and the bodies it connects me to?

Such description begins by necessarily bracketing the understanding of 'the body' that I have inherited from a dominant Western metaphysical tradition (that is, as a bounded materiality and individual subjectivity, and as universally *human*), and becomes curious about the ways in which bodies exceed these strictures, both conceptually and materially. This is a posthuman phenomenological exercise, but as this book insists, it must also be a feminist one – that is one that is also committed to feminist situated knowledge and its careful attunement to difference. Thus, although posthuman phenomenology is scaffolded by the work of Merleau-Ponty and Deleuze, it necessarily relies on feminist theory to resist phenomenology's own tendency towards the 'species error' and an undifferentiated human experience. Chapter 1 thus begins with Adrienne Rich's politics of location as the condition of possibility for posthuman phenomenology, rather than as a mere supplement or optional add-on. As I argue, if phenomenology asks us to understand the world as lived, we can only begin from a situated politics of location – albeit one whose spatiotemporal scale is torqued through posthuman relationalities and becomings.

In a very practical sense, the applicability of the tools of an embodied phenomenological analysis for describing experiences that are below or beyond human-scaled perception may not be immediately clear. How do we experience and describe the workings of our sputum or our watery fascia? How do we hone our attention to the dissipation of our perspiration into a humid forest atmosphere, or of our psychopharmaceutically enhanced urine that flows downstream to find a home in new bodily hosts? My discussion of posthuman phenomenology in Chapter 1 therefore also includes an outline of strategies for *enacting* it: I begin with a practice of embodied intuiting and deep attunement and description drawn from my 'apprenticeship' under the late Sam Mallin, an eminent Merleau-Ponty scholar who was fiercely committed to the value of doing phenomenology, rather than merely studying it. As I argue, however, some aspects of our lived experience – subterranean affect, prehistoric transcorporeality, or planetary toxic dispersals, for example – require proxy stories to amplify the experiences of our wateriness that are latent, too quiet, or too vast to easily grasp. I pay particular attention to science stories as a helpful proxy, and I draw on new materialist feminist engagements with science, and the work of Elizabeth A. Wilson in particular, to help make this case.

Importantly, though, this book does not insist on the 'correctness' of posthuman phenomenology. Whether or not my argument sufficiently deals with phenomenology's ties to subjectivity and intentionality that some argue inseparably tethers it to humanism will likely remain an open question. More interesting to me than whether I am 'right' or not is the question: *what might be activated by calling my practice a kind of phenomenology?* What happens when we claim that dispersed embodiment is also lived embodiment? How might we rethink the history of phenomenology, and the genealogies of posthumanism, by audaciously suggesting that phenomenology might have always been posthuman? In short: *what will it do?* Moreover, while posthumanism pulls us out of the mire of anthropocentrism, my aim in holding on to phenomenology (at least as a starting point) is to insist on our own situatedness as bodies that are *also still human* – insisting that without this close attunement and politics of location, a responsive ethico-politics towards other bodies of water will likely elude us.

As glaciers melt, deltas flood, and we row our lifeboats down the middle of the River Anthropocene, it seems we need any valuable tool we can muster to negotiate the rising tide pushing in from the sea. Bodies of water – as lived embodiment, as figuration, as hydrocommons in difference, and as feminist protest – may not be the paddle that will guide us out of this planetary mess. But I am wagering that this figuration might just help us learn to swim.

1

Embodying Water: Feminist Phenomenology for Posthuman Worlds

A posthuman politics of location

I have no means of knowing the human body other than that of living it.
                              –Maurice Merleau-Ponty (1962: 108)

The human body is the first and the most immediate cultural location of water.

                              –Margaret Somerville (2013: 78)

We are the watery world – metonymically, temporarily, partially, and particularly. Water irrigates us, sustains us, comprises the bulk of our soupy flesh. Yet it isn't easy to begin with a 'we'. Granted, its inclusions are intentionally abundant; counted here are not only humans and other animals, plants, funghi, protoctists, but also geological and meteorological bodies such as oceans, rivers, aquifers, subterranean streams, clouds, storms, swamps, and soils – all dripping or tidal or damp. With this list, the idea of *what a body is* becomes productively, posthumanly, torqued. But in literal terms, this 'we' is too (erroneously) encompassing; there are bodies that it does not admit. Hydrophobic substances such as bitumen, for example, come to mind. In our current age of fossil fuel addiction and concomitant climate change, this antipathy speaks volumes.

But 'we' is not only a question of constitutional accuracy. In feminist political terms, this 'we' goes against much feminist labour to insist on difference and disaggregation. As Adrienne Rich (1986: 225) argued in her (still highly relevant) 1985 essay on the politics of location, 'we' are many, and 'we' do not

want to be the same. Rich learns these insights from Audre Lorde, and other
black feminists and feminists on the margins of a largely white, largely middle-
class, largely straight feminist movement that was claiming the 'we' of women
too readily. In Audre Lorde's (1984: 112) words, the idea that our differences
did not exist, or that they could be shed, was nothing more than a 'pathetic
pretense'. Claiming a 'we' too hastily risks misrepresentation. Thus, to write
'the body' is too abstract a gesture, notes Rich. Her choice is instead to claim
the body as *my body* – as specifically hers, with its own politics of location: 'To
write "my body" plunges me into lived experience, particularity'; it 'reduces
the temptation to grandiose assertions' (215). 'Begin with the material' (213),
invites Rich.

Consider, for example, the materiality of the waters that you are. We could
refer to these as intracellular fluid (all of the waters that buoy your trillions
of cells) and extracelluar fluid (plasma, interstitial fluids, lymphatic fluids,
transcelluar fluids), or we could name them more specifically: cerumen, chyle,
sebum, sputum.... In a different register, we might speak of your humours
(black bile, yellow bile, phlegm and blood), or simply of things like spit, and
joint lubrication, and pee. At one level, such lists can be Rich's 'grandiose
assertions' in another guise, but if you pay attention, these waters also situate
you very specifically. *Begin with the material.* Are your synovia too septic? Is
an accumulation of angiogenic growth factors in your pericardial fluid causing
you heartache? Does your blood clot too easily, or too obstinately? (Or: Does
it contain that monumental 'one drop' of racialization that will situate you in
sometimes incomprehensible ways? Is your blood spilled too readily?) And
also: do your tears flow too freely? Did your eyes water upon finding that old
letter folded in the pages of a book, long forgotten? The saliva that floods your
mouth when your teeth pop the peel of a juicy kumquat; the sweat slowly
dampening the fabric in your armpit, or at the small of your back as you sit
on this bus, on this day, in this too-hot town ... All of these waters are about a
specifically situated you.

Rich's (1986) own account of her location is similarly grounded in an
embodied materiality, inflected with an affective and political subjectivity.
Her white skin is not just an idea that grants her privilege but also a surface
that has been stretched and disfigured, and which becomes the sac of
progressively arthritic joints; she has bones that have been 'well nourished

from the placenta' and the decent 'teeth of a middle-class person' (215). But significantly, the waters that situate Rich in her specificity do so because of their interpermeation with waters and matters beyond her 'own' body: Jewish blood and white skin passed on from other watery bodies; healthy amniotic waters that bred those strong bones. And while the waters that may have spilled down her cheeks, or moistened her sex, may be of 'her' body, they are also symbiotic condensations of bodies beyond hers: a homophobic culture, a long-sought lover. Rich avers that 'the problem was that we did not know whom we meant when we said "we" ' (217). Here she underlines the bad feminist habit of including too many bodies in a cosy togetherness – but her descriptions of her own body also suggest that the 'we' *may not extend far enough*. While the 'we' is insufficient, it is also in many ways inalienable.

In other words, claiming 'I am a body of water' as an alternative to the 'we' personalises and individualizes the claim in a way that is equally inadequate. Bodies of water puddle and pool. They seek confluence. They flow into one another in life-giving ways, but also in unwelcome, or unstoppable, incursions. Even in an obstinate stagnancy they slowly seep and leak. We owe our own bodies of water to others, in both dribbles and deluges. These bodies are different – in their physical properties and hybridizations, as well as in political, cultural, and historical terms – but their differing from one another, their differentiation, is a collective worlding.

An adequate understanding of embodiment, then, is not given by simply asking what 'a body' is. Instead, we need to be more curious about our politics of location: Where is my body? When is it? Why is it – that is, thanks to what, and whom? What are the membranes that separate it or differentiate it from others? Where and how do those membranes break down? Where and when does that body cease to be? And then: in what ways does it repeat? Rich already demonstrates that an understanding of one's body – even a rigorously situated one – is multiscalar and mutigenerational; porous and palimpsestic. It is a congeries of the personal and the political; of the material and the semiotic. It is biological and cultural, and it is never only one thing, in only one place, or only 'itself'. While Adrienne Rich wrote these notes over three decades ago, in many ways they model a feminist posthuman understanding of embodiment, and a feminist subjectivity that is thoroughly materialist. Rich's body thus also suggests the possibility of a posthuman politics of location, watered.

My first objective in this chapter is to suggest how embodiment, and bodies of water in particular, can be understood from the perspective of a feminist posthumanism. This clarifies some key conceptual scaffolds for this book, but also traces a certain trajectory through body-thought. While terms like feminist posthumanism or new materialism may sound very avant-garde, they amplify and orient particular currents in feminism that pre-exist these terms (in a refrain that I come back to more deliberately in Chapter 2, this is difference and repetition; these new trajectories of feminist thought repeat older ones, but differently). Tracing this genealogy is on the one hand a feminist politics of citation: an acknowledgement of theoretical debts as an ethical practice. On the other hand, I want to make a specific argument: that thinking about difference and subjectivity – a key question in contemporary feminist thought – is productively developed when the materiality of the body, and its various porosities, flows, points of stagnancy, and scalar complexities are brought into focus. Furthermore, this attention to bodily materiality connects questions of feminism more directly to environmental concerns – not only as something we deal with, but also as something we embody, intimately and diffusely. The meaning of water as a particular kind of embodied and environmental materiality – with its unique properties and audacious promiscuity, with its spiritual significance and utter banality, as a specific planetary habitat and a species-specific boundary – unfolds in this book's ensuing chapters.

My second objective in this chapter is to insist that posthuman bodies are *lived*. The body that Rich describes is not just an idea but the material substrate that allows that idea to be. Even as intimacy does not confer mastery or transparent access to a body, Rich knows her body (partially and through different kinds of sensory apparatuses and amplifiers) because she *is* that body. Watery embodiment, as I offer it up, is neither speculative fiction nor thought experiment, but a complex description of the ways in which we live as bodies, and specifically as wet and spongey ones. The feminist posthuman figure of 'bodies of water' surfaces from a deep attentiveness to the ways in which I am embodied, and to how this corporeality matters in/as the world. I fill out this figure in the chapters to come by drawing on a variety of resources – philosophical, scientific, storied, artistic – but parse these all through the sensory apparatus that is our watery, never-quite-contained, flesh. What results is a thick, saturated description of lived embodiment unfolding over the course of this book. Like the bodies it describes, this story emerges from multiple directions. My aim in drawing on these sources is to discern how 'bodies of water' as a political-ethical feminist figuration can be activated as a way of living these bodies.

These descriptions are grounded, moreover, in the conviction that all theory is material. Concepts only make sense to us because we can experience them, bodily, even when these experiences are too distant, too small, too large, or too intensive to readily grasp at the surface, where we take up what phenomenologists would call 'the natural attitude'.[1] Our bodies as sensory apparatuses must sometimes stretch and contract in order to access the lived materiality that a concept or a theory proposes, yet we live these concepts nonetheless. To describe the world as it is lived is the work of phenomenology, but in order to account for the ways in which an aqueous perspective torques our understanding of embodiment, we need a different kind of phenomenology – one that can divest itself from some of its implied and explicit humanist commitments. What I propose is a feminist posthuman phenomenology. Elaborating this – as a theory, as a method – takes up the latter parts of this chapter, where I also draw on the conceptual resources of Maurice Merleau-Ponty and Gilles Deleuze. Before turning there, let us return to feminist posthumanism, and bodies of water.

Milky ways: Tracing posthuman feminisms

In 1985 Adrienne Rich's body is lesbian, Jewish, white, feminist, aging, healthy – in different orders, all at the same time, in both more and less metastable becomings. In terms of identity, Rich (1986: 215) acknowledges that 'even to begin with my body I have to say from the outset that body had more than one identity'. She notes how her race and her gender are materialized in concrete ways; she acknowledges where her white skin has taken her, and places it did not let her go (216). She acknowledges her age, her sexuality. She notes the geopolitics that situate her, and the historical flows of global power that imprint upon her skin. While these subject-forming lineaments materialize her very concretely, they also index her multiple belongings, and anchor her subjectivity in multiple places. For Rich, the body is always multiple. In what follows, I want to further explore this multivalency in a posthuman feminist orientation in ways that both amplify and extend Rich's insights.

Rich's body is also situated as a maternal body. In Rich's extended exploration of motherhood in *Of Woman Born*, she describes nursing as a vector of powerful and sometimes uncanny affect: 'the act of suckling a child, like a sexual act, may be tense, physically painful, charged with cultural feelings of inadequacy and guilt; or, like a sexual act, it can be a physically delicious, elementally soothing experience' (36). Breastfeeding connects her directly to her infant, but also to other bodies across time, where the entwining of bodies might stir 'the remembered smell of her own mother's milk' (220–221).

Rich thus describes the transit of waters between bodies as a matter of fact, but also as a matter of feeling, of memory, of gendered and sexual embodiment. The intercorporeal flows of breast milk are also a matter of privilege, and a matter of racialized reproductive politics. Novelist Toni Morrison (1987) taught us that breast milk is yet another matter to be usurped from black women, while long histories of slavery, economic disadvantage, and reproductive classism reveal that breast milk flows through materialisms of nation-building, imperialism, and colonization (Bartlett 2004; see also Gaard 2013). The practice of wet nursing is also steeped in discourses of human privilege and speciesism; science writer Florence Williams (2012: 163) remarks that in certain contexts, wet nurses are 'transformed into virtual dairy cows'. This statement, while intended to (rightfully) incite concern for human milk machines, should move beyond speciesist analogy to direct our compassion towards our ungulate kin as well. Breastfeeding connects Rich more generally to a deep evolutionary past of mammalian adaptation, even if the deep time explanation for lactation has been mostly washed away, and will only ever surface through speculative waters. As Greta Gaard (2013: 603) also notes, the industrialized dairy system 'replace[s] breastfeeding's gift economy and sever[s] the nursing relationship between mammal mothers and offspring'. In the process, Big Dairy also extracts wealth from animals and nature, and concentrates it in the hands of capitalist-speciesist producer owners – thus forging other kinds of subjectivities around labour and class. In all of these ways, nursing is a materialization of a particular but multiply-sited politics of location – of both a 'my body' and various kinds of collective 'we's'.

These politics are moreover shaped by the material composition of specific milky waters. Consider that in addition to fat, vitamins, lactose, minerals, antibodies, and other life-sustaining matters, North American breast milk also likely harbours DDT, PCBs, dioxin, trichloroethylene, cadmium, mercury, lead, benzene, arsenic, paint thinner, phthalates, dry-cleaning fluid, toilet deodorizers, Teflon, rocket fuel, termite poison, fungicides, and flame retardant (Williams 2012: 238). Recent studies (Morgensen et al. 2015) also reveal a troubling transit of perfluorinated alkylate substances – used primarily (and ironically) as a waterproofing synthetic agent – in breast milk, possibly leading to interference in the immune system of the suckler. As Williams notes, if breast milk were sold at the grocery store, in some cases it would exceed allowable levels of chemicals in foods on the shelf next to it (238). Phenomenologist Eva-Marie Simms (2009) echoes these concerns, arguing that the material bond between a lactator and an infant must be understood in the context of the toxic world in which we live, as a matter of embodied ethics.

Not all transits are life-affirming, then. Nor are all poisonous threats new. Historical vectors of (colonial, classed, raced, gendered) power once placed opium on a mother's nipple so that an unwanted child could suckle itself to death (Rich 1986: 261–262), for example. But contemporary forms of environmental pollution that pool in mothers' milk increasingly foreground the need to think about bodies differently – as not at all those discrete, zipped up skins of Enlightenment individualism. In the first place, these toxic transits highlight what Stacy Alaimo (2010) calls our transcorporeality. Transcorporeality refers to 'the literal contact zone between human and more-than-human nature' (2) and insists that bodies are never fully autonomous.

The flows of biomagnified toxins in breast milk also remind us that bodies are both nature and culture, both science and soul, both matter and meaning. As Elizabeth A. Wilson (2015) has compellingly argued, engaging with the biology of bodies is not an alternative nor even a complement to humanistic, cultural, or social constructivist theories; these different processes are rather all inextricably tangled up; attempting to understand one facet without engaging the others will result in an impoverished analysis. Bodies are always, as Donna Haraway claims, natureculture. Trained well in Western dualisms, we might try to parse out the 'real' biological flows of milky intercorporeality (DDT, antibodies, flame retardant, calcium) from affective, even metaphoric ones (bonding, love, revulsion, fear), but such divisions falter. Psyche and soma, biology and affect, dwell in and as our bodies in what Wilson (2015: 61) (after Sandor Ferenczi) calls 'amphimixis', where seemingly disparate bodily factions are nonetheless communicating with each other in empathic relations. Wilson does not claim that our various embodied means of knowing the world (digestively, neuronally, culturally, etc.) are indistinguishable from one another, but rather that there is no 'originary demarcation' between these kinds of organic knowledges. Once we read Williams's shopping list of breast milk toxins and hold a child to our bodies, arguing for a definitive quarantining of feeling from fact would be very difficult, indeed. We could say, using the language of Haraway or Karen Barad, that these various bodily interfaces – biology and mood and culture and context – are always co-worlding the phenomenon we come know as our bodies. Rather than two separate entities interacting, they intra-act; they become what they are only in relation. Co-worlding is always a collaborative process, and always emergent. The thing called 'the body', as Rich has already suggested to us, is a congeries of other bodies, and always on the move. Nonetheless, it also settles down enough to be accounted for, and to give an (always provisional) account of itself. As we shall see, without such accounting, building an ethical relation to the world would be impossible.

While an insistence on amphimixis and naturalcultural worldings denaturalizes a separation between matter and meaning, integrating these orientations with a more common feminist understanding of subjectivity is not without its difficulties. Alaimo (2010: 117) points out, for example, that transits of toxins do not necessarily recognize the divisions of bodies according to race, class, or gender – a challenging insight that sometimes leads to critiques of posthumanism as apolitical, and uninterested in ethics. We might worry that so much attention to the flows that connect bodies begins to dissolve the ways in which these bodies are different in terms of race or sexuality or gender. We could call this a concern about flat ethics that might follow on from such flat ontologies.[2] Feminist posthumanism can attend to these concerns by acknowledging decades-old work in environmental justice. Feminist and anticolonial campaigns for environmental justice clearly demonstrate that while flows of toxic matters and currents of gendered, racialized, and colonial biopower are not synonymous, if we trace both we note important patterns of reverberation. For example, we might consider the differences between Rich's breast milk, and that of women living at Akwesasne Mohawk (Kanien'kehá:ka) reservation a few hours drive upstate from where Rich's children were nursed. Until 1978 when polychlorinated biphenyls (PCBs) were banned, all of the sludge generated by General Motors' massive automotive industry was contained in pits on the 258-acre property adjacent to the Kanien'kehá:ka reservation. Like all bodies of water, those sludge pits were porous; like all bodies of water, the bodies of women, and fish, and infants, were porous too. The Mothers' Milk project spearheaded by Mohawk midwife and activist Katsi Cook revealed that women living on the reservation and eating fish from the St Lawrence River had a 200 per cent greater concentration of PCBs in their breast milk in comparison to the general population (La Duke 1999: 10–23).

The direction of these kinds of toxic flows is not only a human project. In Akwesasne, human decisions resulted in the dumping of PCBs, but the permeability of the ground, the path of the river, the appetites of the fish, all become caught in these currents. And anthropogenically created pollutants such as those that Rich's own breast milk may have harboured travel further still, but thanks to more-than-human travel agents. Hitching a ride on atmospheric currents cycling from more temperate regions to the polar north, many persistent organic pollutants (POPs) settle in the Arctic. Here, thanks to the Arctic's cold climes, these toxins do not readily break down; instead, they concentrate, and they enter the food chain – from plankton, to fish, to large marine mammals. (We should pause here. It is important to note that while the blubber of whale bodies keeps them warm, this insulation also attracts and then magnifies fat-soluble toxins, over the course of a long cetacean life. In the words of Rebecca Giggs (2015: n.p.), 'levels build up over many seasons, making some animals far more polluted than their surrounding environment'. Toxic breast milk, in other words, is also a multispecies issue.) Sea mammal fat is then consumed by humans in Arctic communities as a traditional dietary staple. As a result, the breast milk of

Inuit women in the Canadian Arctic contains two to ten times the amount of organochlorine concentrations of samples from white women hundreds of kilometres to the south; PCB levels are also alarmingly high (Trainor et al. 2010: 146–147). Importantly, this 'body burden' manifests in multiple ways; Trainor et al. remind us that for Inuvialuit, Gwich'in, Dene, Inuti, Innu, and other groups in the Canadian Arctic, the local ecosystem provides physical sustenance, but ensures cultural sustenance, too (145). While health risks are well documented, the psychological and spiritual effects of contamination also inundate these lactating bodies, and the bodies they in turn nourish (147–148).

Posthuman feminism amplifies the politics of location that Rich and Lorde and others have already elaborated. The falsely touted 'faceless, raceless category of "all women"' does not hold for a materialized politics of location any more than it does for other kinds of identity politics (Rich 2003: 219). But instead of only particularizing the body through a closer materialist investigation, feminist posthuman orientations also multiply and expand it. When an Inuit woman nurses her young, her transcorporeal gift is laced with a specific colonial politics of location – but one where the effects of colonial incursion do not require direct proximity to a colonizer. Colonialism is carried by currents in a weather-and-water world of planetary circulation, where we cannot calculate a politics of location according to stable cartographies or geometries.

Time, moreover, is disturbed and redistributed too. Planetary breast milk highlights the uncanny overlap of slow violence (Nixon 2011) and intergenerational violence with the singularity of an infant's hungry yelp that is always insistently *now*. In these milky ways, time is also unevenly metered – now rushing forward, now seemingly stagnantly still. In her recent work on Chemical Valley (not far from Akwesasne), Michelle Murphy (2013: n.p.) describes contemporary toxic transits as structured by a latency, a temporal lag. 'In temporal terms', she writes, 'latency names the wait for the effects of the past to arrive in the present ... [it] names how the past becomes reactivated. Through latency, the future is already altered'. In the context of our water bodies, latency might also be an affirmative capacity to gestate life in the plural; the 'not yet' of latency can also be the unfolding of possibility – a 'potential not yet manifest' that is not necessarily apocalyptic (Murphy 2013: n.p.).

We'll return to this life-proliferating possibility in Chapters 2 and 3. But here, latency describes a more ominous temporality hovering on a threshold between 'maybe not' and 'just wait'. For a posthuman feminism, embodiment is therefore not just about more biologically robust detail. It is about paying attention to the complication of scale, where a familiar deictics of 'here' and 'there', 'mine' and 'ours', even 'local' and 'global', or 'now' and 'then', which might have once seemed relatively securable, are now queerly torqued. Time, place, and bodies are all caught in the warp and woof of planetary colonialities that are naturalcultural and diffracted, but still racialized and gendered, all the same.

As Wilson (2015) also cautions, taking a materialist orientation towards bodies does not mean that biological data should be accepted uncritically, as some kind of full and final arbiter of truth. In the context of our contemporary epistemological paradigms, there is a sense that through scientific knowledge, things (like bodies, like water) might finally become knowable. When described through vectors of performativity, or social construction, or affect, or even a more conservative politics of location, knowing our bodies still seemed like a somewhat (comfortingly, even) speculative endeavour. Once biological materiality enters the flow, however, we might think that the depths of our corporeality can be finally fully plumbed – that we might finally become transparently knowable, to ourselves and others. Yet, as Stacy Alaimo (2010) notes, transcorporeal threats (as well as gifts) are often invisible, and, drawing on the work of sociologist Ulrich Beck, she reminds us that risk is incalculable. How, for example, do we calculate the risks of toxic breast milk, when these flows cannot be dissociated from cultural questions, and other kinds of flows? From an amphimixic perspective, and in a water world of queer time and space, we can never track the trickle, definitively, back to its source. Milky fluids cannot be disentangled from Arctic currents or gastric juices, from amniotic seas or cisterns full of our liquid waste. As Alaimo (2010: 62) puts it, the complexities of transcorporeal embodiment are 'difficult – if not impossible – for individuals to apprehend without access to scientific technology or institutions'. In other words, productive relationships with the natural sciences are necessary in order to map these transits with rigor – for example cultivating literacy in biological data as Wilson suggests. Later we'll explore how these relationships can play out in terms of a phenomenological practice. Importantly, though, such engagement does not aspire to an epistemology of scientific certainty. It rather enacts a tentative collaboration of knowledge projects where any final 'truth' is always elusive (Alaimo 2010: 20). In this context, knowing a body is never an exercise in certainty – certain boundaries, certain relations, certain transits, certain outcomes. A posthuman politics of location must give up the will to mastery, even of our own subject-selves.

As noted however, even within this 'swirling land[water]scape of uncertainty', we still need to give an account (Alaimo 2010: 20). Aqueous transcorporeality therefore demands of us a posthuman feminist ethics – a way of being responsible and responsive to our others, despite (or even because of) this 'ever-changing landscape of continuous interplay, intra-action, emergence, and risk' (21). Before turning to matters of method, then, we might return to the question of 'we', and an account of commonality that still insists on difference.

The politics of location of Rich's body, those of an Inuit woman's in Arctic Canada, or of someone involved in Katsi Cook's activist research in Akwesasne, are all differently assembled. They do not all merge in an amorphous flow. Nancy Tuana describes this as the membrane logic of 'viscous porosity' where viscosity draws attention to 'sites of resistance and opposition' rather than only 'a notion of [porous] open possibilities' that might suggest, again, that undifferentiated 'we' (Tuana 2008: 194). Difference is key to a feminist posthumanism, but at the same time, differentiation is never a decisive severing. We began with the objective of 'describing the geography closest in', as Rich recommends, and we have paddled a great distance while never really leaving this body that is 'mine'. These bodies are all caught up in one another's currents – as they are with the whale's body, the body of the rain cloud, and the body of the increasingly toxic sea. As bodies of water, we are always, at some level, *implicated*.

My point is that these bodies are all collaboratively worlded. For some readers, breastfeeding and breast milk – both literally and semiotically – might represent the quintessence of a humanist, even biologically reductive feminism that implicitly romanticizes and reveres the mother–infant bond as an exclusionary model of ethics, care, or distributed embodiment. For some readers, these bodies and practices might meld too easily with a prioritization of reproductive sexuality, and even a heteronormative one that privileges the cis-gendered feminine body. When paired with concerns about toxic waters, this example also veers perhaps too close to transphobic environmentalist discourses of sex panic, where toxic waters are a harbinger of feminized men and queer amphibians (di Chiro 2010). Even if my example of breast milk does not take up the question of endocrine disruptors, the increasingly discussed transcorporeal pathways along which those chemicals are transmitted are sometimes framed in a similar manner: global flows, latent accumulation, dispersal, and diffraction into and through bodies of the 'innocent'. As Mel Y. Chen (2012) has powerfully argued in a similar vein, toxic panics are also laced with fears both of disability and racialized invasion, and carry troubling undertones that suggest a fabled return to (racialized, non-disabled) purity is desirable. These are not the affiliations that a posthuman feminism welcomes. Nor do I court ways of telling these stories that frame indigenous women as exotic, naively vulnerable Others somewhere 'out there'[3] – another version of the subaltern brown mother-and-child.[4]

I understand these associative risks, but I stick with breast milk all the same because I want to press an understanding of human reproduction and maternal nourishment as part of a broader logic of posthuman gestationality – one that can also be explicitly queer, and anticolonial. My proposition is that specific bodily waters – breast milk here, or amniotic waters as I discuss in the next chapter – are material metonyms of a planetary watery milieu that interpermeates and connects bodies, and bathes new kinds of plural life into being. Human reprosexuality is not at the centre of a gestational logic; it rather repeats an ontologic that it *learns from water*. As watery milieus for other bodies, we are always gathering the debts of the myriad watery bodies that are the condition of our possibility. Eventually, we all give ourselves up to another wet body. We all become with, or simply just become, other bodies of water.

A posthuman feminism reminds us that the waters that we comprise are both intensely local and wildly global: I am here, and now, and at least three billion years old, and already becoming something else. I unpack this understanding of watery gestationality in the following chapters. But acknowledging this broader, more-than-human understanding of gestation is no reason to ignore a specific kind of watery body – a human maternal one, also raced and gendered and subject to colonial logics. Especially given the ways in which these maternal bodies have been scientized, monitored, instrumentalized, and contained across various cultures and times but particularly in the modern West, a specific response to these bodies is demanded. Understanding our transcorporeal implications in the bodily waters of others – human and other animal, but also oceanic, riparian, estuarine, meteorological – should not dilute a feminist politics of reproduction or breastfeeding; it should rather allow us to see how all of us are swimming in these milky seas.

My hope is that by imagining ourselves as all bodies of water, we realize that (in a manner of speaking) 'we are all breast milk'. As Michelle Murphy and her colleagues in the 'Engineered Worlds' project remind us, industrially produced chemicals are found in the blood and breast milk of every single living subject. They persist across generations, forward and back, while the transcorporeal lineaments of accumulation and distribution mean there is no place or time of pure refuge. In this context, the imperative cannot be segregating lactators into 'that' kind of feminism, while the rest of us get on with other pressing environmental problems. We may not all be lactators, but we are probably consumers, or settlers, or policy makers, or actants that are in other ways co-worlding an emergent planetary situation of changing climates, warming currents, and chemical accumulations. While the nursing of an infant begins as a matter of fact for lactating human females (and even some males) as a way to situate that specific body – marked by the pleasures, or burdens, or pains, or scars that accompany that practice – it is evidently a much more dispersed matter of concern. These waters gather and distribute the liquid runoff of a global political economy and techno-industrial capitalism that produces vastly divergent body burdens, but which nonetheless gathers us all. Breast milk is no longer (and has never been) an issue for the biologically essentialized, lactating woman alone. In the words of Karen Barad (2007: 384), a posthuman feminism has an ethical responsibility to take 'account of the entangled materializations of which we are a part'.

How to think (about) a body of water: Posthuman phenomenology between Merleau-Ponty and Deleuze

Posthuman feminism thus provides the theoretical scaffold for articulating what it means to be a body of water – to be always only precariously contained in a skin sac, and instead profoundly distributed, inherited, gestational, differentiated. Concepts like transcorporeality, naturecultures, amphimixis, and co-worlding provide a lexicon for this uncanny mode of living both particularly, with a specifically materialized politics of location, but also collaboratively, as part of an always emergent planetary hydrocommons. Concepts, as Elizabeth Grosz (2012: 14) has argued, are moveable bridges that help us imagine an otherwise; they don't solve problems but provide a way of orienting ourselves towards them.

Concepts might be primarily tools of thinking (Grosz [2012: 14], following Deleuze and Guattari, refers to them as 'immaterial') but thinking is also an embodied act; concepts are also embodied. We understand them because our bodies as finely attuned sensory apparatuses live them, in one way or another. Following this proposition, we have to understand these conceptual frames as somehow also arising from lived experience. Indeed, the figuration of bodies of water also surfaces from a deep attentiveness to the ways in which we, like all living earthly entities, embody water. Such description needs to suspend, or bracket, the understanding of 'body' that we inherit from a dominant Western metaphysical tradition (a bounded materiality that houses an individual subject), and become curious about the ways in which bodies exceed these strictures, both conceptually and materially. If our bodies are mostly water, where does this water come from? Where does it go, and what does it make possible? How does our wateriness condition how we live as bodies, and how we become implicated in the bodies of others? To ask these questions, much less answer them, we need to divest from the idea of bodies as only human, as contained within our skin, as beginning and ending in the 'I'. We have to seek out, in our own modes of living and engaging the world, the ways in which that humanist conceptual apparatus (even as we also 'live' it as a comfortable default) falters. In these ways, tapping bodies of water as figuration is a *phenomenological* exercise – one that, taking heed of Edmund Husserl's (2001: 68) famous dictum, goes 'back to the thing itself' in order to account for things as they appear in experience, once sediments of the natural attitude have been scraped away. Phenomenology is 'a matter of describing, not of explaining or analysing' (Merleau-Ponty 1962: viii); it is achieved through 'a direct description of our experience as it is' (vii). In this accounting, language stretches to accommodate experience. New concepts arise as a result of this grappling. This kind of phenomenological attunement, amplification, and description can loosen what we know and open to what we do not.[5]

Posthuman feminism should not be understood, therefore, as an alternative to phenomenology. I propose instead that these two projects might be brought productively together. Of course, it is possible (and even likely) that like Sara Ahmed's (2006: 2) work in queer phenomenology, the posthuman feminist version I propose here 'is not "properly" phenomenological'. But I persist because this posthuman phenomenology is a way of insisting that our bodies – even and particularly in their posthuman contractions, expansions, diffractions, and collaborations – are nonetheless lived. I want, in other words, to expand how we understand what it means to live as a body in this planetary context. This is not only an ontological imperative, but also an ethical one. Insisting on a posthuman phenomenology means that the hard-to-grasp scales of living in which our watery bodies participate become less abstracted, potentially more sensory. In a context where popular apathy and hopelessness are fuelled by an inability to connect with the more-than-human scales of planetary distresses (Duxbury 2010; Neimanis and Walker 2014), a posthuman phenomenology can put us in better contact with our bodies as implicated in those hard-to-fathom phenomena – climate change, ocean acidification, aquifer depletion, and toxic transits half-way round the world – which we are co-worlding all the same. By deliberately embracing phenomenology I want, moreover, to underline the need to cultivate a phenomenological 'wonder in the face of the world' (Merleau-Ponty 1962: xiii) and a desistance from the mastery of more analytical approaches. I also hope that phenomenology, as attunement, listening, and observation might somewhat temper all the language of agency and acting that infuses much new materialist writing, feminist and otherwise (for sometimes our bodies are quieter than all that). Conversely, I hope that phenomenology might also be reconfigured, so that both description and the world we purportedly describe are productively torqued – where humans are not at the centre of it all, after all. We can't – and I would argue we shouldn't – take ourselves out of the picture, but we can cultivate ways of imagining our lived experience as decentred, if always transcorporeally implicated.

Feminist phenomenologists have been at the vanguard of questioning what 'the body' is and means. Trailblazing feminist philosophers – Simone de

Beauvoir (2010, Luce Irigaray (1985b), and Helene Cixous (1976) – building on and intervening in the phenomenological tradition have long challenged the discrete individualism and phallogocentrism of a neutral body. Phenomenology has also contributed to important, more detailed feminist analyses by thinkers such as Elizabeth Grosz (1994), Margrit Shildrick (1997), Gail Weiss (1999), Rosalind Diprose (2002), Lisa Guenther (2006), and Sara Ahmed (2000; 2006), among others, of bodies as indebted to other bodies—leaky, permeable, and intercorporeal, in terms of both their matters and meanings. This feminist phenomenological work articulates with the posthuman understandings of material, interconnected body-subjects I described earlier, traced through the work of Adrienne Rich and Audre Lorde into more contemporary thinkers such as Karen Barad, Elizabeth A. Wilson, Nancy Tuana, Mel Y. Chen, and Stacy Alaimo. Feminist thinking on bodies, in various guises and forms, thus establishes a fertile culture for elaborating a posthuman feminist phenomenology. In the next chapter, I explore Luce Irigaray's phenomenology of bodies and water as an early articulation of a posthuman orientation. First though, I want to draw additional sources into this feminist conversation.

As a key thinker of both phenomenology and embodiment, French phenomenologist Merleau-Ponty and his work represent one of the most thorough philosophical attempts to understand what it means to be embodied in the context of a shared world. Merleau-Ponty thus provides a compelling way to imagine phenomenology as compatible with a posthuman feminist project. As various commentators have argued, despite his association with existential humanism, Merleau-Ponty offers a 'radical revision of the body's ontological sense' (Barbaras 2004: xxiii). His situation within a project of philosophical humanism is in fact what makes his openings to an intercorporeal, environmentally situated and contingently becoming body so remarkable. Merleau-Ponty (1968, 2003) rejects dualisms in which humanist understandings of embodiment are usually mired, and instead presents us with a body that emerges from various debts and connections to other bodies, whereby bodies are always chiasmically entwined with the world. For Merleau-Ponty, what we can know about things resides neither in a transcendent platonic realm of ideals nor solely in our solipsistic imaginings; it emerges in the ineluctable imbrications of body and world in a lived experience that is necessarily somewhere, sometime, and somehow.

We can understand embodiment as a concept, moreover, because our bodies – watery, fleshy, and otherwise – are a key resource for figuring this out. For Merleau-Ponty, corporeal existence is central: going 'back to the things themselves' is necessarily an embodied undertaking. Merleau-Ponty's detailed theory of embodiment avers that the body is not something we 'have' ('the body is not an object' [Merleau-Ponty 1962: 198]), but is rather something we inescapably *are*. We only have a world because we live as bodies that know the world as an extension of the body's ways of being ('we are in the world through our body' [203]). Merleau-Ponty is thus not only a helpful source for developing a posthuman understanding of corporeality, but also offers a method for getting back to the body through the resources of our bodies and their various kinds of experiential knowledges.

A second source I turn to here is the work of Gilles Deleuze, sometimes in collaboration with Felix Guattari. Deleuze is certainly a major source for contemporary posthuman and new materialist thinking. Despite a sometimes fraught uptake by feminist phenomenology (Deleuze's work does not refuse a feminist politics of location, but neither does it do much to cultivate one), his writings nonetheless provide a rich supporting conceptual apparatus for my experiment in posthuman phenomenology – namely, through the innovative and evocative ways he invites us to think about bodies differently. In Deleuzian rhizomatics, a 'body' is not defined by notions of liberal humanism but rather refers to any metastable entity that has a threshold of endurance, beyond which it ceases to be. We as human bodies do not sit atop and apart from the entanglements of the material world; we are instead consistently pulled out of our place of privilege by our symbiotic relationality to other bodies. For Deleuze, bodies are congeries of all kinds of physical, material, cultural, and semiotic forces, and how they *become* is more interesting than what they are. Particularly useful, as will become clear, is Deleuze's attention to the various strata that a body simultaneously inhabits, or moves across.

So, in many ways, both Merleau-Ponty and Deleuze offer helpful conceptual footholds for thinking what it means to be a body of water, but articulating their work together is not an obvious or seamless task. Deleuze is critical of the phenomenological tradition generally and Merleau-Ponty in particular for being too humanist, where meaning only emanates from a human vantage point. Immanence here can only ever be immanence to a subject (Deleuze and

Guattari 1994: 149–150).[6] It is possible to read Merleau-Ponty, and certainly the larger phenomenological project, in these terms. Indeed, where Merleau-Ponty (1962: viii) claims that 'all of [his] knowledge of the world … is gained from [his] own particular point of view', a suspicion of Merleau-Ponty as human-centric is understandable. But I think there is also a possibility for cultivating a certain space between these thinkers;[7] I am interested in how each provides a way to read the other otherwise. My specific wager: if to be human means also always to leak beyond the limits of that humanity, then our embodiment affords the possibility of more-than-human contact with the world. Put otherwise, if consciousness is embodiment (Merleau-Ponty) and embodiment is more-than-human (Deleuze, feminist posthumanism, and – as I will argue – Merleau-Ponty), then we can also access and live a world that exceeds the bounds of a comfortably human-scaled experience. We will get to the 'how' of this proposition shortly. Before that, let's look to see how Merleau-Ponty and Deleuze help make this case in more detail.

Deleuzian rhizomatics is critical of the metaphysical tradition of individualistic humanism, and of a human subject whose perspective is totalizing. Yet, Deleuze nonetheless acknowledges human subjectivity as one expression, or one capture, of bodies. In Deleuzian rhizomatics, a body is defined primarily by what it 'can do' and what can be done to it, while still maintaining the body's metastability as a whole.[8] While human bodies certainly differ from one another, they are a particular kind of body that exists because of certain thresholds for affecting and being affected; humans are humans because of what, in the most generalized sense, they can do, how they endure, and what it takes to kill them (or dissolve them, to be recomposed as something else). Although more-than-human transfections with more-than-human bodies in various kinds of symbiotic becomings comprise a key element of Deleuzian philosophy, generalized thresholds of affectability are what make humans humans (and not frogs, or glaciers, or can openers). The problem for a Deleuzian view is not the instalment of the human; it is rather the instalment of the human at the centre, with his coagulated, sedimented subjectivity as the 'measurant of all' (Merleau-Ponty 1968: 249).

Another key to Deleuzian thinking on bodies is the fact that these thresholds are determined by myriad forces, which include the 'molar' sedimenting processes of subjectivization. Molar subjects (or the body as a whole, the spatial or temporal aggregate) are forged from and stabilized by social, political, cultural, biological, physical, historical, and other kinds of flows. But a body's persistence is just as dependent on its molecular stratum – a super- or subcutaneous molecularity (the disorganizing parts or pieces) that infuses the human body at every turn: the churning and flowing, the intake and effluence, the trickles that transit into assemblages with other bodies beyond the coherent human subject-self. Bodies demand both processes of deterritorialization and reterritorialization (1987: 57–59, 211).

Our human bodies of water serve as a helpful illustration. As a human body, I am somewhat organized, with seemingly discrete borders and boundaries. My skin gives the illusion of a hermetic seal that keeps my intricate plumbing mostly from view, and thus from my explicit attention. From my human subject point of view, this body appears to me as whole, separate, and organized. But my body of water also breaches the skin sac – regularly, imperceptibly, and also in periodic demonstrative gushes. This might be, as described earlier, in the nursing of an infant; it might also be in an involuntary milking at the sound of a baby crying, or simply when too much time since last nursing has passed. A watery body sloshes and leaks, excretes and perspires. Its depths gurgle, erupt. A body of water also extends, transcorporeally, into other assemblages: watershed, cistern, sea; and other bodies that are human, vegetable, animal, and hydrogeological. My consumption becomes viscera to become, perhaps, toxic breast milk, thousands of miles away. While the individual body might seek to bracket, subdue, or tame these channels and flows, the body could not live without them. They sustain a sense of subject-self as much as they challenge that subject-body's coherence.

In one sense, we can think of this interruptive body of water as Deleuze and Guattari's (1987: 153) Body without Organs (BwO) – that site of experimentation populated by 'non-stratified unformed, intense matter'. Uncontrollable eruptions correspond in some ways to the BwO as escape route, or release valve, for our bodies that are otherwise corralled and contained. This kind of subversive and destabilizing sense of embodiment is perhaps what Deleuzian rhizomatics is best known for, but in Deleuze's view, bodies must also be more than this. Even if Deleuze and Guattari want us to 'make [ourselves] a Body without Organs', they also know that we need to keep some part of our subjectivity intact, or else risk total dissolution.[9] The human body could not survive without this double articulation. The BwO and its molecularities provide us with the possibilities for change, subversions, and partial dissolution (for better or worse); but they also serve as a substrate for an organized or molar body, which is necessary to keep annihilation at bay.

The human nursing body becomes a particular kind of symbiotic assemblage with a nursing infant. While Deleuze is less helpful in terms of illuminating the ways in which this becoming-together of bodies is raced, classed, and gendered, he does provide a helpful conceptual frame for thinking about how this watery body also escapes and repeats differently, its latent potential selected elsewhere, becoming something else: human body becoming weather current, becoming whale body, becoming nursing mother thousands of miles away, downloading organochloride compounds into her nursing becoming-child – or perhaps becoming entirely differently. What Michelle Murphy (2013) describes as latency – that unknowable temporal lag that keeps the materiality of bodies in a suspended and uncertain unfolding – Deleuze elaborates in the concept of virtuality. Bodies, as in part virtual, are also extensive through time. Virtuality, in Deleuze's terms, is that 'indeterminate cloud' that surrounds and coexists with actualized bodies. Virtuality is a body's could-have-been and might-become; it is the zone of potentiality from which bodies are selected, and actualized.[10] Because of their virtual potentiality, 'we do not know what a body can do' – this is Deleuze's oft-cited paraphrase of Spinoza. But nor do we fully know what bodies can withstand, or how they will continue to affect others. The bounds of a body – not only spatially or even temporally, but also in terms of its effects and affectability – can never be fully determined. This virtuality is also another way of describing our bodies of water as always also more-than-human, and human bodies in general as always more-than-coherent, bounded, subjects.

A Deleuzian view of embodiment does not deny human subjectivity, or the existence of human bodies; indeed, it is according to these bodies that we most commonly make sense of the world. But Deleuze's project encourages us to remember that our bodies do not stop at our skin; they are also molecular, extensive, and virtual. This helps us account for the micro-scale hydraulics upon which our molar subjectivity depends, as well as for the oozing, leaking, absorbing, and fluvial ways in which this subjectivity is also disrupted. But when read alongside Merleau-Ponty's understanding of bodies, these multiple strata of embodiment – as is evident in a Deleuzian breast milk posthumanism, for example – refuse theoretical abstraction; this ineluctable more-than-human-bodiedness is necessarily part of our lived experience. Let's go back to Merleau-Ponty to flesh this out some more.

As noted earlier, when Merleau-Ponty (1962: 61) describes his project as 'a study of the advent of being to consciousness', this is always an embodied consciousness. For Merleau-Ponty, embodiment *is* consciousness. But is embodiment for Merleau-Ponty synonymous with the coherent body that Deleuze insists we need to disorganize – the stratified despot and the humanist view of 'Man', that 'molar entity par excellence' (Deleuze and Guattari 1987: 292)? Clearly, for Merleau-Ponty, the body has a tendency towards organization. There is a 'unity and identity of the body as a synergetic totality', he avers, that enables consciousness to comprehend the world and make sense of what we encounter in a synthesized way, across and through all of our various bodily modalities (1962: 317) – cognitive, affective, motor, and perceptual.[11] Without this 'loose unity', our experience of the world would be fragmented and largely incomprehensible. In other words, like Deleuze, Merleau-Ponty (1962) acknowledges the necessity of some organizing subjectivity. We can see this in the many ways that a disorganized body strives to 'right' itself – a phantom limb that still asserts its presence (80–89); a spatial awareness that insists on 'righting' an inverted room (243–254). But what these analyses also reveal is the ways that our bodies are also always disrupting and disorganizing; if they weren't, there would be no reason to strive for (relative) 'rightness'.[12] Planetary breast milk transits and intercorporeal becomings, for example, remind us that we live our bodies not only via a secure command centre that keeps us all together; we live our bodies even as we are falling apart.

Merleau-Ponty (1962: 198) agrees that the phenomenological body is 'always something other than what it is'; it is 'never hermetically sealed'. Bodies are open and permeable, permeated. For Merleau-Ponty, the same operations that enact an embodied consciousness also guarantee that the body is never a static or stable entity; it is constantly transforming. This understanding emerges most strongly in what Merleau-Ponty (1968: 149) calls the flesh of the world – a 'mesh' of elemental being in which all beings participate, entangle, and entwine. Merleau-Ponty (1968: 123) also refers to this intertwining of bodies as chiasm – not a 'fusion or coinciding of' body and world, but rather, an 'overlapping or encroachment' such that 'things pass into us, as well as we into the things'. This, we could say, is Merleau-Ponty's version of worlding – a co-labour of body and world.[13] Flesh, as 'a possibility, a latency', also reveals that for Merleau-Ponty, bodies are not predetermined, but rather emergent in/ as incalculable potentiality (Merleau-Ponty 1968: 133).[14]

For Merleau-Ponty, all of this is phenomenologically evident, and part of the body that we can 'go back to', and describe. Our extension into the world, our latent potentiality, our molecularity, and all of the micromodalities that allow us to become subjects, but also become otherwise, are all part of the lived embodiment that serves as our 'pivot' or 'medium' for knowing anything in the world, at all (Merleau-Ponty 1962: 82). Earlier, I insisted that the idea of watery embodiment is neither an abstract concept nor mere metaphor nor an overlay of scientific fact gleaned from an outside; watery embodiment is something we live, and as such, it is also something that can be *accessed, amplified,* and *described.* But clearly, some of the ways in which we, as bodies of water, exceed a molar, organized understanding of bodies are more available to us than others. Indeed, as steeped in a latency, or virtuality, in Alaimo's 'swirling world' of uncertainty, our bodies will never fully reveal themselves to us either. My proposition is that we can nonetheless access, amplify, and describe a posthuman embodied experience. This, as I've suggested, is not only a methodological experiment (although it is that as well). In an aqueous world where the waters that we are and the waters in which we corporeally traffic are increasingly turning away from us, situating ourselves and describing our implication within a posthuman bodyscape is also a question of ethical accountability. The question remains: how?

How to think (as) a body of water: Access, amplify, describe!

We have a specific politics of location as bodies of water, but as watery, we also disrupt our own sense of embodied self. In the face of fear, the welling up of water in our affective and visceral bodies can result in the sudden and unexpected elimination of tears, or pee, or shit. Such eruptions might seem beyond the control of the disciplining processes to which we usually subject our visceral selves. 'Excuse the outburst', we might say after a tearful breakdown. We might consider involuntary evacuations from below a sign of our animality: 'how unlike me', we apologize. A pressing thirst can similarly disorient the organizing project of our subject-selves. Thirst diffracts me, I lose my focus. I cannot concentrate on the words on the page, or keep my thoughts trained. My throat searches for some forgotten cache of saliva and the incessant attempts to swallow distract me. ('What did you say? What was that again?') In extreme dehydration, the molar body may altogether recede; we edge towards a desiccated sort of bare life. In cases where I pass on my water deliberately and intentionally, what meanings and materialities do I pass on with it? These dissolutions of my self into a watery world may reside below or beyond my direct contemplation, but they extend my body all the same. Or: the tide is rising, we are caught in the waves. Even though our bodies are mostly watery, we hit a plunging threshold that we cannot bear: too much destratification, a flooded thingification.

But is this elimination, withdrawal, transfer, or deluge something other than me? We could call these experiences of our aqueous becomings a *more-than*-human embodiment. They interrupt a comfortable human sense of a bodily self, while also amplifying our very human vulnerabilities – in this sense, human *all the more*. In opening us up to the droughts, seepages, and inundations that are also animal and elemental, we are reminded that our humanness is always more than the bounds of our skin. By tuning into these bodily molecularities as lived, we might also attune ourselves empathically towards other bodies of water, beyond us. This includes those of us for whom our subjectivity has always been situated in/as a more-than-humanness: one might be subjected to a chronic illness that means one's visceral body is perpetually unruly; or one may be dependent on a water source too distant, too polluted, or too costly to respond to one's bodily needs. In these instances, one's assemblage of watery bodiedness can spill beyond the discrete comfort of the human, and in doing so reemphasize the flimsy membrane that just barely holds this conceit together, but which is patrolled all the more for it. Such attunement could also include empathy towards the ocean, forced to carry too much plastic, too little oxygen; or a whale turned toxic vector; or a river, redirected and drained such that it cannot fulfil its responsibilities to provide for its human kin, it is forced to turn away (Povinelli 2015). Or, we could say that in these molecularities, we tune into an originary elemental empathy that is always there, latent, swimming below the surface.

Posthuman phenomenology moves athwart our body-subject's tendency to perceive time, movement, speed, size, and distance as scaled to its own molar experience, even where such extension may seem difficult for our modest human perspective to grasp. In some ways, this project goes against Merleau-Ponty's suggestion of the proximal distance of things. This is the specific distance between the perceiver and the perceived that achieves an optimal tension between the inner horizon and the outer horizon of the thing – for Merleau-Ponty, optimally revealing the thing in its essence. To increase or decrease this distance would mean that we would begin to lose our comfortable grip on things (Merleau-Ponty 1962: 302) – standing too far away from a painting, or trying to listen to the radio with the volume too low. While Merleau-Ponty discusses this proximity spatially, we could also extend this phenomenological proposal to an optimal temporality. A nanosecond may not even seem to 'exist' to us, while deep time is equally hard to fathom. Proximal distance expresses a zone of relation between body and thing that allows the various modalities and interpretive capacities of the body to remain optimally (although always loosely) unified. In other words, for Merleau-Ponty, proximal distance facilitates the cohesion and organization not just of the thing in the world, but of the body as well – its various capacities (movement, perception, cognition) can gear into each other, comfortably. We have already seen, however, that our bodies also experience themselves as falling apart, dissolving, extending into things, and eventually going beyond their own reach. A posthuman phenomenology seeks to acknowledge our sense of comfort with this proximal distance *while at the same time* continuing our investigation of our lived experience beyond this point. When we slip beyond our comfortable proximal distance, we can better attune ourselves to our more-than-humanness.

In the case of our bodies of water, we may perceive the 'time' of this water as immediate, synchronized with our own molar human lifespan. We might anticipate that the water that constitutes our body will cease to exist in time with our flesh and its capacity to imagine a past and a future. Some cosmologies with a stronger sense of intergenerationality clearly challenge such an imaginary, but those of us steeped in a Western atomized ontology – according to which we, for the most part, *live* – find this tricky; it is a stretch to fathom the time of our bodies of water as extending beyond our proximal comprehension. Yet we know that our planetary waters have persisted – nothing added, nothing lost – for several billion years. This water holds in it a past as remote as that gaseous primordial soup, as well as a future, unforeseeable. Similarly, we most comfortably perceive the 'size' of water in relation to our humanist body's relation to it: it is something we drink, in which we bathe, or expel from our systems in relatively predictable (and graspable) quantities. We might, with a little more attention, experience the spatial scale of water at the visceral level, as that which irrigates our own bodily systems and carries away our waste. But what more might we learn about our bodies of water if we could stretch or shrink this proximal relationship?[15]

Posthuman phenomenology suggests that such ancient events, unforeseeable futures, or water too big or too small to easily comprehend, may not necessarily be as distant as one might think. Japanese researcher and thinker Masaru Emoto (2005) takes high-speed photographs of water that capture the unique and revealing structures of water crystals at their moment of freezing, just as the water molecules are crystallizing. His photographs reveal the molecular affectivity of water and its capacity to embody emotion: when water in a glass beaker is exposed to the word 'happiness', Emoto's photograph shows a crystal that is symmetrical, delicate, exquisitely balanced, and beautiful. When exposed to 'unhappiness', the crystal appears out of balance, only partially formed. Exposure to different music – melancholy, discordant, joyous, threatening – similarly results in differently affected crystals. Just a good story? Perhaps. Or perhaps Emoto's photos reveal an intercorporeal (or, following Barad's [2007] insistence that relata do not precede relations, an intra-corporeal) embodiment of affect, experienced at a more-than-human scale. These torqued scales of watery connection appear in a very different, but equally provocative register, in Elizabeth Povinelli's (2015) story of Tjipel, a creek in Northern Australia, but also a young woman, possibly transgender. Despite embodying an entirely more-than-human spatiotemporal scale, Tjipel engages in a relation of responsivity with the human bodies that live beside her and with her. Povinelli describes how some of Tjipel's aboriginal human kin seek to be responsive to her, and how they are certainly affected by Tjipel's own capacity to alter her arrangement of existence (drying up, turning away) as a response to human actions. This too is a kind of more-than-human, inter- or intra-corporeal affectivity. In order to understand Tjipel's capacity to be affected, human bodies require a sensibility of water at a more-than-human scale.

This manipulation of our proximal relationship to things also brings us back to the question of the virtual – that is, a body's indeterminate potentialities that according to Deleuze accompany all of its manifest actualizations. The virtual also relates to those unknowable or ungraspable times and spaces that have not been taken up by our bodies of water – those potential routes that our particular bodies of water did not take, but might have, in a prehistoric past, in an unknowable future, or in a body of water that is too near or too far to seem a part of what I consider my actualized body. All of the potential expressions of a body are latent in one of its actualizations. As such, the virtual is neither *fully* graspable nor describable. But if we apply this idea to our bodies of water, the distinction between the actualized body and this idea of virtuality blurs: are the nanoscopic or prehistoric watery expressions of my body *actual* but ungraspable (by me)? Or are they *virtual*, precisely because they are ungraspable (by me), and because they seem to me more of a 'might have been' than an 'is'? In an open-closed system such as water, where the materiality of water endlessly cycles and repeats, yet all the while becoming 'different' (a point to which I will return in detail in the next chapter), the distinction between 'was' and 'might have been', or 'is' and 'could be' is not clear. If I share one molecule of water with a tsunami that occurred thousands of years ago on the other side of the world, is that tsunami bound up in my own body of water's virtuality, or its actuality? Molecules of material actuality channel through this potentiality. The point is not to quibble with Deleuze's terms. Rather, if we understand Deleuze's posthumanism within a frame of lived bodily experience, the distinction between virtual and actual-but-ungraspable may become less important. Both demand a stretching of my comfortable human scales of spatial and temporal proximity. Both demand a way of tapping into a bodily more-than-humanness that is lived, even if our molar selves have difficulty grasping these experiences. I propose that a practice of posthuman phenomenology can help us contact these experiences, even if only ephemerally, several molecularities removed.

But again: how? A good place to start is embodied attunement. Eminent phenomenologist Herbert Spiegelberg (1965: 659) refers to 'phenomenological intuiting' – the act of utter concentration on the thing 'without becoming so absorbed in it to the point of no longer looking critically'. We might consider this as remaining open to the wonder of a phenomenon, of bracketing the 'natural attitude', yet at the same time sensing a phenomenon's contours, limits, movements, and speeds. This intuiting demands that we tap into a lived experience, albeit one that is mostly covered over or simply taken for granted (and thus dismissed from our attention) by our comfortable corporeal imaginaries. In a practice he calls 'body hermeneutics', Samuel Mallin (1996) adopts this idea as a way of finely honing an embodied attunement to the world and our own bodies, according to the bodily modalities of cognition, perception, affect, and motility.[16] According to these methodological leads, we might begin the business of 'how' by asking: what does the body of water look, feel, or taste like? How do these movements change when we are excessively lubricated, or excessively thirsty? What affect is elicited in our watery expulsions? How do we respond to dehydration affectively, or through our moving bodies? How does a visceral need to pee make the body move? For example, I can try to home in on my molecular body's changes as I drink a glass of water. But at some point, this attention will become strained, and it will probably seem as though the water has moved into the invisibility of what Drew Leder (1990) elaborates in terms of our 'recessive body' – those subcutaneous processes that escape our explicit attention. Perhaps. But what if we pay closer attention, and fine-tune the sensory apparatuses of our bodies more keenly? Don't I also sense a wet weight at my centre? A certain tension in my skull eases. My step is less sluggish. Such techniques require perseverance and repetition. According to Mallin, anything useful or interesting needs to be teased out, poked, prodded, and coaxed through a descriptive practice.

Body hermeneutics and other versions of phenomenological intuition can be a good starting point for thinking *as* a body of water. *Access, amplify, describe.* But in a very practical sense, it is not immediately clear how the tools of an embodied phenomenological analysis would be applicable to experiences that are below or beyond human-scaled perception. How do we grasp the virtual? How do we trace the wateriness of our distant pasts, our unknowable futures, or of our body's own microscopic internal seascapes? How do we map transcorporeal transits that happen out of view or out of focus, beyond the comfortable proximal relation of our body to its parts – the workings of the cerebral spinal fluid that occupies my subarachnoid space, or the journey of my SSRI-laced urine into estuarine communities downstream, or the dissipation of my perspiration into a humid forest atmosphere, to exchange wet breaths with the causarinas? When we move deeper, or further back, or more extensively out, things get complicated.

In these cases, our molar thinking, imagining, and sensing bodies need help. I suggest that 'proxy stories' can be avenues for de-sedimenting our human-scaled perspective. These stories are not substitutes for embodied experience; they are its *amplifiers* and *sensitizers*. Art, for example, is an ampliflier. One experience of water might go like this: between two rooms hangs a curtain – hundreds of strings of crystalline blue beads, plummeting freely but in unison to the gallery floor, looking for the lowest place, the path of least resistance. I position myself in the middle of the curtain, and let this cataract pour itself over me, a baptism of string and glass. I can't move. Beneath its persistent pressure, I am prevented from floating away. I feel the weight of water – the way it grounds me, pulls me down, pulls me under. Even though this 'water' – an installation by Felix Gonzalez Torres in the Koffler Gallery in Toronto, on a summer afternoon in 2002 – isn't 'wet', it activates and amplifies in me the lived experience of water as undertow, as stronger than my own measly self.[17] Or, projected behind a wall of cascading water, Rebecca Belmore gathers the sea in a bucket, and grunting and struggling throws its contents at me, the viewer: a thick ropy red runs down the screen, and I feel the waters of my white settler body flow into the colonized waters of Turtle Island (also known as Canada). Belmore's video installation *Fountain* (2005) allows me to access, and amplify, my own watery politics of location, channelling through my corporeal seas.

Writing, images, objects, and other art forms can work in these ways, giving us access to an embodied experience of our wateriness that might otherwise be too submerged, too subcutaneous, too repressed, or too large and distant (or even too obvious, mundane, and taken for granted), to readily sense: a drought experienced at the back of a parched throat, a fishy ancestor swimming up my unfolding vertebrate body, a glacier melting felt in my gut. The desire to draw on these stories does not represent a failure of phenomenology to get 'back to the things themselves'; it is rather an affirmation that these stories too are pulled from a material world – but then condensed, concentrated, and given back to us such that we can more readily access and amplify them, anew.

I return to art as amplifier of an embodied politics of location (and Rebecca Belmore's work specifically) in Chapter 4. Here, though, I want to explore how science can serve as a different kind of amplifying proxy story.

While notable exceptions persist and proliferate, phenomenologists are critical of the scientific-empiricist view of things. Natural scientific explanations of bodies do not – at face value, anyways – appear to be particularly congruent with attention to *life as it is experienced*. Merleau-Ponty (1962: viii) himself asserts that the reliance on phenomenological description over analysis and explanation is 'from the start a foreswearing of science', even as he engages scientific stories as useful starting points or complements to his own investigations. But posthuman phenomenology affirms that scientific and phenomenological views are not necessarily incompatible. As Ulrich Beck (cited in Alaimo 2010: 19) notes, many of our contemporary embodied experiences 'require ... the "sensory organs" of science – theories, experiments, measuring instruments – in order to become visible or interpretable'. Alaimo further suggests that 'syncretic assemblages' of knowledge are needed to understand the ways in which our bodily matter is implicated in a world that cannot be adequately grasped through one mode of inquiry alone (Alaimo 2010: 19). Even if Alaimo (2009: 23) elsewhere insists that the 'trans-corporeality' she describes is '*not* a phenomenological ... stance', perhaps this surmisal gives short shrift to the value of phenomenological description, and also instates too wide a gap between the attunement of phenomenologists and that of natural scientists to the wonder of the world. I propose that scientific knowledge and phenomenology can be one of these syncretic assemblages.

As I've argued, experiences below and beyond the individual humanist scale – planetary breast milk, but also a gurgling gut, a sweaty dispersal into the fog, even the effect of our ablutions on riparian life and other human life-at-a-distance – are also strata of our lived experience. If some scientific findings – such as those of evolutionary biology, organic chemistry, or molecular physics – may seem too abstract, imperceptible or distant for verification through lived embodied experience, this is mostly a case of the hegemony of a human-centred and human-scaled perception. To assume bacterial life, meteorology, or multispecies biochemistries are not *lived* in some way in and through our human bodies either underestimates the actualities and potentialities of our embodied dispersals or misunderstands what it means to live. Interestingly, despite Merleau-Ponty's (1962: viii) distrust of the hegemony of scientific perspectives, he also states that 'all my knowledge of the world, even my scientific knowledge, is gained from my own particular point of view, or from some experience of the world without which the symbols of science would be meaningless'. This is an opening to posthuman phenomenology, where our bodies parse the findings of scientific knowledge through their various sensory apparatuses.

Even science that seems at the furthest possible distance from our embodied experience – for example science from the oceanic benthos – 'makes sense' because of our embodied capacity to feel, to know, and to understand. As artist Rona Lee (2012: 16) notes, 'despite the seemingly scopic emphasis of much ocean science and its apparent alignment to what might be called an epistemology of distance', 'conversations at NOCS [National Oceanography Centre Southampaton] have revealed the extent to which sensuous understandings; emotional response and imaginative projection inform oceanographic study'. She continues:

> One colleague told me of how the sight of small jellyfish, floating weightlessly along at a depth of 30,000 meters, had led him to reflect on the impact of gravity, as symbolized by the return to earth of death, in shaping our consciousness and how, had we evolved in an aquatic medium, buoyancy would have given rise to an unthinkably different metaphysics. Another of an instance when the temperature of a black smoker (undersea hydrothermal vent) was brought home to him not by the gauges on his instrument panel, but the experience of watching a length of ducting tap, attached to a piece of external equipment, melt away; activating an imagined sensation of the extreme heat involved. (16)

Relationships and processes that govern the world we inhabit, and which are described by various scientific discourses, are all in some way lived – directly or intensively, virtually, and imaginatively – by us. In line with Merleau-Ponty, the world makes sense to us, in all of its wonders, because we are embodied.

Like our bodies themselves, our embodied knowledge of our bodies is always becoming, moving, changing. Advances in the domains of science and biotechnology alter the way in which we experience embodiment, and what a body in fact is.[18] How we exist and understand ourselves as embodied beings is not some inert, static, enduring sort of truth.[19] In these contemporary times, we are increasingly living our bodies as fragmentable, augmentable, extendable, and intelligible in ways that are mostly new, or new incarnations of old tricks. Organ transplantation, biobanking, and assisted reproduction, for example, fragment our bodies in new ways, putting pressures on commonly held notions of bodily integrity (Blackman 2010). At the same time, we are becoming increasingly aware of our embodiment as intimately imbricated in and visited by environmental others – animals, bacteria, and toxins (Alaimo 2010; Simms 2009). The insides of our viscera are now available to us in microscopic detail, and we can trace chemical markers of our psychopharmaceutically enhanced urine, dispersing through our local watersheds. Planetary breast milk transits may not be fully trackable, but we do have access to various kinds of sensory apparatuses that can begin to sketch out these journeys, between species and across geographies and generations.

Again, these changes are not extraneous to our lived embodiment. The ways in which we understand what it means to be a body, the cartographies that our bodies chart, and our inextricability from complex webs of relation are all *lived* by us, in phenomenologically relevant ways. (Put otherwise, it would be absurd to think that our 'bodies' somehow change, while our facultings and means for knowing those bodies – a mind? a tongue? a language? – are somehow untouchably static.) The miniature videocamera inserted down one's throat creates a new relation to one's stomach (Sawchuck 2000); the implantation of another person's kidney shifts and radicalizes the experience of intersubjectivity in significant ways (Waldby 2002); 3D ultrasonography inaugurates new configurations of the maternal 'I' (Mitchell 2001).[20] Could we not imagine a similar sort of reconfiguration – one that stretches and disperses our bodies – when we read how our human wastes and emissions are transforming entire oceanic ecosystems? By paying attention to the measurement of water levels in aquifers, reservoirs, or lakes, might our own thirst be imagined as a more extensive, collaborative gullet? Our bodies of water clearly demonstrate the 'I' as both technological and ecological, connected up with other bodies of all kinds, and lived at diverse levels of sensory perception. The sensorium that opens to us through technologies and other types of monitoring and assessment apparatuses *changes* how we actually experience our bodies because we take on these schematizations, and integrate them into our ways of being in the world. In other words, once the mediating tools of science and technology are brought into our sphere of experience, they cannot help but impinge upon the ways in which we experience ourselves and our bodies. Information gleaned from these tools does not 'interfere' with our knowledge of bodies, as though that knowledge were a stable and determined thing; this information participates in the worlding of bodies, and our ongoing, unfolding, experience of embodiment. Merleau-Ponty taught us that existence *is* embodiment – that we only know the world through our experience of being embodied. But as that experience shifts – as it inevitably does – our methods (and epistemologies) for understanding that experience need to be adequate to that shifting.

The use of biological, chemical, or other scientific tools and information to amplify and extend more human-scaled experiences not only reconfigures our understanding of 'embodiment' and 'the lived', but also makes available to us resources that can help us access and describe our posthuman corporeality. Because scientific accounts either stretch or shrink our human proximal relation to certain matter or forces, by grappling with such accounts we can nudge ourselves closer to appreciating those dimensions of experiencing the world that do not easily conform to a human-centred one, but which we nonetheless live, skimming across, journeying through, gathering up, and nestling inside our own lived embodiment. What scientific perspectives teach me about the mechanics of fluids, the chemical composition of water, the ecological hydrological cycle, and the necessity of water for the gestation of all life can facilitate contact with my posthuman corporeality. For example, while it may seem that I lose my grip on the water that I drink from a glass as it travels deep into my viscera, pharmacokinetics helps me perceive the mechanisms, times, and processes of absorption. Or, while the fleshy buoyancy that cushions my bones has little need for words such as *intracellular fluid (ICF)* and *extracellular fluid (ECF)* to experience the fluvial passages and watery buffer zones that facilitate every movement my body makes, scientific explanation can nonetheless help me understand the workings of my motile body's water as I bend to lift a book or bump my hip into a chair. Or, evolutionary biology can amplify the time of my waters far beyond my proximal grip on them. A mammalian diving reflex allows me to dive to depths much greater than most animals, thanks to a marked reduction in heart rate and cardiac output that reduces my body's consumption of oxygen (Morgan 1982: 77). Scientific explanation of this reflex does not *invent* the sensory experiences of my body in a transition from land to deep water – these are embodied knowledges, too. Such scientific stories, however, help me to tap into the phenomenon, already there, swimming in my waters and burrowed in my flesh.

These conversations, these reciprocal but always imperfect dialectics between scientific knowledge and phenomenology, reaching towards greater understanding, are tools of phenomenological attunement. Again, when such 'wonder' is brought together with the serious acknowledgement of the biological substrata that one finds in science, this can shift the experience of our own humanness. The edges of our discretely bounded selves begin to blur, and our skin becomes increasingly transparent. While phenomenology may not *require* this amplification, these amplifiers can enhance, rather than annul, phenomenology's insights into what it means to be human.

Posthuman phenomenology's feminist orientation also reminds us that engaging science is not without risk. Scientific schematizations can overtake the body-as-lived, in all of its fluctuating and interpermeating complexities. (Science, after all, is not a 'God Trick', as Donna Haraway (1988) would say, but articulated by situated bodies.) As explicitly feminist, posthuman phenomenology must also be attuned to criticisms of specific aspects of applications of biological and other scientific thought on additional terms, namely, that it can wrest this knowledge and power from us, by congealing, reifying, or essentializing aspects of our embodiment in ways that oppress. We know that treating science as the new, all-knowing god can have disastrous effects, not only epistemologically but also practically, in the lives of women, people of colour, indigenous peoples, queer people, people living with disabilities, and others.[21] In this context, a feminist posthuman phenomenology does not simply hand the reigns over to scientific data. While phenomenologists in the tradition of Merleau-Ponty distinguish their work from empiricism because of the latter's claim to absolute and unambiguous truth, the feminist tradition I am invoking here is concerned with the false objectivity of empiricism, and the power of the purportedly 'neutral' scientific knower to determine the fate of those bodies it marginalizes.[22] Moreover, as I mention above, while Elizabeth A. Wilson (2015) cautions strongly against failing to engage with scientific data (this will only lead to impoverished feminist analyses, she argues), she is equally as critical about simply accepting science at face value – as a final arbiter or truth. She advocates instead for taking scientific data 'seriously but not literally, moving them outside the zones of interpretive comfort that they usually occupy' (13).[23] While Wilson's method is not phenomenological, posthuman phenomenology shares this objective. In a feminist posthuman phenomenology, to amplify is neither to corroborate nor justify – nor certainly to set the bar. It is rather a rendering of an experience more accessible, more graspable, more intelligible, in a desire to experience more deeply, more subtly, more intercorporeally.

If phenomenologists are troubled by the use of proxies and syncretic assemblages such as science as ways of getting to 'experience' or going 'back to the things themselves', it bears remembering, as Donna Haraway (1988) taught us many decades ago, that all vision is prosthetic; all knowledge is mediated. We only know the world through the mediation of prosthetics – there is no 'pre-mediated' state to get back to. In this sense, no less than the specific powers of our primate retinas and optic nerves mediate what we are sure we perceive, microscopes and telescopes similarly give us access to certain visions while they hold others at bay. Both a tongue and a water quality autosampler, both a sensitive fingertip and a DNA sequencer, are sensory apparatuses that give us information about the world. *This holds for all sensory apparatuses.* Language, cosmology, ideology, and corporeal imaginaries equally serve as mediating prostheses that open certain experiences for us, but foreclose or restrain others. All such apparatuses create an interface of experience; all are fallible, variable.

This realization brings a key point home: phenomenology always comes from somewhere. Our own politics of location, and our bodies in all of their prosthetic interfaces, co-world the phenomena we describe. Again, this does not mean that phenomenology fails to engage 'the thing itself'; it only underlines what Merleau-Pontian corporeal phenomenology and feminist posthumanism have already stressed: that all 'things' are co-worldings, all essences provisional, and that as bodies, we are always chiasmically making the world. This is not solipsistic relativism; this is 'feminist objectivity' in Haraway's (1988) words. Or put otherwise, this is the only world there is. Insisting on Haraway's prosthetic vision as a way of approaching phenomenology reminds us that our embodiment and becoming-with other bodies are an inescapable co-constitution of nature and culture, of imagination and matter. On such a view, we might even say that *phenomenology has always been posthuman.* All existence is cyborg. Any 'thing' we 'get back to' – in a humanist or posthuman orientation – can be accessed only through mediated perception.

A posthuman phenomenological method exerts a two-way pressure: first, upon phenomenology to understand that all perception is mediated, and getting 'back to the things themselves' will always require something like Haraway's prosthetic vision. But secondly, a posthuman phenomenology also reminds posthumanists that the embeddedness of bodies within contexts, within specific possibilities and matrices of power, cannot be transcended. A posthuman method can no more easily escape the situatedness of the practitioner than a phenomenological one can. Here, as noted earlier, feminist and anticolonial corporeal phenomenologies are particularly instructive in reminding us how the differences of racialized, colonized, and gendered bodies need to be specifically traced, not erased (see Fanon 1986; Ahmed 2006; Shildrick 1997; Irigaray 1985a; Trinh 1989; de Beauvoir 2010). Flight from one's specifically situated human body is not feminist posthumanism, but rather an arrogant fantasy (Åsberg 2013). Situated knowledges and politics of location *condition* the kind of posthuman phenomenology I am advocating. The problem with phenomenology was never *description by a body,* but rather the assumption that description only issues from certain kinds of bodies, and is only about certain kind of bodies. A feminist posthuman phenomenological method must insist on describing the (social, morphological, cultural, biological, structural, imaginative) conditions that enable certain experiences for some bodies, but foreclose others for other ones. To do so, we begin with our (situated, posthuman) bodies. Recall Rich's imperative: begin with the material; describe the geography closest in.

Not only do we require the syncretic assemblages of science to find our posthuman phenomenological bearings, we also need to attune ourselves critically to the differences of bodies that together world our planetary hydrocommons. The kind of posthuman phenomenology I am advocating must be committed to feminist, but also anticolonial, anti-racist, queer, and crip futures. Even – *especially* – as our bodies molecularize and destratify, and defy and interrupt our sense of coherently bounded self, the flows of power and restratification are hardly washed away.

Posthuman ties in a too-human world

Importantly, a posthuman phenomenology does not dispense with the human; this is neither possible nor desirable. Accessing, amplifying, and describing the body of water as a feminist figuration – like any critical-creative undertaking I engage – is still something I do with my very human body. But that doesn't make this figuration, or this method, irredeemably humanist. Theory, concepts, description: all these are made by human bodies for human bodies, even if these bodies are also more-than-human, and even – especially – as they are sometimes rendered inhuman. This posthuman methodology (of scholarship, maybe also of living) asks the phenomenologist to activate and amplify the more-than-human modes of living *that are also always part of existence and part of our 'own' corporeality*, and which emerge from our particular politics of location. A feminist posthuman phenomenology is a methodology that challenges a too-easy 'we', but won't remain tethered to a bounded 'I', either.

While the human body is indeed a convenient 'resting place' from which to engage in philosophical practice,[24] the refusal to abandon one's human molarity is not only a question of ontological adequacy; it is also an ethical consideration. To ignore or discount ourselves as specifically human bodies would mean that we would also have to ignore or discount those many ways in which we as humans act upon other bodies in specific ways. (A body, remember, is defined not only by its capacity to be affected, but also by its capacity to affect.) If we consider our world's water-related ecological crises, inextricably linked to our other human projects of dam building, factory fishing, and the theft, capture, and sale of ancient aquifer stores as privately owned commodities (to name only a few), the urgency of acknowledging how human projects affect other bodies of water in the world becomes clear. This imperative intensifies the more we account for our posthuman politics of location: as white or brown; as male, female, or otherwise gendered; as settlers, as travellers, as migrants, as deeply rooted in place. The ways in which specific bodies are seriously implicated, while others bear the heaviest burden in relation to our planet's troubled waters, requires ongoing and increased attention. A close attunement to our posthuman embodiment of and as water reveals that 'responsibility' is not a simple thing to allocate, nor an easy thing to shoulder. We need to keep looking for ethical responses that can be adequate to these questions.

A feminist posthuman phenomenology also helps us realize that this kind of accountability, or response, is not merely a question of 'the right thing to do', as some kind of categorical moral imperative. Our human bodies are *materially* composed of water in ways that inextricably link our human, specifically situated bodies to other bodies – sea, whale, human in the distance. Our human projects – fossil fuel burning, plastic consumption, infusing all things in our homes with flame retardant – may be dreamt up and executed by our human subject-bodies, but all of us as an embodied hydrocommons materially live these effects, in one way or another. The planetary hydrocommons is not outside of us, but quite literally channelling and cycling through us. Even if it may seem as though I have little to do with multi-million dollar hydroelectric dam projects on the Peace River in northern British Columbia, or the water of the Flint River travelling through corrosive lead pipes and into the taps of residents in Flint, Michigan, or indeed, with biomagnifying levels of toxins in Arctic human and more-than-human animals, we need to torque this proximal distance. This is the ethical imperative.

If the aim of feminist posthuman phenomenology is to attune ourselves differently to a world in which we are implicated, and to experiment in modes of worlding *otherwise*, then the question remains: what do these descriptions do? What can they change, and how can they illuminate and produce more ethical accounts of living well together? Posthuman phenomenology can be a tool for thinking with environmental matters, such as water, in order to transform the contours and limits of humanist modes of inquiry, but also of its ethics. Refiguring ourselves as bodies of water is thus not only an experiment in human embodiment, but also a feminist commitment to following the flows of marginalization and injustice, as well as those of connection, empowerment, and joy that our watery corporealities collaboratively engender.

Posthuman Gestationality: Luce Irigaray and Water's Queer Repetitions

So remember the liquid ground.

– (Irigaray 1991: 37)

Hydrological cycles

Our bodies are hydrophilic, through and through. This should hardly come as a surprise. It is almost too cliché to say these days that 60–90 per cent of our bodies is constituted of water, but perhaps it is the only reasonable place to start this chapter. About the same percentage of the earth's surface is wet and blue. Water infiltrates and inhabits the vapour we breathe, the land we work, the animal, vegetable, meteorological and other earth others with whom we share this planet. As embodied beings, we are, primarily, bodies of water in a watery world.

Yet our bodies of water are neither stagnant, nor separate, nor zipped up in some kind of impermeable sac of skin. These bodies are rather deeply imbricated in the intricate movements of water that create and sustain life on our planet. We all feel these movements viscerally, in the superabundance, acute paucity, or mere banality of the rain, sleet, and snow that dominate our weather reports; we have all learned of the cycles of transpiration, evaporation, and condensation to which these precipitous movements belong. However, while we might understand such traversals and transformations of water upon the Earth according to a high-school science classroom's version of 'the hydrological cycle', this water is in fact engaged in a multiplicity of complex and co-implicated cycles, about which more nuanced stories can be told. Within that overarching hydrological cycle, water moves neither at a uniform speed nor as a coherent mass, but rather is differentiated, in space and in time, all the way down. When it rains, or snows, some water will soak into the ground, replenishing the surface soil for several months before rejoining the cycle; other water digs deeper – settling into subterranean aquifers for thousands of years. Some watery weathers will forego such percolation and infiltration altogether; some water evaporates almost immediately back into the skies. Other kinds of wet opt instead for a quick getaway, running along the Earth's surface towards rivers, lakes, and seas where they may finally take a breather, perhaps for a hundred years, or only several days. Frozen, some surface water becomes glacial, holding out against the warming creep of the thaw.

And still, all of these different watery routes do not account for the smaller yet immensely significant amounts of surface water that are absorbed by living beings. Biological water is in turn inaugurated into its own series of cycles – becoming plant breath, seed bath, muscle lubricant, protein folder, the fluid in your inner ear. While only comprising 0.0001 per cent of the earth's water, biological water is also the most restless, often moving on to new pathways and fresh bodies at breakneck speed (at least from a planetary perspective). Yet, these life-animating waters are perhaps what we humans know most intimately, if only ever ephemerally. These biological processes are in turn maintained by their own water relays. For us humans, this includes the collection and expulsion of maternal amniotic waters, the absorption and circulation of water within our gestating bodies, and the flow and flush of waters in the various bodily fluids that intercorporeally sustain our bodies – all of which are part of the biological and meteorological cycles of water that extracorporeally nourish our bodies.

These varied speeds and slownesses, multiple movements, and diverse incorporations of 'water' belie the difficulty of speaking of water in the abstract – as though it were one undifferentiated and amorphous thing, the same everywhere and all the time. But, undeniably, this is all *water*. *We are all bodies of water*. In fact, paying attention to hydrological cycles presents a rather queer notion: water is evidently both finite *and* inexhaustible; both the same and always becoming different, too. Our planet neither gains nor relinquishes the water it harbours, but only witnesses its continual reorganization, redistribution, and relocation. This means that the water that temporarily comprises and sustains all of these bodies brings with it a history that is at least 3.9 billion years old and will continue far beyond the span of our own lifetimes, and the lifetimes of all those other bodies, too. So, just as our bodies find a thread of commonality and connection in and through this seemingly 'closed' system of water, we are constantly confronted by difference – the different rates, speeds, pathways, and bodily expressions that water takes on. This variability is then diffracted through vastly different ways in which water affects our (different) bodies, and how we, in turn, affect the waters with which we live. We could even say that water can only serve as a connector *because* it expresses or facilitates difference. Through the continued expression of watery difference, bodies proliferate and transform – always seeking out new expressions of watery embodiment. This 'closed' system is not really that closed after all.

In this chapter, I want to continue unpacking this seeming contradiction – that water is both exquisitely specific, yet also entirely mundane, and ubiquitous, and common. In doing so, I'm hoping we humans might better understand what it means to be implicated in this stuff. Water is not only something we take in or use (drinking, bathing, cooking), as our relation to water is usually considered when we think about the human right to water, or water justice more generally, but something we embody in a posthuman sense, too. I am interested in the swampy saturated ecologies that our bodies inescapably *are*; I want to think more about the sea inside, bodily tides, and human plumbing. How might both our difference and commonality as bodies of water help us cultivate more attentive relations to other bodies of water, both connected to and different from us – those bodies to whom we are indebted for our material existence, and to whom we pass on our own bodily matters, in turn? If we are implicated within these hydrological cycles, from where do we gather our own waters, and to what or whom do we bequeath them? With whom do we share them? My interest is in how these questions are not just matters of fact, but matters of concern – for politics, ethics, and living well with others. Negotiating an ethics of embodied difference is a resolutely feminist issue. The question that follows, however, is: how might we refract these feminist concerns through an ecological, and specifically hydrological, situatedness, too?

'Remember the liquid ground', writes Luce Irigaray (1991: 37), so the watery works of this French feminist philosopher seem a good place to begin. Irigaray is well known for her explorations of sexuate difference[1] and the articulation of ethical relations that can be cultivated when we attend to such difference. In describing how these differences manifest, however, Irigaray simultaneously offers a phenomenology of elemental and material embodiment. I am thus curious about what Irigaray can offer to a theory of embodiment that begins with our watery constitution, particularly when the difference of bodies is a priority concern. In this chapter, I propose that we might think of Irigaray as a posthuman phenomenologist – that is, I suggest how her work on sexually different bodies might be parsed through a framework of posthuman phenomenology, providing a sort of posthuman or new materialist feminism *avant la lettre*. Her attention to materiality alongside an insistence on the becoming, unfolding and facilitative capacities of such matters reveals a fecund way of thinking embodiment that pays attention to both the material realities of fleshy bodies, while also refusing a biological or material essentialism. In doing so, Irigaray offers a helpful scaffold for elaborating the figuration of 'bodies of water' – my project in this book more generally.

In Luce Irigaray's (1991) most watery text, *Marine Lover of Friedrich Nietzsche,* she implores her (masculine) interlocutor not to forget the waters that made him possible. This provocation also includes an attentive description of the ways in which waters animate, connect, and facilitate watery bodies that are also different. Irigaray's phenomenology thus suggests a specific onto-logic of bodies of water. Here, I refer to this onto-logic as an 'amniotics' – my way of naming the logics that entangle bodily waters in both commonality and difference. Water is articulated as always both 'being' and a process of 'becoming' – gathering water from certain bodies and flowing back into others in return. According to this onto-logic, water is also both body *and* milieu; water is what comprises bodies but also that which bathes bodies into being. Being and becoming are also proliferations of the different, and the new. To further elaborate these ideas, I also return in this chapter to the work of Gilles Deleuze, specifically his work on difference and repetition. Water, in its amniotic onto-logic, materializes this movement: it repeats, but always differently.

What emerges is an operative concept for my larger project in this book, namely, the idea of posthuman gestationality. Posthuman gestationality is a facilitative mode of being, *but one that is not necessarily tied to the female human.* My insistence on the posthumanism of gestational waters also underscores my desire to read Irigaray beyond humanism – beyond the anthropocentrism that seems to spill at times from her pages. Moreover, athwart some of her more explicit proclamations on sexual difference and the binaristic and even heteronormative essentialism with which her work is sometimes associated, her posthuman phenomenological description of watery bodies also suggests a different kind of theory of sexuate difference – one of desirous becoming that cannot be tied to a binaristic logic of two. From this desire flows my rather queer reading of Irigaray, perhaps against her own intention. Water seeps into Irigaray's work, stealthily making it strange.

Just as significantly, I wager that posthuman gestationality asks an ethical question of us, in all of our common wateriness: if we are all watery, then we all harbour the potential of watery gestationality within our corporeal selves. Again, this gestationality need not take the form of a human reprosexual womb: we may be gestational as lover, as neighbour, as accidental stranger. We learn gestationality from water; we repeat its potential in and as watery bodies, too. In the context of our world's pressing water crises, this lesson can encourage us to be more thoughtful, and more responsive, in terms of what we give back to water in all its forms, but in particular to those planetary water bodies that we (as always differentiated) currently exploit, pollute, and instrumentalize. How might we, in a partial dissolution of our own sovereign subjectivity, also become gestational for this gestational milieu?[2]

Elemental bodies: Irigaray as posthuman phenomenologist?

For Luce Irigaray – one of the twentieth century's key philosophers – water is paradoxically a 'liquid ground', both essential to life *and also* always shifting. Water is at once the originary condition of all possibility, but also its force of differentiation and wellspring of unknowability. Indeed, the multivalence of Irigaray's 'liquid ground' epitomizes the notable difficulty many commentators have had in coming to terms with her philosophy. Both poststructuralist and essentialist in her view of bodies, both retrograde and avant-garde in her theories of sexual difference, both celebrated for her embrace of ambiguity and dismissed for her contradictions – it is no wonder that many of us just don't know what to do with her. At the same time, this difficulty is precisely what makes a reconsideration of her work compelling. New interests and emphases within feminist theory provide fresh ways in which to understand her writing, which makes this rereading more interesting still. Parsing her work through frameworks of posthuman embodiment, new materialisms, and feminist phenomenology not only provides the terms that help me make better sense of her project but also helps articulate 'bodies of water' as a figuration and ethical project more broadly.

Irigaray's contributions to a feminist thinking with matter arise most obviously in her attention to sexuate (*sexué*) difference and body-morphological phenomena – genital lips, mucous, womb and intrauterine space, breath, placenta, amniotic fluid, saliva – as potential sources for a rematerialized feminine subjectivity, and a revised understanding of the ontological more generally. Irigaray's insistence on sexuate difference as ontological (that is, as conditioning the possibility of existence, rather than just one variation of beings, among many) is strongly linked to a key concept in her work, which I refer to as the gestational.[3] Irigaray most often presents gestationality in terms of the feminine-maternal. For Irigaray, understanding the foundational nature of sexuate difference means we must acknowledge the maternal as that which allows any other being to be. For Irigaray, maternity is a facilitative, gifting force that is not abstract, but located in and as material bodies of sexuate difference (as Braidotti [2002: 23] reminds us, the root of 'materialism' is 'mater'). Irigaray insists that if we ignore this gestational materiality, masculinist and phallogocentric ontologies of sovereign beings and subjects inevitably crumble; they would seemingly come from no place, indebted to no one. This reminder not only calls phallogocentric philosophy to task but also affirms the unacknowledged potential of the feminine. Irigaray contends that because of the phallogocentrism that has dominated philosophy and language since Plato and before, we have yet to experience sexual difference *as* difference; thus it is *yet to come*. Irigaray (1993c) presents intrauterine space as a place of fecundity that can empower and enable women to proliferate beyond the confines of their representation in phallogocentrism. Through attention to a necessarily material gestational maternal, Irigaray hopes that sexuate difference will be able to realize its difference as difference. Such difference, contends Irigaray (2002b: 171), is 'the condition of presence'. 'Sexual difference', states Irigaray

(1993a: 5), once we allow it to be *as* difference 'would constitute the horizon of worlds more fecund than any known to date – at least in the West'.

Unsurprisingly, this focus on feminine morphology, and the maternal in particular, has raised more than a few feminist eyebrows through the years: isn't this just another repetition of woman as womb – uncontainable and abjectly excessive (see Showalter 1981, de Lauretis 1987)? As Elizabeth Stephens (2014: 188) reminds us in her appraisal of Irigaray's matters, 'feminine materiality and biology are not simply or unproblematically a source of difference or resistance; they are also the rationale for women's historical silencing and exclusion'. For this reason, any celebration of bodily matters needs to consider carefully the histories that it inadvertently repeats. Serious engagements with Irigaray's work have mostly come to reject reading her attention to female bodily morphology as naive biological essentialism whereby women are defined by their anatomies,[4] but this does not mean any kind of consensus about how best to conceptualize her project has been reached. Some have suggested, for example, that the use of female bodily morphology in Irigaray is instead a clever rhetorical strategy, that is, either synecdoche or catachresis that does not *really* equate woman with her anatomy (see Gallop 1988), or similarly, as a 'strategic essentialism' (see Whitford 1991; Braidotti 2003; Butler 1993) that offers a resymbolization of the female body, as a 'tactical intervention' (see Lorraine 1999: 93). These readings of Irigaray certainly do not deny that the materiality of feminine bodies matters, yet the mattering of that matter is still not fully accounted for. In calling attention to women's material bodily difference as primarily rhetorical, strategic or tactical, it seems that these readings acknowledge the difference of feminine embodiment only reluctantly, for effect, without true commitment. Relegated to such a position, how can materiality be fully embraced as a teacher and a guide?

Another way of rejecting a biological reductionism in Irigaray has been to focus on her invocations of 'woman to come' and to read these through a Deleuzian framework of virtuality.[5] Despite Irigaray's rejection of Deleuzian thought, there is a strong resonance between her descriptions of feminine embodiment and Deleuze's concept of the virtual.[6] We recall that virtuality is not a wide open 'anything goes', but rather the cloud of indetermination that hovers around an actualized body (Deleuze and Parnet 2002: 148; see chapter 1). For some commentators, this is the way in which Irigaray figures 'woman'.[7] For Irigaray, 'woman' means both woman as we know her and woman in her potentiality. Even as virtual, however, Irigaray's woman is still connected to her fleshy matter, where that virtuality inheres in woman's specific material embodiment. We see such an understanding of woman, for example, in Irigaray's (1985b: 120) insistence that the question 'what is a woman?' cannot be answered, even if we can describe or map her current situation.

These Deleuzian inflections help shift our understanding of Irigaray's project towards a more posthuman reading, but the real, lived matter of Irigaray's bodies still requires an adequate account. Some suggest accounting for this materialization demands rethinking what we mean by essentialism. This is partly what Alison Stone (2003, 2006) is up to in her appraisal of Irigaray's 'realist essentialism', while Helen Fielding (2000) and Gail Weiss (1999), each in her own way, suggests that essentialism, when read through the phenomenological experience of the body, posits a female body or morphology that is far from determinate, stable or reductively biologized; the open-ended becoming-ness of bodies, in other words, does not have to contradict their matter. Kirby (1997: 69–81) expresses a similar dissatisfaction with the dualistic treatment of material bodies in commentaries on Irigaray's work, while Braidotti (2002) and Grosz (2004, 2005) both find in her writing a strong resonance with process ontologies of becoming, and a productive elaboration of sexuate difference as an engine for the material proliferation of life-in-the-plural. In a particularly prescient early commentary, Margrit Shildrick (1997) notes that a key element of Irigaray's strategy is dismantling the nature/culture dichotomy 'that positions the biological as static, ahistorical and determinate, and culture as representative of development and change'. Shildrick continues: 'Against the convention, what her work stresses consistently is that culture also demands – indeed, depends on – constant repetition and sameness, while the biological is inherently interactive and dynamic' (177). Many other commentaries have taken on and explored Irigaray's notion of the 'sensible transcendental' to suggest that unlike other posthuman theories of immanence, Irigaray eschews abstraction and remains committed to lived experience (see Haynes 2012). And, as Rachel Jones (2011) comprehensively elaborates, the key to understanding the ways in which Irigaray's matters are not just naive biologism lies in her insistence on the term 'sexuate' – a deliberate blurring of the binaries of mind/body and nature/culture. On Jones's reading, 'sexuate difference...articulates both nature and culture, and the relations between them' (6). In short, the biological is also always semiotic – inscribed and inscripting.

I will return to pick up on the implications of many of these readings throughout this chapter. In the meantime, the point is that all of these readings reject matter in Irigaray as inert, or deterministic – yet nonetheless hold that it is 'real'. While themselves emerging from a variety of theoretical orientations, these conversations collectively offer a provocative way to think through Irigaray's bodies that doesn't sidestep the matter of its matter.[8]

Irigaray's writings predate feminist posthumanism or new materialisms as named theoretical orientations,[9] yet the above readings of her work also anticipate these more recent feminist theoretical frames. They place Irigaray convincingly within the (multivalent and transversal) genealogies of posthuman and new materialist feminisms,[10] which are emerging as another way of interpreting Irigaray's work within some new scholarship (see Stephens 2014; Parker 2015; Jones 2011, 2015). Making these connections reminds us of the thick temporal foldings of feminist thinking and acknowledges the debts that the proclaimed 'new-ness' of these theoretical orientations can sometimes paper over. Reading Irigaray through posthumanism and new materialism can thus potentially inflect a genealogy of posthumanism with an important feminist difference, but also give us helpful theoretical scaffolds for explaining Irigaray's relation to matter. Instead of falling back on dichotomous positions (essentialist *or* constructivist; biologically reductive *or* virtually to-come), we can read Irigaray's work as prefiguring matter as dynamic and facilitative, while still attentive to semiotic systems of power. The being and becoming of bodies in her work – lips that touch, placentas that welcome, breath that connects – could be understood in Barad's terms of matter's 'agential realism' or Bennett's 'vibrancy'. Matter, in other words, is engaged in both 'bringing new things into the world' and the 'reconfiguring of that world' (Barad 2007: 170); it is hardly the 'dead or thoroughly instrumentalized' (Bennett 2010: ix) stuff we might imagine it to be. (After all, it is Irigaray [1985b: 115] who first laments that 'certain properties of the 'vital' have been deadened into the 'constancy' required to give it form'.) Alongside the more recent work of Vicki Kirby (2013) and Elizabeth A. Wilson (2008), Irigaray posits embodied matters as problem-solving and responsive, where their engagement in a body's becomings is never teleological or deterministic, but like the 'woman' Irigaray interpellates in her work, is always still 'to come'.

Again, this doesn't mean that matter (for Irigaray, or in the world at large) can do or be anything. Specific matters gather their own chemical, physical, and biological properties that limit the ways they can act in the world at a given time, or become as and with other kinds of bodies. Similarly, the cultural meaning of woman is not arbitrary; it tends towards certain engagements and unfoldings that are in part oriented by woman's specific embodied matters, such as the genital lips or the placenta. But crucially, this meaning is neither locked nor fixed. (A penis is not a vulva, but in a nice paraphrase of Spinoza, we still don't fully know what either can do. Moreover, as trans* embodiment demonstrates, nor is the link between woman and placenta, or even vulva, a foregone imperative, even if this connection is a *tendency* in our contemporary moment that meaningfully participates in securing a particular symbolic order.[11]) This indeterminacy is not a problem for Irigaray, but precisely an engine for her theory of difference and differenciating becoming. It is precisely because of the open possibilities afforded by this specific biological matter (e.g. the placenta's gestation of life-in-the-plural; the erogenous flesh that enables woman to 'touch herself all the time' [Irigaray 1985b: 24]) that woman remains ultimately unknowable. In short, the matter of the body is not a static trap but an opportunity and a generative force.

Reading Irigaray's matters through a posthuman or new materialist ontological orientation begins to untangle some of the problematic ways in which her work has been received. On such a reading, matter and meaning can be understood as always entangled – emerging from a persistent mangle of ideas and material properties, both of which exert limits and neither of which can tell the whole story alone. Here, materiality is not essentialized, but as Irigaray (1985b: 51) herself insists, '*Matter* ... [is] what always begins anew to nourish speculation, what functions as the *resource* of reflection' but also as its 'waste' or 'discard'. Matter is what makes thinking possible, but is too often then quickly forgotten, or reduced to instrumentalized resource or finite facticity.

I wonder, though, if we can push our interpretation further still. What if we read Irigaray as practising a kind of *feminist posthuman phenomenology?* That is, what if we understand Irigaray as a posthuman phenomenologist, whose theoretical and methodological orientations are not unlike the trajectories I describe in Chapter 1? To understand her, first, as phenomenologist is not a stretch: like Maurice Merleau-Ponty (whom I discuss in the previous chapter as a key precursor for posthuman phenomenology), Irigaray insists that our bodies are our best teachers in terms of finding the means for scraping away at this sediment. She tells us, for example, that 'our body, right here, right now, gives us a very different certainty. Truth is necessary for those who are so distanced from their body that they have forgotten it' (Irigaray 1985b: 214). She insists that one 'pay attention' to oneself, 'without letting convention, or habit, distract you' (1985b: 206), and that this requires 'a certain recourse … to the phenomenological method' (Irigaray 2000: 156). Moreover, it is 'a cultivation of our sensory perceptions with a view to paying a greater respect to the world and to the other(s)' that provides the methodological orientation for an ecological ethics and ethics of sexuate difference (Irigaray 2015: 102). As Alison Stone (2015: 117, 118) points out, Irigaray 'returns to the world' in a kind of 'everyday realism' (2015: 117, 118) – a key premise for an embodied phenomenology like Merleau Ponty's – and that this return demands our perception as specifically *bodily* beings. Stone, too, makes explicit the resonance between Irigaray and Merleau-Ponty and suggests that as phenomenological, their work depends upon an entanglement of perceiving bodies and contextual worlds, both dependent on one another: 'To perceive things and the world', explains Stone (2015: 119), 'is to apprehend them through the sense that we have only as embodied beings, while, being embodied, we are inescapably located within the world.'

But if we are to take on board the above understandings of Irigaray's matters as aligning with posthumanism, and if, as our own bodily waters suggest to us, we understand bodies in a posthuman vein, then any descriptions of them and by them should also strive to push beyond the borders of humanism. In other words, to accept Irigaray as phenomenologist also demands that we affirm a posthuman understanding of embodiment. And – as I hope will become clear – if Irigaray is a phenomenologist, then she makes the case for posthuman embodiment all the more strong: bodies are not only beings but intra-active becomings, and any essential qualities and boundaries that we might ascribe to them are always provisional and open to revision. Bodies will always exceed what they 'are', across time, space, and species.

My aim here is not to classify Irigaray 'once and for all', or to find the 'right' way to read her. Rather, I am interested in how considering her in these terms can both activate a different kind of phenomenology and also insist on a kind of posthumanism that is necessarily embodied, sensible, and lived. My parallel objective is of course to see if reading Irigaray in this way can also help us better imagine and understand our own posthuman embodiment as not only virtual, becoming, or materially intra-active in general; I also want to see what this can teach us about living as watery bodies in a watery world. Given that we humans are composed mostly of water, it seems imperative to ask how our theories of embodiment might foster (or hinder) care, concern, and responsibility towards the diverse planetary bodies of water that sustain us.

We'll get to all this. But first, we might slip into these questions by noting that Irigaray's phenomenologies are also elemental conversations – and thus already pushing beyond humanist understandings of embodiment. Irigaray's attention to matter is not limited to the human body; she is also explicitly interested in elemental phenomena – such as air and breath, the earth, fire, water, and the sea.[12] Irigaray not only provides deep descriptions of the way our bodies are in the world, but at the same time follows the rhizomes that travel between and through the phenomena she describes. Thus, she accounts for our bodily extensions into – and their indebtedness to – other bodies. As bodies of porosity, we are constantly interpermeating our surroundings. Irigaray's (1992: 39) is 'a body of air filled by palpitating blue', 'eating the sun' (43); a body 'animated throughout' and 'changed by a cloud' (99); a body that is an 'atmosphere of flesh' (24). In these ways, we can begin to see Irigaray's phenomenology as also an ecological and elemental one.

In some instances, these connections of our human bodies with other natural bodies do indeed seem metaphorical – that is, descriptions of the way that the sexuate difference of bodies is mirrored in (rather than contiguous with) the nature of weather, plants, and animals (see Stone 2003, 2006). Yet crucially, the language Irigaray deploys always remains connected to the materiality of the phenomena she describes. Take breathing, for example. When Irigaray (2002a: 80) suggests that woman engenders with her breath and shares her breath even before she shares the nourishment of her body, this is a true description of some women's bodily experience, even as Irigaray's prose opens to a broader metaphorical or metonymical significance.

As always more than metaphorical, we can trace in Irigaray's work a contiguity or continuity (rather than analogy) with the elemental. She writes that 'we are made up of these elements [air, water, fire, and earth] and we live them' (Irigaray 1993b: 57); she reminds us that the gift of breath comes not only from human bodies but from vegetable bodies as well (Irigaray 2002a: 51). As elemental bodies, human bodies drink the rain and feel the drought; the winds that bend tree branches strengthen and make supple our own swaying spines; the warmth of the sun encourages our growth, as it does algae on a pond's surface, or seeds germinating in the soil. In other words, we might more accurately say that Irigaray's attention to bodily matters is *also* an attunement to the matter of our elemental milieus.

Between Irigaray's attention to the elemental, on the one hand, and her concern for the distinctly feminine morphological body, on the other, a certain slippage emerges. The image of mucus, for example, can be mapped both according to a female morphology and a mechanics of elemental fluids, while the air that masculinist philosophy forgets is both an elemental milieu and the fuel of human lung-power. Her descriptions of fleshy human corporeality in terms of 'elemental passions' can be read as an extended material metaphor that is effective precisely because our physiological reality is intimately connected to a meteorological and geophysical one. To use posthuman feminist theorist Stacy Alaimo's (2010: 2) term, Irigaray's phenomenology of embodiment is thus fundamentally *transcorporeal*, where 'the substance of the human is ultimately inseparable from "the environment"'. By describing bodies in these terms, Irigaray's phenomenology becomes posthuman, as the bodies we live are porous and reciprocally indebted. Human embodiment is always more-than-human too: we are imbricated with elemental and environmental matters in relations of contiguity and belonging, rather than hierarchy.

Within a feminist posthumanism, however, transcorporeality is never 'merely' a matter of physical or chemical exchange. Gathering up feminist theoretical insights on embodiment across decades, we know that matter is never 'just' brute matter; when matters of the body overlap with and transit through a more expansive elemental milieu, this transcorporeality is also a semiotic and symbolic one. Meanings ebb and flow, gather and disperse. Matters organize along, align with and push against vectors of power and subjectification that are also embodied. Matters remain hybrid mixtures of world and word. In short, this would mean that any posthuman phenomenology of embodiment that acknowledges the transit of matters between human and more-than-human bodies would also need to account for the flows of significance, too. We might ask: what kinds of ethics and politics, alliances and relationalities, are materialized in these transcorporeal tangles of embodiment? What might acknowledging these transits as a mode of living our elemental embodiment open or invite, in terms of our relationships to different kinds of bodies? And, if we already recognize that water is both common and intricately different, how does Irigaray help us parse these material meanings?

My suggestion is thus to turn to Irigaray's phenomenologies of watery embodiment more specifically to see what they might teach us about the logics of difference and connection – across materially but also socially, culturally and otherwise situated bodies. An ineradicable alterity that is also sustained and gestated by an aqueous commonality is, I propose, what rethinking Irigaray's bodies of water can help us to imagine.

Love letters to watery others: *Marine Lover of Friedrich Nietzsche*

A key element of Irigaray's descriptions of both the elemental and the bodily-morphological is the notion of fluidity. Arguably, fluidity is the clearest way in which Irigaray fuses her elemental philosophy and philosophy of sexual difference into a cogent theoretical position. Some commentators thus focus on the seeming dichotomy that Irigaray installs between the fluid feminine and the static, solidified masculine (see Caldwell 2002; Olkowski 2000). This attention is hardly surprising, as Irigaray's writings on fluidity certainly gesture in this direction. For example, in 'The Mechanics of Fluids', Irigaray's (1985b: 112) focus is on the 'flowing' and 'fluctuating' woman, while in other texts, she accentuates the feminine who describes her body as 'fluid and ever mobile', and 'secreting a flow' (1992: 25, 15). For Irigaray, feminine bodies are fluid, both figuratively in their non-subsumability into a masculine paradigm, and literally in their genital mucosity, their placental interchanges, and their amniotic flows. This leakiness is what makes woman always a woman-to-come. The feminine cannot be known as feminine (as sexuate difference) within a phallogocentric logic because this logic is predicated on rigid and static forms, solid truth and knowable entities. Because the real properties of fluids cannot be accommodated within phallogocentrism, neither can the (virtual) reality of women and the feminine.

The 'fluid feminine' is not, however, a source to be uncritically celebrated. As Elizabeth Stephens (2014: 193) points out, for Irigaray, fluidity as an aspect of feminine biology is also 'the very category by which the exclusion of the feminine is effected'; that is, it is the same phallogocentric logic that labels women as unruly and uncontainable. Yet at the same time as the fluidity of the feminine keeps women outside of hegemonic ontology, this fluidity is also what we need to embrace, posits Irigaray, if we are going to move towards a future of sexuate difference that serves as a mutually loving and respectful source of fecundity, creativity, and support for both the masculine and the feminine. Moreover, while the fluid passing between the two sides (two lips) of the woman engenders her continual becoming, this passage of fluid between 'me' (feminine) and 'you' (masculine) is also crucial for the mutual sustenance of both[13] sexes (1992: 15). The fluid can engender positive sexuate difference and hold the masculine and the feminine in a respectful relationship that evades comparison and subordination. Subsequently, if a fruitful and fecund relation of sexuate difference depends on fluidity, clearly the fluid must also have a distinct relation to the masculine. Sexuate difference according to Irigaray's own logic cannot be cultivated by women alone, because the very basis of this difference is a positive (rather than comparative or subordinating) relation between others.

This brief introduction to Irigaray's fluids highlights two key things: first, the material and the semiotic are always intimately imbricated; and second, the relationship between fluidity and sexuate difference is not … cut and dry. The ways in which materiality works with, athwart, against and through meaning-making, are more complicated than saying we all just need to 'go with the flow'. Simply focusing on the relation between fluidity and the feminine is not enough; we also have the challenge of acknowledging both a feminine material fluidity and a masculine one, but also of accounting for the difference of a feminine fluidity without reifying the ways in which the fluid underwrites exclusion.

One way to begin parsing this complexity is to switch focus from fluidity to *water*. While these two ideas can easily be (and often are) elided, they are not synonyms. For some critics, fluidity is a quality that encompasses the whole of Irigaray's ouevre – a way of thinking elementality more generally, as a material-semiotic philosophical proposition (see Stone 2015). To think Irigaray with water, however, demands a more vigilant attention not only to the materiality of bodies, but to the ways in which these bodies comprise an elemental-environmental hydrocommons. In other words, I am more interested in water as materiality, than in fluid as a property. Water, as we know, is a shape-shifter – moving from solid to liquid and gas, and taking up residence in and as bodies of all kinds. Water is undoubtedly related to the fluid, but as the materialization of an abstract property, it allows us to think the mattering of this matter in more specific and situated ways – in terms of the bodies it animates, the operations it makes possible, and the limits it encounters. We can begin this exploration by diving into Irigaray's (1991) immemorial waters in *Marine Lover of Friedrich Nietzsche*.

Marine Lover is an 'amorous dialogue' between the textual avatars (presumably) of Irigaray and Nietzsche. In it, Irigaray illuminates how Nietzsche's concept of the eternal return betrays a fear and disavowal of the watery element to which his birth is nonetheless indebted. As a result, Nietzsche's eternal return will never be able to return difference *as* difference. On Irigaray's reading, Nietzsche tethers himself to a desiccated future of the self-same, where death and entropy are the only outcomes.[14]

Such are the themes aswim in this most aqueous text of desire and disavowal. But waters in this text flow multivalently, with various depths and registers. Perhaps most obviously, water is used in this text as a way of situating multiple 'feminines'. In *Marine Lover*, we encounter women as beings-in-the-present, but we also encounter a woman-in-the-future, whom we do not yet know and who is 'still to come'. In other words, the text describes both an actual woman – that is, the specular woman of Nietzsche's eternal return who is refused admittance into his 'echonomy' (Lorraine 1999: 66) – and a virtual woman – the woman demanding a different potentiality than the possibility offered to her by the eternal return of the self-same. Alongside these two feminines we also encounter some sense of a 'first woman', a maternal primordial feminine who engenders and gestates both the actual and the virtual. In Irigaray's original French text, of course, this connection is highlighted by the homonymic relation between 'mer' (sea) and 'mère' (mother). This multiple-woman is then diffracted through the multiple ways in which the fluid, water, and the sea figure in *Marine Lover,* as these move between descriptions of waters that are feminine, waters in which the feminine lives, and womb-like waters both feminine and maternal. The feminine is the rapturous sea that moves about endlessly (Irigaray 1991: 13); she is the maternal waters out of which the Overman and the masculine are born, and whose depths they now fear (52, 67), yet she is also the fluid woman whom man uses, unacknowledged, for sustenance, and whom he attempts to solidify in his image. So, on the one hand, we see how Irigaray uses water to mark off the qualitative difference of the feminine – even in her own differing. While in man's world, 'it is always hot, dry and hard' (13), the feminine sea is multiple, flowing, gestating, and sustaining.[15]

Yet, on the other hand, while these waters seem mostly feminine, the masculine is aqueous too, even in his fearful forgetfulness. In these pages we glimpse how the masculine variously emerges from the water, is afraid of and repulsed by the water, depends physiologically upon water, and is returned to the water. While clearly the masculine comes from and is indebted to the forgotten sea/the fluid feminine, no clear moment of separation of the masculine from his immemorial waters, and no clear renunciation of his watery beginnings, is offered. The masculine returns to the sea too; as phallogocentric fisherman (48), as a drowning man engulfed by waters he cannot escape (66–67), as a swimmer-to-come once he stops resisting the current (37). The sea is both danger and saviour, a threat and a buoy. And to complicate the watery figuration further, the narrator describes the masculine as not only *in,* but *of* water, too. She acknowledges the saliva in his mouth that enables him to speak, even as it/she is forgotten once speech is underway (37), and asks, 'where have you drawn what flows out of you?' (38). In other words, while it is the sea to which the masculine must return for sustenance, this sustenance not only immerses him, but permeates him as well, an incorporated and intimate aspect of his bodily being. Even when he would prefer to 'freeze rather than flow' (33), the watery element is still a part of the masculine, despite its tendency to solidification.[16]

And how could it not be? As a phenomenologist, Irigaray describes our bodily waters as lived. The masculine, too, experiences embodiment as a composition of blood, bile, tears, saliva, perspiration, ejaculate, urine, and breathy vapour. The masculine, too, flows with and interpermeates the elements.[17] No matter what disavowal is enacted, water comprises and is required of all biological bodies. Water is necessary for maintaining our cell structure, for facilitating necessary chemical reactions in the body, for physically transporting nutrients and oxygen through the body, and for enabling waste elimination. We drink, we move, we urinate, salivate, ejaculate, perspire; intake, movement, output.[18] Whether masculine or feminine, we are all in debt to this water, for it is only because of it that we move, we grow, we live, we have a body at all. Irigaray's descriptions subtly remind us of these material necessities.

As posthuman phenomenologist, Irigaray is also interested in the symbolic economies of these waters, and their latent potentiality. Similar to her remarks in 'Mechanics of Fluids', where Irigaray (1985b: 113) considers the fluid potentiality of sperm that has been coopted and reified in a logic of solids, in *Marine Lover* her descriptions of a frozen and solidified masculine implicitly ponder the masculine's fluidity-in-the-future: What might water mean for the ethical and political potentiality of the masculine, Irigaray leads us to wonder, if it were acknowledged and mobilized rather than disavowed and feared? In short, while Irigaray's references to the watery masculine in *Marine Lover* are not as prominent as the connection of the fluid to the feminine, and while we must, following Irigaray, always pay attention to the *difference* of feminine and masculine waters, it is clearly not only the feminine that is caught up in these watery currents. While what Irigaray's interlocutor thinks he fears is drowning, Irigaray reminds him – quietly, almost imperceptibly – that what he should really fear is thirst.

Such thirst, Irigaray moreover suggests, can only be slaked through a meeting of the sexually different. 'Between you and me, me and you', *Marine Lover's* narrator hence laments, 'you want me to make a dam' (Irigaray 1991: 56). This dam would halt the flow of water between the masculine and feminine, the flow that is vital, Irigaray suggests, both for the maintenance of sexuate difference in a respectful relation and also for the continued fecundity, development and growth of both. Sexuate difference needs to be facilitated, gestated by this watery transit. This alerts us to a third way in which *Marine Lover* mobilizes the aqueous: water is also productive of difference. Water, we could say, *gestates* difference. For Irigaray, not only are the masculine *and* the feminine both of water, but water also comprises the watery gestational element that conditions these sexually different beings in the first place. This third aspect of watery embodiment – as productive of difference – is especially alive in Irigaray's descriptions of the sea. In *Marine Lover*, the sea engenders both the feminine and the masculine; out of the sea they both emerge.

Of course, this 'third' body of water – the gestational – is thus not exactly a 'third', for it distinctly overlaps with the feminine fluid and comprises one of the manifestations of feminine waters which we encountered above. Might Irigaray be asking us to consider our bodies' watery origins as both maternal womb and watery element more generally?[19] This connection is most helpfully explored through the way in which both the sea and the maternal womb are described by Irigaray as abyssal, unknowable depths, a bottom that 'has never been sounded' (60–61). Irigaray, for example, asks her interlocutor in *Marine Lover* whether his 'most dangerous beyond' is not in fact 'the unexplored reaches of the farthest ocean' (38). These unknowable depths are also 'that dark home where you began to be' (57).

While on the one hand this unknowability gestures towards the 'mystery' (40) or inability of a masculinist philosophy to contain or definitively represent the feminine, it also references the resistance of oceanic abyssal depths to full representation. Our watery beginnings – maternal or planetary – will never be fully or definitively revealed. As Irigaray writes elsewhere, we do not *see* our first beginnings in our maternal amniotic habitat,[20] and the moment at which this watery world passes from the realm of the concealed to the realm of the revealed for us will always be ambiguous. Even in an age of new digital imaging and obstetrical technologies, 'the origin' is always just a matter of telling the story one way, rather than another. All of our apparatuses of knowledge[21] – our new technologies, but also our cultural or religious inheritances, our languages, our sensitive guts, and our delicate hearts – will select and enact separations between one body and the next, but the precise moment of passage remains obfuscated. And, like the maternal abyss, the sea is also a kind of mystery that can never be definitely captured by any apparatus of knowledge. The deepest reaches of the Pacific in their darkness, in their inaccessibility, are less known to us than the moon. Even recent footage of these depths gathered in bionic submersibles can only illuminate with their spotlights one small patch of this darkness at a time. What could stitching these moments together in some ocular patchwork reveal? Again, nothing definitive; as the next moment is revealed, the previous one is already becoming different. Over 60 per cent of the earth is covered by ocean more than a mile deep, which makes it by far the largest habitat on earth; yet, what lies beneath the surface of our oceans remains largely unknown.

A material feminine womb thus reverberates in and with the unknowability of planetary waters more generally. In this unknowability, the potential for difference and the birth of difference lies latent. This, Irigaray tells us, is Nietzsche's oversight. Yet, to conclude our reading of *Marine Lover* here – with waters that are both feminine and gestational – might be too hasty. Doesn't this just retie a phenomenology of watery bodies to the feminine, and to a reprosexual feminine womb at that? Charges of biological essentialism seep slowly back in. What happened to the potential of masculine waters? What of the waters in-between? As I've already suggested, the slippage between the feminine maternal womb and the sea more generally might be about *more than the actual feminine-maternal*. To move beyond a biological or essentialist reductionism, however, requires a posthuman, transcorporeal reading of this relation.

In the first place, this means paying attention to how the gestational in *Marine Lover* is not simply overlaid upon the maternal-feminine as either perfect coincidence or convenient analogy. These maternal origins are rather *contiguous* with deeper and wider seas. If we were to trace a genealogy of our own gestation, it would have no definitive starting point, no clear beginning of beginnings. The waters that gestate one body have come from other bodies, gestated by earlier waters, gestated by waters that precede those. Aqueous origins are diffuse and multiple. As such, gestation cannot be reduced to a single instance in an actualized female womb. Although Irigaray makes clear in *Marine Lover* (and elsewhere) the undeniable relation between the maternal and the gestational, the sea is not simply a metaphor for the female mother or the womb; it has also provided the womb's very condition of possibility, and continues to leak into our human wombs, in various extended traces. This phenomenological realization is accounted for by environmental activist Sandra Steingraber, who muses about her own amniocentesis procedure: 'I drink water and it becomes blood plasma... Before it is drinking water, amniotic fluid is the creeks and rivers that fill reservoirs... The blood of cows and chickens is in this tube. The nectar gathered by bees and hummingbirds is in this tube. Whatever is inside the hummingbird eggs is also inside my womb' (Steingraber quoted in Alaimo 2010: 104). These insights are implicit in Irigaray's own descriptions of our immemorial waters.

Moving beyond a naïve biologism also means more deeply considering the implications of the unknowability that Irigaray describes in relation to both maternal and planetary seas, and the difference these watery bodies gestate. Near the end of her love letter, Irigaray rhetorically asks, 'Where does difference begin? Where is it (elle)? Where am I? ... How can one master that dark place where you find birth? Where you begin to be' (67). With these questions (and tellingly, the last one is an affirmation rather than a query), Irigaray reminds us that difference begins in the sea: I (the feminine) begin in the sea; you (the masculine) begin in the sea; and difference/it (elle) also begins in the sea. Irigaray thus seems to be suggesting that while the gestational is feminine, the copula in this formulation does not invoke a reciprocal symmetry; the gestational is more (and perhaps less) than the many manifestations of the feminine that Irigaray describes. And this observation in turn brings us back to the flows of water between the feminine and masculine traced already above. Irigaray (1993a: 5, 1993b: 15, 2002b: 128) insists repeatedly that the fecundity of gestation is not limited simply to the moment of birth, but is rather an ongoing regeneration. This is why, as cited above, the narrator of *Marine Lover* laments the move to erect a dam between 'me' and 'you': the gestational, remember, is also a connecting flow between the sexes which ensures their mutual sustenance and proliferation.

Could it be, then, that through her descriptions of our bodies of water in *Marine Lover*, Irigaray queers the simple relations between the feminine and the fluid that are too easily extrapolated from her work? Irigaray invites us here to think more deeply about these bodies, their difference in relation to their interconnectedness, and their gestational capacities alongside the obfuscation of any definitive origin or starting point. We are furthermore invited to consider how water is the element that crucially underpins these relations: as we are created and gestate in an amniotic sac, nutrients are delivered to us by water that enables us to grow. Our waste is removed by similar waterways, and we are protected from external harm by our amniotic waters, waters that are not disembodied or neutral but are themselves in a body of water, a body that is specifically a maternal one.[22] How is our experience outside of our amniotic beginnings any different? Water continues to be our buffer, our vital conduit, our solvent, our gestational medium. The maternal waters in which we as bodies are created and nurtured are a part of the greater element of water which continues to sustain us, protect us, and nurture us, both intra- and intercorporeally, after we emerge from these wombs. We might understand this passage as one from a smaller womb to a larger one, or from one tiny sea to a greater one. Yet this is a passage of neither severance nor separation, but rather one of diffusion, evaporation, condensation, incorporation … We are created in water, we gestate in water, we are born into an atmosphere of the same water although more diffuse, we take in water, we harbour it, it sustains and protects us, it leaves us … at the same time as we are always, to some extent, in it. The passage from body of water to body of water (always *as* body of water) is never synecdochal or metaphoric; it is radically material. These complex and shared cyclings – body, to body, to body – comprise our planetary hydrocommons.

Gestationality is a watery key. We have used it to untie waters from a limited biological/symbolic feminine. My next proposal is that we can turn it further still, to unlock a reading of sexuate difference that is not only released from a heteronormative binaristic view of bodies, but which also opens to something generatively posthuman. Turning with this posthuman turn, however, requires first a stronger scaffold for elaborating water's queer logic of difference and repetition, and its connection to sexuate difference.

Gestationality as (sexuate) difference and repetition

For Irigaray, difference begins in the gestational watery elemental. But our bodies of water also tell us that this 'beginning' is already always part of overlapping and interconnected cycles of repetition: we know that water on the earth is finite. Except for perhaps some minute amounts of vapour that may enter our atmosphere from the cosmos, all the water that is here, on, in and hovering above our planet, has always been here. *Each watery singularity has been somewhere, sometime before.* Yet, while the water that moves through these cycles is always 'the same', it is by no means undifferentiated. What repeats is always difference.

That this suggestion of the difference and repetition of our bodies of water should emerge from a reading of Irigaray's love letter to Nietzsche is hardly surprising. *Marine Lover* expounds a critique of Nietzsche's concept of the eternal return, whereby in his elision of the feminine, the masculine philosopher enacts a forgetting of where he comes from and his own conditions of possibility. As a result, all that can return is the self-same.[23] Irigaray instead calls us to remember our gestational waters – a gestationality that is enacted through a repetition of waters that engenders difference. We could say what she articulates is the repetition of difference.

However, read alongside Irigaray's philosophical commitments to the unknowability of the feminine body – that is, its perpetual yet-to-come – the entire notion that difference could *repeat* as anything other than 'itself' may seem jarring. Does not the very notion of unknowability suggest something that has never been before, something unfamiliar and surprising? And does not repetition suggest the return of the same? Certainly, this would be a commonplace understanding of repetition according to representational logic: repetition re-presents, re-capitulates, re-states. The same old story, over and over again. This is precisely the 're-turn' that Irigaray criticizes in Nietzsche. My proposal for thinking with this seeming incompossibility is to return to Deleuze. I noted above that despite Irigaray's own rejection of a Deleuzian mode of thinking, the concept of Deleuzian virtuality is a helpful way to understand her figuration of woman, and for understanding the way that materiality can also gather latent possibility – even unknowability. Here, I suggest that Deleuze's own explicit challenge to the logic of representation in his theory of difference and repetition can also help us make sense of Irigaray's gestational waters.

In the first place it is worth noting that Deleuze's theory of difference and repetition is heavily indebted to his reading of Nietzsche's eternal return (see Deleuze 1994, 2002). According to Deleuze, the eternal return is a question of selection among differences. The eternal return is a dissolution of identity and representation and instead is the affirmation of difference. Freed from representational logic, the only thing that can truly return is the will to power, or the force of differentiation. Deleuze takes these primary ideas from Nietzsche. Building on them, he shows us how through distribution and temporal displacement, difference is all that could ever truly repeat.

Repetition produces a spatial and temporal force of differing-from-itself (e.g. Deleuze 1994: 220), whereby differenciation – that is, an internal, intensive force of differing – can emerge.[24] This leads directly to Deleuze's (1994: xiv, 28–29) challenge of our commonplace understanding of difference, which we normally posit in terms of an original that would provide the basis for what is (oppositionally, analogically, comparatively) different. Just as our common understanding of 'bare repetition' leads us to conceptualize repetition primarily in terms of the identical (or: what repeats is the 'same', only at a different time, perhaps in a different place), difference is only ever thought secondarily and negatively as a 'not-this'. Deleuze challenges us instead to think difference *in itself* by ungrounding the notion of the privileged model that would mediate difference. Through repetition, difference is selected and distributed, again, always differing from itself. Accordingly, there is nothing that unifies 'the different' except its repetition or force of *becoming* or capacity to produce (28, 41). For Deleuze, then, the eternal return is necessarily the eternal return of the different (41–42; 241–244).

In Deleuze's terms, the hydrological cycle we described as multiple in terms of its embodied strata (the maternal amniotic waters, the waters within the gestating body, the waters that intercorporeally sustain the body, the waters that extracorporeally nourish the body, and so on) might be understood as a 'system of simulacra'. Deleuze (1994: 278) describes such systems as constituent of series that communicate through their differences, and display linkages and internal resonances: 'none is either opposed or analogous to another. Each is constituted by differences, and communicates with the others through differences of differences'. Among these various series, because there is no original that enjoys a privilege over others (278), origin remains an open question, since 'the sole origin is difference' (125). In terms of water, then, these moments or expressions of water (what gestates us, what sustains us, what surrounds and connects us) all coexist. The movement of water holds the *was*, *is*, and *yet-to-come* together in its materiality. This means we can understand water as not only engendering difference (as the gestational 'was') but also as its expression (the gestated 'is') and its potential (the unknowable 'yet-to-come').

Because a differentiating movement is always at work, water's continually unfolding embodiments as expressions of water's 'eternal return' are hardly instantiations of 'the self-same'. Water takes up singular expressions: evaporation, condensation, precipitation, transpiration; the water I drink, the water that carries nutrients to my foetal body, the water that cushions my body as I bump into a chair, the water that protects the body within my body (which in itself is its own singular body of water); the water we excrete and expel, and which returns, always differing, becoming different, to other strata – ebbing, dripping, raining, flushing. As mentioned, our planet produces no water in addition to that which was always already here, yet it is not in spite of, but rather because of, water's closed system that the difference of water continues to generate itself, to differenc/tiate itself. At the same time, however, it is only the *actuality* of water that is a 'closed system'. Because of water's latent virtual dimension, the potentiality of water's expressions can never be fully known; because water is always becoming (drawing on its latent virtual potential), it is always seeking out differentiation. As much as it may repeat the morphological blueprint, genomic pattern, or chemical structure of its 'parent', every gestated body of water is a unique iteration. This difference implies the radical unknowability of the 'not yet'. In this sense, water is always an 'open system' as well.[25] And let there be no mistake about this differentiation: our own lived experiences as human and more-than-human bodies remind us at every turn how my womb is different, how your tears are different, how the Pacific ocean, the mud on my shoes, the drops of fog that are collected by nets in the mountains of Chile to quench the thirst of bodies on her arid coastal plains – how all these waters are different. Even, or especially, as they repeat.

Despite their different appraisals of Nietzsche's eternal return, both Deleuze's and Irigaray's accounts of difference and repetition resonate in their rejection of representational logic and insistence on the creative force of repetition to produce something different – something yet to come and never fully knowable in advance. Yet, what Deleuze's theory at first glance seems to leave out is sexuate difference. Irigaray, however, figures this difference in relation to our bodies of water in three possible ways. To recap what we found in *Marine Lover*, sexuate difference might, first of all, manifest in the actualization of water bodies. For example, semen is not female mucus – neither in semiotic nor in physiological terms. Whereas feminine waters tend to flow and connect, masculine waters tend to freeze, harden, and evaporate. These qualities and processes, she argues, certainly link the sedimentation of phallogocentrism to the necessary disavowal of the feminine discussed above, but they are also grounded in materiality. As Irigaray describes, feminine genital mucous remains fluid in its continuous passage between her two lips; meanwhile masculine semen, if not passed on to another living body, becomes sticky until hard.

Feminine waters highlighted by Irigaray also include cyclical menstruation and amniotic waters. These point to the second possible way in which waters are for Irigaray sexually different, namely, in the maternal gestational waters of the feminine. As humans, our very becoming relies on water, but significantly, one specific singularization, one specific moment of water is needed for this: we require a watery gestational medium of the feminine-maternal that is not possible without sexual difference. Despite all of our new reproductive technologies, the elaboration of human life still requires a certain feminine water, a certain gestational medium.[26] As Irigaray reminds us, only because of sexual difference can our hydrological cycles of difference and repetition, at least in the human realm, continue.

A pause is called for here, before moving on to sexuate difference's third aspect. As various commentators have argued, Irigaray's work, particularly in its more recent articulations, can be understood as espousing a certain heterosexism and deepened reification of binaristic gender and sexuality. As she herself claims, an ethical relation of immanence calls for a triple dialectic: 'One for the male subject, one for the female subject, and one for their relationship as a couple or in a community' (Irigaray 1994: 39). Or: 'the most fundamental locus of irreducibility is between a man and a woman' (Irigaray 1996: 139).[27] Not only does this entrenchment provide little consideration of bodies that do not align simply with either of the gendered sexual poles that Irigaray presents, but Irigaray's position also treads upon dubious ground in concomitantly arguing for the primacy of sexual difference amongst other expressions of difference. In Irigaray's (2002a: 98) words, sexuate difference is 'insurmountable', and 'unsurpassable': again, 'the most universal and irreducible difference... is the one that exists between the genders'.[28] Given these important criticisms, how are we to understand the first two ways in which sexual difference might play out in relation to the difference and repetition of our bodies of water, outlined above? In highlighting how the feminine *differs from* the masculine fluid, and how one actualization of the feminine fluid – the maternal – requires specific attention, do not these two proposals also enact an entrenchment of sexual difference as binaristic, materially reified and comparative – thus propping up precisely the kind of dualistic thinking we're hoping water can help us dissolve? Even though, according to Irigaray, feminine waters hold a virtuality in respect to themselves (that is, they include a dimension of the 'yet-to-come'), the virtuality of masculine waters still requires affirmation within a theory of sexuate difference. But even more significantly, the virtuality *of sexuate difference itself* would appear on this understanding to have no place at all. Put simply, *sexuate difference itself*, in respect to the relation between the sexes, seems to be for Irigaray an actualized, sedimented relation through-and-through – a relation between the a priori poles of 'masculine' and 'feminine'.

I'm not hinting that a comparative difference of feminine and masculine has no political value. As Braidotti (2002) quite rightly points out, these kinds of differences still matter in our current social, political, economic, and cultural contexts, so to disembed any theory of sexual difference from such considerations (including the everyday misogynies and gender-based violences as which they can manifest) is absurd.[29] Moreover, in these same contexts where the labours of maternal bodies are still undervalued and denigrated, where these bodies are still and increasingly subject to marginalization and technologized colonialism, and where they still enact a profound material connection between a present life and a becoming life in an (as of yet) non-substitutable way, there is still reason to attend to the specificity of maternal bodies within a broader ethics of responsivity to other kinds of life.[30] In other words, I am unwilling to enact yet another effacement of the maternal, even if – as will become clear – I don't want to hold it up as the essentialized model of gestationality.

Still, while these two initial proposals of how sexuate difference might proliferate and repeat through Irigaray's bodies of water can be illuminating and are politically vital, these proposals are coming up against a critical limit, in the possible solidification *of sexuate difference itself*. So, unless we want to expunge questions of sexuate difference from a discussion of the political and ethical potential of all bodies of water, then we need *more* than a comparative analysis of the sexuate difference of bodies of water that holds the masculine and feminine infinitely apart. Our task: How might we think about the sexuate difference of our bodies of water beyond the dichotomous chasm that Irigaray's descriptions seem to suggest?

Again, I propose that the germ of such a way of thinking can be found in Irigaray's own posthuman phenomenological descriptions, even if some of her own pronouncements on sexual difference (particularly in her later work) seem to contravene this notion. Reading Irigaray alongside Deleuze, once more, can help not only acknowledge a theory of sexuate difference within watery embodiment, but in fact offer one that is decidedly posthuman, on a number of levels.[31] We can start by looking more closely at the idea of sexual reproduction. This will lead us to a third way in which difference can be configured as sexuate – thus both affirming Irigaray's insistence on sexuate difference and amplifying how this aspect is also nascent in Deleuze.

The feminine-maternal is required for the gestation of difference for the simple reason that as humans, in a biological sense we reproduce sexually. Our early experiences of gestation are within feminine-maternal waters, as Irigaray repeatedly describes. Sexual reproduction, it would therefore seem, is the repetition that engenders difference. But does sexual reproduction demand sexuate dualism? What if sexual reproduction were more inclusively thought of as the meeting of at least two bodies of difference in order to proliferate further life?[32] What if such reproduction were thought as gestationality – as the giving over of one's own materiality for this proliferation of further life, different to one's own?

Despite my suggestion that Deleuze's theory of difference and repetition eludes these questions, a closer look at his ideas on sexed reproduction provides some interesting possibilities along this line. In *Difference and Repetition*, Deleuze (1994a) links his conception of sexed reproduction to an explanation of embryology. On Deleuze's explication, the embryonic egg or larva is not a less-differentiated blob that becomes increasingly more differentiated as it progresses, but rather the egg is the virtual subject; the egg holds all the potential only a fraction of which will ever be actualized in the subject: 'Every embryo is a chimera, capable or functioning as a sketch and of living that which is unliveable for the adult of every species' (250); 'there are systematic vital movements, torsions and drifts, that only the embryo can sustain' (118). In other words, the virtual precedes the actual, and the virtual is always in excess of the actual, despite being materially tied to it. Because the egg is already part of the interpermeating cycles of difference and repetition, this egg is already differentiated. But – and this is the key point – as egg, sexual difference is at the threshold of the virtual. More accurately then, it is *both* differentiated (as an egg, as a body) *and also* still becoming differentiated – the source of latent potential and virtuality. The egg expresses a kind of material virtuality, condensed and intensified, within/as the actual. This is not the same as saying that the feminine is virtual, as is the masculine. Instead, it suggests that *sexual difference is itself virtual*. Sexuate difference, in this respect, is not only an accomplishment (as it can be, in the case of actualized, sexually different bodies), but perhaps more importantly is also *an always-yet-to-come*. To think *sexuate difference itself* as virtual does not tie us to sexual duality and dimorphism, but nor (crucially) does it efface sexual difference altogether. Sexuate difference is rather in excess of this actualized dimorphism (currently) required for sexual reproduction. We do not (and should not, as Braidotti reminds us) do away with sexual difference, but we should be wary of pinning down too precisely what it is, what potential it holds, what it means.

Could Irigaray's phenomenology accommodate this proposal towards which Deleuze gestures? Again, this possibility returns us to an expanded understanding of gestationality. Although Irigaray's later work does indeed seem to argue for the primacy of this sexual dimorphism, we recall that her descriptions of the watery gestational in *Marine Lover* nonetheless invite us to consider sexuate difference itself as more than reproduction by sexually dimorphic bodies. Her descriptions of the (explicitly material) watery flow *between* the sexes, we recall, suggest a kind of material virtuality not unlike Deleuze's egg. Irigaray's proposition is, however, a better expression of the lived *transcorporeality* that such gestation demands. While Deleuze's description of the egg, or the larval subject, provides the opening to rethinking sexual difference and gestation as virtual, it is Irigaray who insists most adamantly that gestationality is a co-creation between at least two. Deleuze, after all, bases his theory on the image of a rather lonely and singular egg. Feminist philosopher Tamsin Lorraine (1999), too, has noted this nuanced difference: while 'Deleuze's images of a line of flight and the highly populated desert are oddly solipsistic', she argues, Irigaray, on the other hand, insists on incorporating 'the participatory communion of mutually constitutive creativity'; Irigaray's version 'attends to how her line of flight implicates and forms a web with the lines of flight of others' in an act of co-gestation (163–164).[33] Irigaray (1991: 38), in other words, foregrounds the necessity of *co-creation* in repetition and difference;

her concern is with the flow between others of (sexuate) difference: 'Where have you drawn what flows out of you?', she asks. Irigaray's careful attention to what both facilitates and thwarts relationality between two not only makes this mutual imbrication clear; it also foregrounds gestationality *as a becoming between bodies,* or in excess of actualized bodies, as an ineluctable condition of the proliferation of difference.[34]

Irigaray, admittedly, still seems to insist that this force of becoming happens between the specifically masculine and the specifically feminine, but this insistence has no option but to begin to dissolve, if we are to take seriously her phenomenological proposition that gestationality extends beyond the human reprosexual womb.[35] Moreover, if 'woman' (and thus 'man') are still to come, then we must admit the possibility of sexuate difference composing itself in ever new ways – indeed, this is a future of sexuate difference that is already clearly in the making, and one that Irigaray's thought must accommodate in order for it to retain value as an ethics of sexual difference. In other words, I find it exciting to swim with Irigaray beyond the bounds of where she may have intended I stop. Gestationality as difference and repetition is also clearly about sexuate difference, but this difference holds no guarantees for what, where, how, or when this difference might become. Sexuate difference, too, remains an open question.[36] Reading Irigaray attentively, we discover that thinking through the maternal-feminine is necessary in our current social, cultural, and political epoch, but there is nonetheless still a watery space for a deeper and less determinate understanding of gestationality. In fact, if we wish to extend Irigaray beyond humanism, such an understanding is vital. We'll return to consider how this expanded view of sexuate difference as gestationality has implications for a posthuman ecological ethics at the end of the chapter.

The onto-logic of amniotics (queering water's repetitions)

We could also tell the story this way: water connects bodies – across times and spaces, through various complex movements and cycles to other bodies and beings in diverse exchanges, gifts, thefts, and forsakings. We could think of this work of water as flow, or more specifically, as a logic of connection or communication. Drawing on posthuman feminist theories of embodiment, as I described in Chapter 1, this is the movement most closely associated with transcorporeality, to use Stacy Alaimo's term, where transit occurs as and by means of fluidity. While a dominant post-Enlightenment Western epistemological ocularcentrism suggests that bodies are (and should be) separate and discrete, water is in fact digging stealth channels through us all. This connection may be immediate and direct, or delayed and removed, but it nonetheless reveals itself as a thread of interpermeation and commonality that facilitates the possibility of something like an *embodied hydrocommons*. But this word – interpermeation – already alerts us to the idea that connection is not just about the pathways that might join up separate nodes in network. Through interpermeation, all bodies are changed. Water, as we've noted, also facilitates the becoming of bodies; it literally bathes them into being. A transcorporeal interpermeation is not only a transit across bodies in space; it is also a transcorporeal gestationality across times. Water not only flows between, and connects bodies; it also facilitates new kinds of bodies. And in this engendering of new watery bodies, water becomes difference. In other words, instead of simply 'flowing', water suggests a more complex logic of interpermeation, gestationality, and differentiation.

Significantly, these interpermeations and differentiations also affirm that water, while proposing an elementality in common for all bodies of water, is not some amorphous matter. Just as bodies need water, water needs a body – it needs to take up expression as bodies of water that are specifically situated, even in all of their porous transits. This suggests that water must also embody a kind of membrane logic. One way we could think about this membrane logic is as something I'm proposing to call amniotics. An amnion is the innermost membrane that encloses the embryo of a mammal, bird, or reptile (animals otherwise known as amniotes), and it contains the amniotic fluid that surrounds the gestating foetuses of these amniotes. In other words, the amnion facilitates the watery world necessary for the gestation of all life for those creatures who have left that water in favour of a terrestrial habitat (even if, in the case of some of these beings, like whales, they have since returned to the sea – a journey I examine more closely in the next chapter). The amnion literally establishes the watery environment, the fluid gestational habitat, necessary for the proliferation of life. But it also establishes a separation between one body and its gestating other. This is not a definitive separation; the amnion is a membrane that facilitates and in fact demands the interpermeation and passage of life-proliferating matter and force.

In one sense, these are the facts that comprise the stories of biology. The importance of water for the gestation, maintenance, and proliferation of bodily life is hardly news to anyone with a rudimentary understanding of the life sciences. But water's biological workings also reverberate in an important philosophical proposition – in an *onto-logic* – that helps us rethink dominant Western ontologies that privilege a static and separated way of bodily being. An onto-logic is a common way of being that is expressed across a difference of beings.[37] As opposed to the way in which 'ontology' might be traditionally understood, an onto-logic does not propose to solve the question of 'Being', nor does it purport to reveal or describe all of being's facets or potential expressions. An onto-logic can rather gather or highlight something that helps us understand a common *how, where, when*, and *thanks to whom* that certain seemingly disparate beings share.

Western metaphysics has long disavowed its debt to what allows being to be in the first place (the maternal, the feminine, the other, the natural). Feminists and other philosophers in the margins of canonized Western philosophy have proposed various reconceptualizations of ontology to account for this disappearing act – sometimes circumscribing 'the ontological' as specifically phallogocentric (or otherwise hegemonic), and bringing to light what is cast beyond such understandings of being. Calling philosophy to task for this 'forgetting' is Irigaray's project in *Marine Lover* and other texts, too. Her insistence that woman is yet-to-come since she has never yet been allowed 'to be' on her own terms seems to suggest that woman (as we do not yet know her) lies beyond the bounds of ontology. But another way of reading Irigaray's relation to ontology is possible, whereby rather than pointing out the limits of what can be gathered by a phallogocentric conception of 'the ontological', the category is instead exploded. This is how we might understand her descriptions of watery embodiment. In describing watery bodies for us in terms of what I'm calling an onto-logic of amniotics, Irigaray also intimates that the ontological might be widened, and significantly rethought.

The onto-logic of amniotics does not suggest that all bodies of water are the same in terms of their being, but rather that bodies of water share a *way* of being because they are bodies of water. The amnion materializes a mode of relational being that is certainly transcorporeal – transiting across and between bodies – but a kind of transit that also nurtures and facilitates other bodies, while also differentiating them. Amniotics thus articulates three modes of watery embodiment, in a common logic: first, bodies of water as facilitative and gestational; second, bodies of water as differentiating, as well as the material accomplishment of this differentiation; and third, bodies of water as necessarily interconnecting and interpermeating, all at the same time. Amniotics asserts an aqueous logic that is at once *of*, *in*, and *between*, while at the same time requiring a force of *becoming*. My wager is therefore that water, as simultaneously that which gestates beings, that which is gestated as difference, and that which interpermeates and connects beings, might teach us something about an expanded understanding of the ontological.

Water, in all of its repetitions – in fact because of its compulsion to repeat – is in the first place facilitative and gestational. Each moment of water will inevitably give itself over to the elaboration of something different, something new. As we've already explored, this is linked to the exuberant idea of sexuate difference described above, where sexuate difference is a general facilitative capacity engendered by the meeting of different bodies, in the production of the 'not yet'. Such a reading of gestationality is owed, primarily to the fact that we all begin as bodies *in* water. Like the amniotic environment, water instantiates a milieu for the gestation of life – a life whose originary becomings float in a never-pin-pointable thick past of gathering materiality-duration. This illuminates the first important step towards an explosion of the ontological: significantly, the ontological comes to include not only 'what is', but *the condition of possibility of that becoming being in the first place*.

At the same time, according to these particular amniotics, what is ontological is always becoming different. The second key dimension of an amniotic logic is differentiation. Every repetition enacts difference. Because, as Deleuze describes, the egg/larva gestates in but also comprises a watery element, it can undergo torsions and movements and express a virtuality that only the embryonic or larval subject could withstand. This virtuality is then actualized as necessarily different: there is no pre-programming, but rather a selection of difference from the virtual. As a result what is gestated is not a reproduction or an eternal return of the self-same, but always necessarily different because of this selection. Again, we can find here resonances with contemporary posthuman explorations of matter and difference. In Karen Barad's (2007: 176–177) terms, differentiation can be thought in terms of 'agential separability'; in matter's ongoing intra-actions, cuts between bodies are continually enacted.[38] These cuts produce bodies of difference, not 'once and for all', but always contingently and changeably so. Similarly, in Irigaray's phenomenology, difference isn't something that 'is', but rather something that is gestated – here, beginning in these immemorial waters. And this differentiating moment further differentiates and repeats.

Anticipating Barad's concept of agential separability, Irigaray's figuring of waters that make a difference also suggests that there is always a membrane that separates the gestational body from the body it proliferates ('between me and you …'). This membrane is not a divisive barrier, but an interval of passage: solid enough to differentiate, but permeable enough to facilitate exchange. Importantly, although science may make a cut that identifies the amnion in a specific time and place, Irigaray has already described (and we have recalled above) how the separation between the amniotic and maternal body is always obscure. The membrane is not divisive, but nor is it decisive. This brings us back to the idea of communication, or the flow between bodies. Alongside difference, then, is the third aspect of an amniotic onto-logic, namely interpermeation. Because of the repetition of water, even the singular and differentiated expressions it gestates are nonetheless connected to one another by way of their materiality. Here, an onto-logic of amniotics makes a contribution to other feminist theories of relational bodies, as well as broader cultural theories of networked and distributed bodies. In biological terms, the amnion (which as living matter is *itself a body of water*) is a permeable and regulating membrane. Water flows from one body to another in various passages of exchange and distribution. Importantly, in an amniotic relation, the membrane that separates the gestational body from the proliferating body of repetition and difference allows passage, and serves to connect. Moreover, the water that one body gives up through gestation and facilitation of another watery being is never directly or symmetrically returned. Such debt is only repaid through the diffuse cyclings of differentiating waters. The very asymmetry of these relations is what accounts for the necessary difference between bodies, and the active proliferation of life that accompanies their relation. As such, gestation is always part of an asymmetrical relation of giving that therefore sustains difference at the same time as it participates in material interpermeation.

Our bodies of water thus ask us to consider how the ontological expresses a multiplicity of being that extends into and through other beings in an intricate and intimate entanglement of relationality – that is, an elemental and multispecies hydrocommons of water –, while never collapsing this interconnectedness into an undifferentiated mass. The onto-logic of amniotics which we can read out of Irigaray reveals a body that rejects discrete individualism, but whose difference is never washed away. This is a crucial point; a proposal of passage and an elemental commonality of bodies alongside differences that are enacted (rather than simply 'existing') does not have to negate Irigaray's claims of ontological difference as the necessary *ground* of embodiment. To say that difference becomes is not the same as saying that there is something – a neutral, undifferentiated body, say – that precedes difference. Difference has always been underway. Membrane logic, or the onto-logic of amniotics, is originary. As such, sharing a common elementality across difference is also an 'always already'. *Remember the liquid ground* – a precondition that cannot be pinned down.

And again, while Irigaray insists on sexuate difference, we have already been pushed to imagine difference in itself as always holding a latent fecundity that I've described as a kind of sexuate difference as differentia*ti*ng. I call this gestationality. But importantly, this fecundity *is called out only in our interpermeation with watery others* – an interpermeation that also generates difference. While difference may be Irigaray's primary concern, in highlighting interpermeation as a necessary part of this onto-logic we also temper her claims about irreducible difference. We must come to understand bodies of difference *as also* bodies that flow into and through one another. In a posthuman feminist move, this is a logic of the 'both/and' rather than the 'either/or'. On an amniotic understanding, this interpermeation of bodies and their necessary difference is no longer a contradiction. *Water both connects us and makes us different. As water we are connected, we are different.* Our difference is not undermined but in fact engendered by the water that we also always carry with us, that we relinquish, share, exchange, gift, and receive.

Amniotics does not solve the question of being, or claim what being is, definitively. Amniotics can rather highlight something that helps us understand a common *how*, *where*, *when*, and *thanks to whom* that certain seemingly disparate beings share. My aim in elaborating this onto-logic is, in the first place, to show how human bodies share a common way of being in the world with all kinds of other bodies of water. The point is not just that 'we are all 60–90 per cent water'; the brute materiality is not the real take-away here. More importantly, as bodies of water we share a common way of relating to other bodies – and this means that our beings and becomings are bound up in one another's materiality, in specific ways. My second aim (particularly in calling this an onto-logic) is to follow Irigaray in exploding certain understandings of 'the ontological'. What does it mean to say that the ontological is not just 'what is' but what allows another being to be, and that which connects beings to one another?

Let's review how this rethinking of the ontological happens in my reading of Irigaray. First, as many commentators have made clear, the 'interval' is a key concept in her work and allows us to acknowledge the importance of difference in the maintenance of ethical relations between bodies. Bodies depend, in fact, on the difference of others. In her posthuman phenomenology, this interval is ontological. In other words, being and becoming do not exist in hierarchy. The interval is not subordinate to the bodies it articulates; and interpermeation, as a key aspect of amniotics, is not subservient to the bodies that interpermeate. What *Marine Lover* makes clear, however, is that this interval is not 'just' an idea, but is always materialized. The interval *is* the water that flows between 'you' and 'me'. The membrane, we recall, *is* also water – enacting a cascade of watery nesting dolls, all the way down. Hence, water blurs the discrete compartmentalization of 'entity' and 'relationality'. This stages a significant challenge to dominant Western understandings of ontological subjects as sovereign entities in their own right. While we may live as bodies in a relatively discrete way, we also live as bodies that are always gathering and dispersing our embodiment within currents of relation. This is not just an 'idea' that Irigaray suggests; it is gestated within the bodies she describes, with phenomenological attentiveness.

This dissolution of the ontological subject as whole or discrete is intensified further when we overlay the materiality of interpermeation with gestationality and difference. We recall that Irigaray figures gestational waters as some kind of 'first' waters. On this understanding, the gestational element may seem primordial because it precedes that to which it gives life. But – and this point is crucial – the gestational element is woven into the puddle of life that is gestated. As bodies of water, we carry our gestational element with us, always, beyond the gestational habitat and return it there in a series of differentiating manoeuvres. While we are 'of' water, in the gestational sense (i.e. we emerge from it), we are also always 'of' water, in the material, constitutive sense (i.e. we are comprised of it). Water can thus illuminate a way of being that is, on the one hand, derived from the disavowed gestational element that allows it to be in the first place. Yet, on the other hand, this onto-logic requires that the gestational medium persevere as constitutive of these same material beings.

Irigaray illuminates this, for example, in her description of life as 'already happening' in the gestational element. Her descriptions remind us that the liquid element is not outside of 'what is' (i.e. the real), but carried and choreographed by it, composed of it, at every instance. Her descriptions of the watery gestational sea reveal a distinctly material gestational element, despite the fact that this 'origin' is at the same time always obscured and never fully knowable. As Irigaray (1991: 61) notes, 'before coming into the light, life is already living. It is germinating long before it responds to your sun's rays.' Life is already always happening in water; what conditions us is itself always already shot through by the materiality of a lively, material real. Water here is a doubly articulated 'life force', for not only does it 'force' (gestate or engender) 'life', but it is also a 'force' that *is teeming with* 'life'. This seeming 'preontological' is one that endures, one that always, necessarily inhabits us: if we can talk about a primordial gestational element at all, it is one that we (literally) in-corp-orate. The obscurity of the gestational membrane or aminon is repeated (but differently) in our own material bodies of water. Irigaray's insistence here on the materiality of the gestational that we carry with us, that is always teeming with life before 'responding to your sun's rays' shows that the virtual gestational capacity and the body of the gestated 'to come' are always intimately, and materially, bound up in one another.

By suggesting this palimpsest of onto-logics that inhere in us, as watery subjects, reading Irigaray queerly also opens up an important ethical proposition: if the relational and the gestational are folded, as a material possibility, into the bodies that relate and are gestated, it means that we, just like all bodies of water, embody the same possibility to relate to others and proliferate new instantiations of the 'not yet'. As Mielle Chandler and I (2013) have argued elsewhere, water as gestational enacts a mode of sociality that we, as human sovereign subjects, repeat. As bodies of water, we exist as 'sovereign bodies' but as water this sovereignty is also always dissolving – as it relinquishes waters to others and gestates new possibilities. In these ways, we become responsive to others, both human and more-than-human. Because of the onto-logic of water that we share with other watery bodies, we all – each of us within this more-than-human community of watery bodies – carry this capacity for facilitative responsivity, and for proliferating life yet-to-come, in our own wet materiality. Mielle and I have referred to this as 'becoming-milieu': Becoming-milieu for an other demands a reorientation of oneself as existing also for what is beyond oneself. Becoming-milieu does not entail total desubjectification (as Deleuze notes, to desubjectivize oneself completely only results in annihilation), but it does require that we loosen our commitments to our own sovereign endurance. The watery potential that we enfold within our own seemingly discrete bodies is a watery offering to unknowable futures.

Once more, this notion fundamentally challenges a dominant Western understanding of ontology that holds up the sovereign ontological subject as self-preserving (again, see Chandler and Neimanis 2013).[39] It also challenges the habit whereby any sense of self-effacement must be tethered to a reprosexual maternal body. Rather, water demonstrates that this gestational capacity belongs to all bodies of water. Some of us might become milieu as womb, but we might also become milieu for multispecies ecologies in our guts, or milieu for gardens that will grow from our deathly and discarded matters.[40] We can also be milieu as ally, as neighbour, as passerby, as teacher. While this might sound metaphorical, we are literally the condition for one another's possibility, as demonstrated by our watery interpermeations. In each of these relations, we have the possibility of dissolving our own sovereign self-preservation, and instead creating the conditions for an other to flourish. In this way, we repeat the lineaments of water's gestationality, differently. Water gifts us this capacity.

Reading Irigaray alongside Deleuze helps us articulate this gestationality as a material possibility and helps us untether it from a reprosexual female body. Irigaray, however, reminds us that gestational bodies are also always specific in their sexuate difference, and that the ways in which these bodies are symbolically inscribed matters a lot. Gestationality is not just a brute capacity of wet matter; it is oriented and thwarted by the flows of power, meaning, and values in which we all swim. In other words, Irigaray reminds us that our capacity to differentiate, to become milieu for an other, also depends on our ethico-ontological imaginaries. In this sense, the actualizations of difference – as woman or man, or as beyond this binary logic; as straight or queer; as human or non-human animal; and as saturated with the weight of all the meanings those bodies gather and materialize – bear directly on our gestational capacities. To become milieu as womb, we know, is not just a question of biological proclivity; it is also bound up in questions of which bodies get to birth children, and under what circumstances. Similarly, to become milieu as companion, or host, or lover, is also a matter of which bodies we deem acceptable to be welcomed in our communities, our nations, our beds. Irigaray does not allow the force of a symbolic economy to be washed away in our enthusiasm for matter. Becoming milieu demands careful considerations of the ways in which our material generosity is oriented. It is also crucial that we always remember that these transcorporeal transits – in their material-semiotic inextricability – may not be benign. Not all gifts are life-affirming. As bodies of water, our capacity to proliferate the not-yet is also always bound up in our capacity to bear toxic messages. Gestation is always non-innocent.

So: what will we bequeath to these others to whom we are connected, and what will we take? How will we negotiate the levees and dams, sluices and tributaries, that guide these dissolutions-for-the-other? These are the questions that figuring ourselves as 'bodies of water' can ask of us, and questions that I hope we can aspire to rise to. Irigaray, in her reconfiguring of ontological subjects as gestational milieus, and as bodies of water that are both in common and also crucially different, helps us understand this proposition more deeply.

Bodies of water beyond humanism

*And in order to speak the meaning of the earth, is it necessary to exhaust
all her stores?*

– Irigaray (1991: 18)

Our planet's life-proliferating and life-sustaining gestational milieus are
wounded. Aqueous habitats – in the Great Barrier Reef, in the Gulf of Mexico,
in the Alberta tar sands, in the Niger Delta – are sacrificed to human fossil
fuel dependency, while rain and snow become poisonous messengers to Arctic
food chains. Seas, both tiny and grand, suffer from slow suffocation. Ancient
aquifers are pumped out of the earth to be bottled and sold for profit – most
recently under the banner of 'life'.[41] We slake our consumerist thirst with
melting glaciers, to end up rowing lifeboats down the middle of our flooded
streets. Monolithic megadams displace humans and other animals to radically
reshape riparian ecosystems. New islands of plastic rise out of the sea, while old
caches of chemical warfare agents lie patiently beneath, slowly releasing distant
memories. Understanding how water has reached this state of degradation
and exploitation asks us to carefully consider our own implications within
this hydrocommons – in terms of not only what we do 'to' water but as water
bodies ourselves.

Irigaray invites us to consider ourselves not only as bodies composed of
water but as watery bodies that have a gestational capacity to proliferate the
not-yet. And, she implores us not to forget the waters that are the condition of
our own possibility. Where our early twenty-first-century planetary waters are
increasingly polluted, redirected for profit, and otherwise instrumentalized,
Irigaray's plea seems all the more pressing. She insists that 'the first ecological
gesture is to live and situate ourselves as living beings among other living
beings' (Irigaray 2015: 101). Such a situation depends, for Irigaray, on a
deep respect for sexuate difference where 'the sexuation of the living is thus
an essential key to an ecological ethics' (101); 'if we consider ourselves as
neuter individuals, we cannot behave in an ecological way' (103). The deep
ethics at the heart of Irigaray's work thus reinforces the need for work in
the environmental humanities, as well as in feminist new materialisms and

posthumanisms, not to forget the ethics of sexuate difference that Irigaray's philosophy has so carefully staked.

We might still ask, however, whether Irigaray's bodies of water move sufficiently beyond an anthropocentric view. While Irigaray offers a radical rethinking of the embodiment of difference through invocations of a kind of elemental materiality, she herself clarifies that a 'decisive aspect' of her work 'is precisely to define what could be a really human sexuality' (Irigaray and Parker 2015: 116). The achievement of 'our humanity' (Irigaray and Parker 2015: 116) and 'the life and culture of the human species' (Irigaray 1992: 3) are her focus. She does not dismiss concern for the more-than-human – and her work is certainly *elementally grounded* – but it is hard to ignore the ethico-ontological hierarchy she seemingly installs: 'Cultivating our sexuate belonging inclines us to respect and cultivate transcendence, first, towards a differently sexuate human and, then, towards any sort of otherness, especially that of living beings' (Irigaray and Parker 2015: 116).

Moving beyond anthropocentrism would not be a simple turn towards geophysical bodies of water. As many kinds of environmentalisms have demonstrated, we can express concern for a lake or a river without fundamentally challenging the environmental ontological imaginaries that allow those watery bodies to be resourced and exploited in the first place. Such concern is no better than a band-aid (which we all know comes off most easily in the bath). No, what we need is to move beyond humanism as the anchor of ontology and ethics – that is, we need not only to extend care beyond human bodies of water but to challenge the commitments of humanism more generally. This would mean dissolving the ground of who gets to count as human in the first place, and the order of things that accompanies any such proposition. This would mean destabilizing Self-Sufficient Man from his place of ontological authority, and recasting the terms of sovereign ontological subjectivity. Such a concern would be both against anthropocentrism and also against phallogocentrism and related instantiations of what Val Plumwood (1993) has called the 'Master Model' – an order of things built on dualisms, hierarchy, and chains of meaning. Moving beyond humanism would require committing not only to other kinds of elemental and ecological bodies of water but also in general to queer ways of being, and to swamping the solid ground of Western ontological frameworks.

Caring for water requires thinking with water's rich biodiversity in all of the bodies as which it lives – human and more-than-human. Irigaray (2015: 103) insists that 'sexuate difference is the first biodiversity that we must take into account'. My proposal has been that thinking with water as gestational of difference and also the actualisation thereof (both being and becoming, both body and milieu) makes it impossible to compartmentalize sexuate difference within discrete bodies. A posthuman theory of sexuate difference shows that difference is a capacity, a tendency – even a desire – to differ, more than it is any actual outcome of that desire (an idea I will return to in the next chapter, in relation to water and evolution). Moreover, as we saw above, rethinking sexuate difference according to broader terms of gestationality refuses a synonymous or entirely overlapping relation to the feminine-maternal. The maternal seas are *diffracted through* an elemental gestational milieu (rather than overlaid in a one-to-one relation). Taking the lineaments of gestation as paradigmatic need not be a 'biologically essentialist' or heteronormative move. Sexuate difference as gestationality could suggest instead a queer, multispecies, posthuman, and elemental proliferation of life-in-the-plural.

All living bodies of water–amniotes and also birds and reptiles, fish, insects and anthropods, plant life, fungi, bacteria and protoctists – owe their corporeal existence to gestation in a watery milieu, which is evidenced in a plurality of processes that extend beyond human wombs. This extension of what might count as a logic of 'amniotics' is even more radical when we include all of the bodies transiting and transforming in our planetary hydrological cycles: ocean, aquifer, hailstorm, morning dew. Each of these watery bodies dissolves for-the-other. Gestationality is posthuman. Making this claim challenges the idea that corporeal generosity, or even ethical orientation, originates and ends with the human. Rather, like *and as* water, we take up and repeat water's logics, differently.

I do not intend to suggest that Irigaray offers us a fully developed theory of posthuman gestationality in this sense, but by inviting us to think about our own bodies of water in the context of deeper, more-than-human gestational waters, where the human body of water is contiguous with rather than analogous to these gestational species-seas, nor does her philosophy necessarily refuse this possibility. Such posthuman intimations, in fledgling form, can be found in Irigaray's references to a gestational element that continues to be carried, as water, within the differentiated-gestated, and the ongoing process of gestation that is required for maintaining the fecundity of sexual difference. We might even push the amniotics we read in Irigaray to make room for the human genderqueer bodies, sexes, and sexualities that already exist as actualities in the present – also gestated in water, also embodying this water, also proliferating and facilitating new forms of being. In turn, considering Irigaray's 'liquid ground' in the context of more-than-human life proposes the possibility for extending such an ethics of difference beyond human sexuate difference, and towards our planetary waters. While Irigaray's work may only be suggestive in this sense, it nonetheless opens a path for thinking through life as not only our own, but as distributed through, indebted to, and facilitative of lives that reach far beyond the bounds of our amniote skin.

3

Fishy Beginnings

Our ancestor was an animal which breathed water, had a swim bladder, a great swimming tail, an imperfect skull, and undoubtedly was an hermaphrodite! Here is a pleasant genealogy for mankind.

— Charles Darwin in a letter to Thomas Huxley
(cited in Zimmer 1998: n.p.)

The oceans are where life was born and the salty fluid that courses through our veins is a reminder of our aqueous origins.

— David Suzuki (2006: 11)

When the seas dried, the primitive Fish left its associated milieu to explore land, forced to 'stand on its own legs', now carrying water on the inside, in the amniotic membranes protecting the embryo.

— Deleuze and Guattari (1987: 55)

But just at that time the differences among us were becoming accentuated: there might be a family that had been living on land, say, for several generations, whose young people acted in a way that wasn't even amphibious but almost reptilian already; and there were others who lingered, still living like fish, those who, in fact, became even more fishy than they had been before.

— Italo Calvino (1965: 61)

We are rather fishy, we humans. We pretty much swam our way here, if not on the outside, then at least on the inside. We are all still, necessarily, treading water. As the above four epigraphs, by a naturalist-cum-evolutionary biologist, an environmentalist, a pair of philosophers, and a fabulist, highlight, we are intimately linked to our evolutionary beginnings through water. Our being as bodies of water has been facilitated by water – that is, by other bodies of water that have preceded us.

Indeed all biological life – animals, plants, and fungi, as well as protoctists (single-celled organisms including slime moulds and some simple algae) and monera (the simplest forms of life such as blue-green algae and bacteria) – depends on the existence of water. This is why our home planet is, from what we know so far, unique within our own solar system. This is also why discoveries such as ice on Mars carry such monumental implications (Whitehouse 2002). Right back to the first signs of life on earth at least 3.9 billion years ago, when small organic proteins likely interacted with their habitat to produce the first bacterial life forms, water has been necessary for the gestation of all living beings. Our earliest ancestors were all apparently water babies, squirming, scuttling, or swimming around their respective watery worlds.

Yet, between 380 and 360 million years ago, a 'fabulous shape-shifting' occurred, in the words of evolutionary biologist Carl Zimmer (1998: 5). A certain lineage of fish decided to evolve legs and feet, lose their gills, hook their aortas, and venture onto dry land. As Zimmer describes in his detailed account of this terrestrial invasion, such a major transformation demanded countless changes in the bodies of these animals; this was not an overnight phenomenon, but rather a macroevolutionary process that lasted over 100 million years. After musing on an underwater encounter between a snapper (a fish who never left the sea), himself (descended from tetrapods who left the sea perhaps 360 million years ago), and a dolphin (whose ancestors left the sea, only to return there about 30 million years ago), Zimmer remarks, 'we three animals live in separate countries divided by a fatal boundary' (4). He refers here to the boundary between air and water, two elements which Zimmer notes are so different 'that you might as well be comparing life on two different planets' (6). But at the same time, Zimmer also concedes that the three participants in this underwater encounter are not 'complete strangers' (4). In their fundamental difference, he nonetheless catalogues their undeniable similarities: skulls and spines, muscles and eyes, embryos that share a strikingly similar pot-bellied, hunchbacked appearance. Not only does water facilitate the being of all three, but this facilitation is a debt from which none can escape.

In this chapter, I continue to explore the idea that we are all 'bodies of water' and as such, implicated in a common way of being and becoming, in relation to others. In the previous chapter, I described this as an 'onto-logic' of amniotics – a mode of embodiment that highlights water as that which both connects us and differentiates us; as that which we both are and which facilitates our becoming. Philosophically speaking, this ontological proposition joins other feminist and posthuman interventions in challenging the idea that ontology first and foremost interpellates sovereign, self-sufficient beings. Amniotics highlights passages of connection (for better or worse) across membranes of difference. Most importantly, though, amniotics foregrounds the idea of gestationality: we owe ourselves to others, and in various ways, we all eventually pass our watery selves on. As bodies of water, we rely on water for our continued proliferation, but we are also reservoirs for this proliferating force of life-in-the-plural. I described this, drawing on Irigaray and Deleuze, as a watery kind of difference and repetition. Our planetary hydrocommons, in this sense, is not just a network of interconnected geophysical and meteorological waters; it is also made up from all bodies that materialize and transform these waters in their own fur and flesh, and in their celled and cyborg forms. Here, I further this proposition in relation to the tri-species encounter that Zimmer describes. How does water help us think about gestationality across species, in a more-than-human frame? And how can we keep not only Zimmer's 'fatal boundary' of difference, but also our watery commonality, in the picture?

My wager is that evolutionary tales, like the one Zimmer tells, provide a lively illustration of the naturalcultural matters of these debts and differentiations. In evolution as elsewhere, our biological matters are always storied, and our knowledges are always situated and contingent. In thinking along with various accounts and interpretations of evolution, I aim to exemplify posthuman feminist phenomenology at work, where scientific knowledge acts as an amplifier of embodied knowing. Rather than either accepting the Word of Science wholesale or alternatively rejecting these accounts due to an ingrained (yet understandable) feminist scepticism of 'objective data', scientific explanations of our watery debts join other kinds of origin stories in a thick elaboration of bodies of water as figuration, as embodied imaginary. Coming to a deeper understanding of this figuration, and how we as bodies of water can live out its promise, is the more general project of this book. In reimagining our bodies as indebted to all kinds of bodies that condition our possibility, I hope we might also consider how, and to whom, we pass our own watery bodies on. If evolution is composed of inheritances and exchanges of all kinds, what do water and our watery kin inherit *from us*, in the context of late capitalism and the Anthropocene?

My concomitant aim is to broach the question of how we know water, and the epistemology of wet. What Zimmer alludes to, after all, in evoking that 'fatal boundary' of species differentiation is a geographical consideration, where our embodied orientation towards water underlines an enduring unknowability. Origin stories, as we saw in the last chapter, have no clear beginning. Similarly, our own embodied limits in relation to living in/with water point to limits of ever knowing, or mastering, water – something I explore by considering our strange kinship with aquatic species and a certain 'fishiness' we all harbour (even though not all of these kin are technically 'fish'). Tales of lungfish, whales, and Aquatic Apes set the stage for thinking about watery embodiment as an epistemological question. How do the stories we tell, and the knowledges we draw on to tell them, work to establish certain kinds of ethical relations with our watery others? How does watery bodiedness demand attention to situated knowledge as an onto-ethico-epistemological matter? This is to say, as we move below the surface, how bodies are *in* water also matters. We cannot survive in the worlds of some of our closest kin, even as they swim within our own deep embodied channels – and we in theirs. *Intimacy is not mastery*. This claim frames the final section of this chapter, where I draw on the postcolonial theory of Gayatri Spivak, and in particular, her theory of planetarity. Here I describe the conceptual apparatus of unknowability as an onto-epistemology and an ethics, which we learn from a feminist posthuman phenomenology of bodies of/in water.

Other evolutions

Into the sea (you) are returned... Why leave the sea?

– (Irigaray 1991: 12)

Feminist transcorporeality reminds us that our amniotic waters are not *like* our planetary waters, but continuous with them. As philosopher Luce Irigaray (1993a: 5, 1993c: 15, 2002a: 5) maintains, and as we explored in the previous chapter, the fecundity of gestation is not limited simply to human gestation and the moment of birth, but is rather an ongoing proliferation of life-in-the-plural. In Chapter 2 our exploration of *Marine Lover of Friedrich Nietzsche* (Irigaray's amorous dialogue with the philosopher that chastises him for forgetting the bodies and waters of his birth) suggested that our gestational milieu might thus be understood as the contraction of a greater ocean into a tiny one, and our birth as the passage from a smaller womb back to a larger one. There, I focused on how gestational waters introduce a continuity between planetary and maternal waters, suggesting that bodies of water partake in a relation of amniotics in the most general sense. But in that text, Irigaray (1991: 57) also subtly indicates to us that the abyssal, unknowable depths that gestate us – 'that dark home where you began to be once upon a time. Once and for all' – posit a transcorporeal stretching of species across planetary time. Bodies of water are themselves aqueous milieus for the facilitation of new kinds of life in the proliferation of evolutionary entanglements.

Despite Nietzsche's rejection of Darwinism, the evolutionary tones of *Thus Spoke Zarathustra* (the text to which Irigaray refers in her own *Marine Lover*) are well noted (see Deutscher 2011). In Nietzsche's text, Zarathustra explicitly invokes his evolutionary ancestry and that of the townspeople he addresses.[1] Picking up on these evolutionary undertones, Irigaray (1991: 12) notes that her interlocutor in *Marine Lover* knows not 'if [he is] descended from a monkey or a worm or if [he] might even be some cross between plant and ghost'. But importantly, Nietzsche (1982: 123) also notes that Zarathustra emerges from the sea. He drags his body ashore, and then immediately disavows these beginnings as he pledges his allegiance to the earth (Nietzsche 1982: 125). This is why Irigaray also underlines that Nietzsche/Zarathustra's 'forgetting' is a specifically watery forgetfulness: just as he forgets his watery maternal gestational element, so too does he disavow his watery evolutionary gestational element – that primordial evolutionary soup that gestated us all. Granted, the evolutionary undertones are subtle in Irigaray's text, and she certainly isn't an 'evolutionist'.[2] Her references to our evolutionary debts nonetheless invite us again, and in an expanded register, to understand gestationality in Irigaray's work in terms beyond the human maternal womb. Irigaray's criticisms of Zarathustra's preference for terrestrial animals give us an opening for thinking about evolution in terms of species genealogies and kinships. In thinking specifically with evolution's watery tales, we will also see how Irigaray's interest in the elemental cannot be fully separated from a concern with other animal bodies (Deutscher 2011: 71). As Irigaray (1991: 13) herself notes, 'as a companion' her interlocutor never chooses 'a sea creature. Camel, snake, lion, eagle, and doves, monkey and ass, and... Yes. But no to anything that moves in the water. Why this persistent wish for legs, or wings? And never gills?' In invoking our soupy, even *fishy*, beginnings, Irigaray suggests that transcorporeal cycles of gestationality echo not only across human bodies and maternal wombs, nor only between human bodies and watery habitats, but across species, symbiotic becomings, and evolutionary times.

When it comes to evolution, it certainly matters what stories we tell (Haraway 2008, 2015), and how we tell them. Phenomenologist Maxine Sheets-Johnstone (2007) has discussed at length the 'surprising' fact that evolutionary biology and continental philosophy have not formed much of a relationship. Without taking into account the evolutionary continuities of the embodiment which so fascinates them, she notes, phenomenologists in particular forgo any sense of history; 'they pretend as if we all just got here – bees, chimpanzees, and what have you, which is by no means the case' (334). Sheets-Johnstone makes the important point that theory in the humanities and data from the sciences have important knowledge to share with each other; her criticism of the lack of attention to evolution within philosophy, however, is not entirely founded.[3] Many major philosophers – such as Nietzsche, Henri Bergson,[4] Merleau-Ponty,[5] Deleuze, and Guattari,[6] and including feminist theorists such as Elizabeth Grosz, Donna Haraway, Claire Colebrook, and Rosi Braidotti, among others – clearly contradict this claim.[7] Collectively, they demonstrate how evolution and the humanities interrelate in fascinating and game-changing ways. My particular interest here is in those contemporary theorists and writers who engage evolutionary science neither as wholesale critique nor, as Sheets-Johnstone seems to suggest we should, as uncritical acceptance of 'the facts'. Things get far more interesting (and provocative) where evolutionary science is not so much an object of study as it is a co-traveller – something good to think with, to wrestle with, to get inside of. What might we learn in terms of the stories we tell about ourselves, and how we might tell them differently?

The critical 'thinking with' evolution embraced by thinkers that I've mentioned above (among others) happens in all sorts of ways, not reducible to each other. Yet, a common thread in many of these stories (and one helpful for me in thinking more about watery bodies) is the challenge that many of these thinkers pose to popular Darwinism – that ruthless teleological process of linear, filial descent (whereby species 'improve' over time), accompanied by a notion of the 'survival of the fittest'. Evolution, it turns out, can be understood as multivalent – moving in several directions at once. The 'tree of life' image (where origins seem clear) becomes murkier the more closely we look. Random crossings undermine the comfort of teleology, while individual variation meets external force in patterns of unevenness and unpredictability. For example, in rereading Darwin's theory of natural selection, Elizabeth Grosz (2004: 97–98) demonstrates that natural selection cannot be understood as some transparent notion of fitness, but is rather a complex set of two parallel processes – one, a force of 'internal dynamism within living beings', and the other, the assertion of external forces and influences. Both 'interfere' randomly with one another such that any sense of ordered teleology is disturbed.[8] Chance, in terms of both individual variation and external force, undoes the notion of evolutionary change as unfolding according to a predictable pattern (see Grosz 2004: 92; Deleuze and Guattari 1987: 54), while symbiotic transfer, lateral mixing, cross-species contamination, and viroid life all hack a popular Darwinism of descent by filiation in key ways (see Deleuze and Guattari 1987: 234–235; Ansell Pearson 1997: 187–189; O'Toole 1997: 164; Haraway 2007; Helmreich 2009: 80–105). In Helmreich's (2009: 81) words, we find the tree of life 'in a brambled state'.

Moreover, these evolution stories are not just biological tales. As Haraway (2004: 2) writes: 'There is no border where evolution ends and history begins, where genes stop and environment takes up, where culture rules and nature submits, or vice versa. Instead, there are turtles upon turtles of naturecultures all the way down. Every being that matters is a congeries of its formative histories – all of them.' Nature and culture are not dichotomous entities, and the former is certainly not the brute or inert matter that is inscribed or made meaningful by the latter. Using feminist philosopher Vicki Kirby's (2013) terms, we might instead think of evolutionary natures as always 'writing themselves' – reading, writing, and rewriting in an ongoing biography. For these thinkers, evolution mixes our categorical separations and certainties rather than reaffirming them.[9]

Evolution is also, as we shall see, where a phylogenetic memory rests in the spleen, where an ancestor is gathered up in a carrier bag, where whales and fish swim through our flesh in lost, loving echoes. In short, evolution is hardly a grand design of transparent improvement. It is complex, multivalent, and often ambiguous. If reading various evolutionary stories teaches us anything, it is that life evolves according to a multiplicity of processes, interconnected, certainly, but by no means uniformly sourced or directed (see Oyama, Griffiths, and Gray 2001). As Stefan Helmreich (2009: 76) reminds me, 'any origin story has multiple – even contradictory and mutually exclusive – versions'. Or we could put it like this: 'The attempt to develop a general theory of evolutionary systems is entirely dependent on the kinds of problems being set up' (Ansell Pearson 1997: 182).

The problem – if indeed you can call it that – I want to set up concerns our watery inheritances. I am interested in how focusing on our evolution as bodies of water might help us understand what it means to be a human body, trying to live ethically with the human and other-than-human watery bodies with whom we share this earth. I'm specifically interested in whether and how we can extend our sense of strange kinship to the planetary waters in which we variously swim and sink, and what work this kind of kinship imaginary might do.

Dissolving origin stories

Life began in the sea. While these swampy beginnings seem to comprise the main storyline of origins, Darwin's animation of life's first bubblings in an oceanic benthos only really surfaced in the late nineteenth century. Stefan Helmreich (2009: 73–74) reminds us that other narratives – of a static and barren dead ocean void of life, or of an abyss of serpents and dragons – have also held sway throughout human history. Yet, despite the fact that the Darwinian primordial ooze imaginary is relatively recent, there are plenty of other stories that have long affirmed the connections between water, beginnings, and life. In Australian Aboriginal cosmology, the Law understands the stream of life as generated by water (Strang 2013: 189), while the image of parting waters figures within a number of creation stories, from the Hindu goddess Bindumati who divides the Ganges to the Egyptian goddess Isis who divides the river Phaedrus. In Judeo-Christian creation stories, water exists before light. In others – stories of Acuecucyoticihuati, Aztec goddess of oceans, of the oceanic and menstrual Sumero-Babylonian goddess Tiamat, and of Hindu goddess Kali – water is often connected to a feminine fecundity, understood as a sacred source of creation (Gaard 2001: 160).

You have probably heard all this before. Indeed, these deep watery roots power the enduring allure of a return to the feminine seas, seemingly always swimming in the margins of our collective unconscious. In pointing this out, I do not mean to suggest that these myths have constantly 'led us astray'. Quite the opposite: their staying power signals something to be reconciled with our current moment. Are we telling different stories now, with the onset of late capitalist science? Unlikely. In many ways, the compounding context of contemporary water crises – ocean acidification, the draining of aquifers, the rising sea levels, and the traces of climate change in all of this – are *re*installing the imaginary of feminine, aqueous origins at every turn. In a special essay for National Geographic, Barbara Kingsolver (2010: n.p.) refers directly to 'Mother Water', and notes: 'Water is life. It's the briny broth of our origins, the pounding circulatory system of the world, a precarious molecular edge on which we survive.' But from another perspective, one could also argue – as does Stefan Helmreich (2009: 99) – that contemporary understandings of life's beginnings in deep sea thermal vents also install new imaginaries of biogenetic kinship which work to 'unsex' this idea of Mother Sea: 'If the sea was once a chaotic and cosmic amnion, an archive of life primeval and life to come, those pasts and futures nowadays read more like a mix-and-match database' of gene-trading microbes written in 'informative language'. Yet, even this story can't fully wash away the undertows and undertones of life-giving, gestational waters. As Helmreich recounts the message of *Volcanoes of the Deep Sea* – a 2003 IMAX film that tells of a possible hyperthermophilic origin for life in the hottubs of the ancient oceans – this narrative nonetheless still offers us 'the deep sea as a motherly matrix and nursery for life on Earth' (72).

What are we to take away from these tales? While Helmreich underlines the ways in which the Mother Sea narrative leaks out, pierced by the hypertext kinship narratives of the new technosciences, the maternal overtones of gestational waters are not easily flushed. Rather than arguing against the association of the feminine with water's gestationality, then, my goal is to expand our understanding of gestationality into posthuman waters. As we already saw in Chapter 2, all bodies of water are gestational. Keeping the feminine in the picture is not the problem (indeed, in many ways this non-forgetting is also a political imperative). The challenge is rather to see how maternal bodies are just one actualization of a more expansive gestationality as a capacity that all bodies of water share. Gestationality does not begin and end with the human, nor with a (heteronormatively inflected) female one at that. Gestationality is something we learn – something we repeat, differently – from water. This is an argument I make in various ways in this book, and which I explain in considerable detail in the previous chapter. Here, I want to focus on it in an evolutionary guise: as evolutionary bodies, water teaches us to repeat a proliferative capacity to gestate life, over and over again, always differently.

But the other point about these origin stories is precisely their divergence from one another. All origin stories – even the most carefully articulated scientific ones – are at some level speculative fabulations. While we may be able to pinpoint an individual parent-womb, the waters that gestate that body, and the body before that, inaugurate us into a watery cascade with no clear beginning. (Scientific accounts of the 'beginning' of planetary *water* are certainly far from definitive! See Kandel 2003, chapter 1.) This is not an epistemological deficiency, where just knowing more, or knowing better, might solve the problem. It is rather an opening to thinking about unknowability as another one of water's lessons. I'll return to this point at the end of the chapter. For now, let's stick with origin trouble, and some of the things we've forgotten.

Elizabeth Grosz (2004), in her recent work exploring the connections between Darwinian evolutionary theory and feminist politics, also notes the connection between our maternal beginnings and our evolutionary beginnings. 'We have forgotten where we have come from', she writes, but '[t]his is a double forgetting: of the elements through which all living things are born and live, a cosmological element; and of the specific body, indeed a chain of bodies, from which we come, a genealogical or maternal element' (2). In fact, the debts to which Grosz alludes here are three: first, to our material constitution that we too often forget to acknowledge in our ontological musings, but without which we could not *be* at all; second, to the specific maternal individual body that gestates us, which was arguably the primary focus of Irigaray's descriptions in *Marine Lover* (see Chapter 2); but thirdly, to the evolutionary bodies beyond our specific maternal gestational habitat. Grosz does not mention water specifically, but we might think more about how water ties these debts together.[10] We are of water, both in the constitutional sense and in the gestational sense, but the nature of gestation is now itself diffracted through the specific maternal body and the collective history of bodies in a watery 'politics of citation'.[11]

Yet despite her attention to the implications of our forgetfulness, Grosz carefully avoids referring to these debts as *origins*. These debts are indeed 'where we have come from', they are 'chain[s] of bodies' and 'elements through which all living things are born and live', but they are not causes or prime movers. She notes, '[t]he origin [of species] can be nothing but difference!' (Grosz 2004: 21). She concludes this from a nuanced reading of *The Origin of Species*, where Darwin never posits what 'the' origin might be. Instead, he produces a theory of descent with modification that is not predicated on distinct groups or identities of species, but rather considers, as Grosz puts it, 'how any provisional unity and cohesion derives from the oscillations and vacillations of difference' (21). Difference itself can be the only basis for the production and proliferation of difference. Grosz (2004: 26) elaborates further:

> Life 'began.' This origin, as much fable as strategic assumption, is not only obscure, conceivable only through abstract reconstruction or speculative genealogy, but is in a certain sense impossible to understand as a locatable or knowable entity, a definite point in time, a single chemical reaction, for it is an origin 'that is not one' that is always already implicated in multiplicity or difference, in a constellation of transformations, an event that imperceptibly affects everything.

The obscurity of these origins is like Irigaray's sea that we explored in Chapter 2, where it figured as an 'origin' whose depths cannot be definitively plumbed. Life's beginnings teem below the surface, but they cannot be pinpointed or isolated. But Grosz's comments here also remind us that gestationality is also always an operator of difference: even the beginnings of life in a proverbial primordial soup require a differenciation—that is, some intensive shift in material choreography such that the limits of affectability of this water are dramatically altered. This 'origin', then, must have already been a multiplicity, which is Grosz's point.

Here we could revisit Deleuze's understanding of the larval subject which I briefly expounded in the previous chapter. In Deleuze's notion of embryology, he argues that the larval subject, or egg, holds an unknown latency – a potentiality for expression that may never be expressed. Of interest to us here is that for Deleuze (1994a: 118–119, 214–217, 248–250) embryology is overlaid with theories of embryogenesis and evolutionary biology (see also Deleuze and Guattari 1987: 46–47). Deleuze implicitly takes up biologist Ernst Haeckel's 1866 (long since debunked) claims that 'ontogeny recapitulates phylogeny'. In this theory that remained popular in evolutionary circles for decades, Haeckel asserted that the growth of a human embryo is a miniaturized mirroring of phylogeny. This supported a teleological version of evolution, whereby development from amoeba, to invertebrate, eventually to tetrapod human was the destined course of progress. Deleuze rejects this. For him, evolution does not move from a more general possibility to a less general realization, as in the undefined embryo that develops more individuality as it progresses, or the simple amoeba that accrues more advanced and individualized traits as it 'evolves up' through species. Instead, evolution unfolds from virtuality to actuality. The embryo 'lives the unliveable', in Deleuze's words; the embryo holds all the potentiality that would rip an adult apart.[12] In order to grow from larva to adult, the adult must select what it can withstand. In other words, the emergence of specific bodies is not a given, but rather an active result of the forces of selection and differenciation. This reading of evolution, like Grosz's, is arguably close to Darwin's own. Evolution, like embryology, does not map a predetermined course where the 'more evolved' species (or adults) simply add complexity on to the 'less evolved' ones (or larvae). Both map a process whereby one body gestates another, who selects (or is gifted) something from the virtual potentiality teeming below the surface of the gestational body's materiality, in movements of difference and repetition that have no determined origin. Even as Grosz and Deleuze (here) focus on evolution by descent and natural selection, the origin of life is not a simple trickle to be tracked back to a clearly identifiable source.

The tree of life becomes even more obscured when we hack evolution in a lateral orientation. Cross mixings, lateral transfers, and symbiogenesis are a more direct concern for Deleuze and Guattari in *A Thousand Plateaus*, whose discussions of the orchid and wasp, and other lateral becomings, are widely known. These becomings are also at the core of Stefan Helmreich's (2009: 81) investigation into the dissolution of the tree of life, in the hot water of deep sea thermal vents. Contemporary microbiological studies of hyperthermophiles do not draw a clear line of descent at all, but instead reveal 'genetic trajectories pointing every which way'. In following these extremophiles, Helmreich discovers how 'lateral gene transfer in microbes places in jeopardy the vertical inheritance needed to root the tree of life' (87). Helmreich's focus is on how new paradigms of science – biogenetics, in this case – are finding new ways to break down life and build it up again, and what this might mean for how we understand kinship and ourselves (these ocean microbes, he concludes, are both 'a primordial version of ourselves' and also an 'alien' – an 'unfamiliar interloper'). But his other point is specifically about how lateral crossings disturb both linear genealogies and evolutionary timekeeping (105) – and, we should note, how these strange kinships are blooming in the sea. Below the surface, the origins of life are murkier than ever.

But even if life began in the sea, what happens to water as a gestational milieu, once we cross Zimmer's 'fatal boundary' that separates watery and terrestrial proclivities, divest ourselves of scales and fins, and learn to stand on our own two feet? Given this tendency to forget our watery beginnings, perhaps we need to pack a bag – a souvenir of sorts – and take it along for the ride.

Carrier bags and Hypersea

In 'The Carrier Bag Theory of Fiction', feminist writer Ursula LeGuin refers to Elizabeth Fisher's 1975 discussion of human evolution where she claims 'the earliest cultural inventions must have been a container to hold gathered products and some kind of sling or net carrier' (Fisher, quoted in LeGuin

1989: 166) – and not a sharp, pointy weapon, as the more popular story goes, at all. Carrying, in other words, is the first trick that we learned to do. For LeGuin, a key point here is that she can recognize herself in this story; in place of sagas of Man the Hunter, she finds a more capacious tale in which to root herself. It 'grounds me, personally', she writes, 'in human culture in a way I never felt grounded before. So long as culture was explained as originating from and elaborating upon the use of long, hard objects for sticking, bashing and killing, I never thought that I had, or wanted, any particular share of it' (167).

Again, it matters what stories we tell. Fisher and LeGuin's story makes sense ('If you haven't got something to put it in, food will escape you' [166]). It is also a more feminist origin story with no need for the biological essentialism of feminine docility (as LeGuin notes, she is often angry, and she'd happily club a hoodlum over the head with her handbag). For LeGuin, the point is that the carrier bag theory is more inclusive and does away with tired hero narratives. This in itself is a good reason to retell it (and, as we'll see below, offering origin stories that start from the place of sexual difference can result in all kinds of productive work). But as LeGuin also notes, a carrier bag holds things, and more than that it 'holds things in a particular, powerful relation to each other and us' (169). This leads me to wonder: what if we push LeGuin's tale even further? I suggest that we *ourselves,* as bodies of water, are also evolutionary carrier bags – facilitating the proliferation of the new by holding water and becoming literal gestational milieu for the other. What we hold is this potential for diffractive relationality.

The water that gave us life is also the water that we humans in turn carry with us, in us. We have literally incorporated this water, as Deleuze and Guattari remark in their epigraph above; the evolutionary emergence of terrestrial life depended upon this. Our own human bodies are approximately three-quarters water, but even life forms evolved to survive in the driest of conditions, such as desert plants, are still at least half soggy. Moving to a new terrestrial address meant that evolving life had to invent creative means for dealing with the threat of desiccation. One of these inventions was the amniotic egg, which kept amniote embryos perpetually in water thanks to their hard, calcium-rich shells. (This liquid insurance replaced the jelly encasing that surrounded fish and amphibian eggs, necessarily laid and gestated in a watery habitat in order to survive.)[13] Other innovations included the various salt and water uptake mechanisms that guaranteed sufficient quantities of both substances, for while aquatic animals were constantly immersed in water and appropriate amounts of saline, terrestrial animals had to actively seek these out. Such mechanisms range from the infiltration of the porous oral and anal surfaces of terrestrial woodlice (Little 1990: 204) to the dew-collecting innovations of a certain Namibian desert beetle who, when fogs are dense, scuttles to the top of a sand dune, stands with its head down and belly up, and drinks the water that condenses on and then flows down its body toward its mouth (205). Other specific innovations include the production of tough skin (to prevent excessive water loss), absorptive intestines (to allow water in), big lungs (to replace oxygen intake through water), and tears (to keep exposed eyes moist and allow vision to become acute) (Zimmer 1998: 109). All of these adaptations, of course, involve a negotiation of our bodies specifically in relation to their watery topography.

But a final innovation reveals the role of water in these adaptations as not only a tool for self-survival, but as a mechanism for the gestation and further proliferation of other life, too. This is what evolutionary scientists Mark and Dianna McMenamin call Hypersea, that is, the interconnected system of terrestrial life that has extended the sea and taken it along for the ride. The McMenamins (1994: 25) elaborate the fascinating process to which Deleuze and Guattari allude: 'The land biota represents not simply life from the sea, but a variation of the sea itself. Acting over evolutionary time as a rising tide, the land biota literally carries the sea and its distinctive solutes over the surface of the land, into some of the driest environments on Earth.' They elaborate: on land, the life sustenance that was passively accessible in a marine environment has to be actively facilitated through increasingly complex networks of microscopic organisms, fungi, and plants, as well as the animals – both human and otherwise – dependent on symbiosis, physical connection, and proximity. In Hypersea, life nests within other life on land like sets of Russian dolls. Or, one species visits another, bequeathing to it new species who seek out new routes of fluid fecundity in a novel other-species internal habitat. Without the sea to serve as a prime communicator and facilitator, life on land needed to chart its own watercourses – most available in the watery tissues and body fluids of other life forms.[14] This is how we became carrier bags.

Hypersea can also serve as an example of the kind of lateral process of evolution that disturbs teleological views of evolution by filial descent. For example, arthropods (likely the first terrestrial animals) invited fungi and other microbes into their bellies to help them digest plant matter. As the McMenamins note, 'indeed, a large living millipede is a virtual walking eco-system of gut-associated organisms', while 'such a level of gut diversity is unknown in the sea' (199). Or consider the case of the pentasome, an internal parasite of land vertebrates, with the following life story:

> (Pentasomes) attach to the host tissue by a row of hooks on their heads and feed on the blood and tissue fluids in the lungs and air passages of the host. (…) Pentasomes typically have two hosts during their life cycles. Male and female pentasomes mate within the final (or definitive) hosts. Their eggs pass out through the host's saliva, mucus secretions, and feces; the eggs are eaten by intermediate hosts, which can be fish, amphibians, small reptiles, small mammals, or insects. Inside their intermediate hosts, the pentasome eggs hatch into four- to six-legged larvae. The larval form bores through the gut of the intermediate host and enters vital organs, where it feeds and grows. When the intermediate hosts (possibly weakened by the infection of the parasite) are captured and eaten by a predator, such as a snake, the predator becomes the final host. The young pentasomes attach to the nasal passages and lungs of the predator and complete their life cycle. (200–201)

While there is speculation about the precise evolutionary history of pentasomes, the McMenamins argue that the internal, watery habitat of land animals, and the network of direct physical connection that the pentasome was required to invent on land, ensured this particular species', and associated species', further terrestrial proliferation. As they put it, 'the body fluids of land vertebrates ended up serving as an evolutionarily important reservoir of Hypersea' that 'makes a significant contribution to the total species diversity of organisms on land' (McMenamin and McMenamin 1994: 204). In other words, in symbiotic evolutionary processes, water is essential not only for the ongoing sustenance of any organism but also as a conduit for life-in-the-plural.

This is another way of imagining Hypersea as the kind of posthuman gestationality we explored in Chapter 2. In Hypersea, not only does the water that comprises us extend in and through other beings, but this extension also facilitates the gestation and proliferation of others – that is, we are carrier bags not only of our own 'descendants' in whom we may have a sovereign vested interest, but also for entirely different and 'distant' species. For example, it is quite likely that the Cretaceous dinosaur *Baryonyx walkeri* facilitated the proliferation of the pentasome parasite on land by ingesting, but not digesting, its marine-dwelling ancestor attached to the skin of the dinosaur's fishy prey (McMenamin and McMenamin 1994: 209). The watery body of the dinosaur thus gestates an other life, *with which she has ostensibly nothing in common.* She gestates the differentiation not only of her own repeated, filiative offspring but also of an other body of water who will nonetheless carry traces of that dinosaur to its next host body.

Posthuman gestationality extends gestational relations beyond 'growing a life' within a human mammalian womb or other amnion to include a more general gifting of one's own materiality in various ways, to different effects (not all of them happy, or innocent, to be sure). From the perspective of the dinosaur, we might refer to such relations as 'parasitical' (with all of the concomitant connotations). However, if we include the perspective of the pentasome, these relations are certainly gestational as well.[15] These 'webs of physical intimacy and fluid exchange' are not exceptional; they are a dominant feature of land-based life (McMenamin and McMenamin 1994: 15–19). As the ephemeral containers and conduits of Hypersea, Le Guin's carrier bags take shape as the bodies of terrestrial beings themselves.

Hypersea, like Helmreich's stories of hyperthermophilic microbial beginnings, cautions us against blurring the specific maternal body of gestation too facilely into a gestational chain of bodies that is evenly selected and descended. Helmreich, we recall, even suggests that new stories of symbiogenesis and lateral gene transfer might 'unsex' our evolution stories altogether, leaving Mother Ocean to be swept away in an incoming tide of bioinformatics. Helmreich's proposal makes once again visible the question of sexual difference, breathing just below the surface – especially as an enduring gendered imaginary of life's beginnings also seems to persist, despite this potential 'unsexing'. From the perspective of posthuman gestationality, however, the question here is not one of either keeping the maternal version of 'sexed' origins *or* flushing her away; it is rather one of thinking sex and reproduction differently. What if sexual difference in these evolutionary tales did not begin and end in the sexual dimorphism of bodies? Sexual difference can be rather a way of figuring the promiscuous fecundity of water more generally. Here, gestationality is always bound up in differentiation and dependent on the interpermeation of watery bodies of different kinds.

Wet sex

In *The Nick of Time* (2004) and *Time Travels* (2005), Elizabeth Grosz seizes directly on the suggestion that sexual difference is necessary for the proliferation of life and claims that sexual difference is ontological – that is, sexual difference is not 'a' key force of differentiation, but is in fact the key force, and the irreducible condition for life. According to Grosz (2004: 31), 'Darwin provides an ironic and indirect confirmation of the Irigarayan postulation of the irreducibility, indeed, ineliminability, of sexual difference [...] He makes sexual difference one of the ontological characteristics of life itself, not merely a detail, a feature that will pass.' Grosz points out how, according to Darwin, sexual differentiation must have occurred before the intricate splitting of species into plants and animals and before there was much detailed differentiation between animal species. Hence the variation introduced with sexual differentiation is responsible for the subsequent explosion of different life. Like Deleuze's explanation of the larval subject – the egg that holds an unknowable potential for proliferation and differentiation – Grosz's reading of evolution emphasizes that the proliferation of life depends upon a sexual difference which is 'incalculable' (67). According to Grosz, this is a 'difference which, in the future, will have been expressed, will have articulated itself' (67). At the same time (like Irigaray), she insists that this difference is one of 'two nonreducible forms' and makes repeated references to 'bifurcation' and 'dimorphism'.[16]

Grosz's insistence on two forms raises many of the same questions that Irigaray's writings on sexuate difference raises (see Chapter 2). Why only two? Why this clinging to a presumed cis-gendered dimorphism, when bodies clearly live and proliferate in other forms and serve as carrier bags of new and futures kinds of life all the same? Or, put otherwise: why insist on such a reductive understanding of *actualized* sexual difference and mechanisms of sexual reproduction? While bearing these critiques in mind, there is still something immensely (and even contradictorily) valuable in Grosz's reading of Darwinian sexual difference. For Grosz (2004: 69), sexual difference is an incalculable engine of the new, but one which produces difference that still carries a debt to the bodies that gestate it: '[Sexual selection] is a mechanism that ensures exponentially increasing variability, that necessitates that the heritable structure from each individual is different from that of each of its parents while in some respects resembling them both'. Those resemblances play out here as a watery feminist politics of citation, burrowed in the watery flesh of the yet-to-come. This is a sexual difference that requires difference itself as an engine – but even in Grosz's reading of Darwin we see that this does not *necessarily* require a masculine/feminine dimorphism. For example, Grosz also acknowledges that 'sexual division, with its correspondingly different reproductive capacities and morphological variations, entails potentially ever more divergent morphological structures' (Grosz 2004: 70). Grosz doesn't really emphasize what I read as the most exciting implication of her reading of Darwin: if sexual dimorphism burst onto the evolutionary scene as an ingenious way of proliferating life, there is nothing to prevent further mechanisms for expressing sexual difference from likewise emerging.[17] Pointing to this unknown future of sexual difference does not deny the role of sexual dimorphism as an important moment in the proliferation of life; it rather stresses that this dimorphism is an already actualized expression of sexual difference. As Grosz (2005: 67) also insists, sexual difference will not go away, but that doesn't mean it will stay this same; it will likely be complexified, elaborated, and developed further.

And of course, in many ways, that future has always already been here. In *Evolution's Rainbow*, evolutionary biologist Joan Roughgarden (2004) produces an impressive catalogue of the ways in which the existence of species in 'two nonreducible sexually reproducing forms', as Grosz puts it, is complicated. While sexual reproduction (compared to budding, fragmentation and parthenogenesis) produces a 'more balanced portfolio of genes' for better long-term survival (Roughgarden 5), even sexual reproduction is far from Boolean. Sex – that is, gamete size – may be mostly binaristic among sexually reproducing species, but there is no corresponding binary in body type, behaviour, and life story (26). Instead, we find various mechanisms for gestating and proliferating life and expressing sexual difference – little of which is particularly neatly binaristic. This includes: all-female species; species with two kinds of females; bodies that change from male to female, or are both, at different times in life; males that gestate eggs and bring offspring into the world; no chromosome difference between males and females; blurred female and male morphologies, or multiple males where one more closely resembles the female; females with phalluses and males with milk-producing mammary glands; and sexual power and dominant behaviours all over the sexually different map. Myra Hird (2004: 85–86), among others, has queered the sexuality of life more radically still, reminding us that most reproduction, in most species, has nothing to do with sex. And, as she has famously underlined, *Schizophyllum* fungi have more than 28,000 sexes (86)! For Hird (2004: 40), troubling our binaristic understandings of 'normal' sex is also about cross-species sexuality: sexual behaviour between flowers and various insects is so common, she notes, that it rarely even recognized as a queerly trans kind of sex.

Again, the point here is *not* to insist that these complex expressions are all necessarily appropriate for humans. Many, of course, are – but the point is rather that sexual difference is neither simply nor fully knowable, but rather open to new possibilities and recombinations. Evolution is one way in which this sexual difference is materialized. Evolution stories remind us that sexual difference as incalculable is not a culturally constructed queer utopia, but the very matter of the world we live in and as. As Roughgarden (2004: 18) notes, the purpose of sexual difference is probably not reproduction as such, since asexual species are perfectly capable of reproducing. Sexual reproduction is an engine of life because it generates increasingly greater diversity in species, and diversity is itself life-proliferating – but importantly, we do not know what life, or evolution, has in store for our future. The morphologies, behaviours, and stories attached to sexual difference will remain open.

But something else curious is going on here – and here, we finally return to the encounter that Zimmer sets up for this at the opening of this chapter. Let's take the dolphin that Zimmer encounters in his underwater meeting. According to common biology, 'male' dolphins and whales are described as having no external genitals, but rather a pair of testes located within their body cavity. The penis is found in a 'genital slit' that (unless erect) is covered by flaps, and male cetaceans have no scrotum (Roughgarden 2004: 40). The purpose for this architecture is hydrodynamic streamlining, but it also demands an innovative circulatory rerouting to keep the gonads cool enough to remain fertile (Zimmer 1998: 123). Roughgarden notes, however, that the rechoreographies required to maintain this genital architecture, although 'normal' in dolphins, would be considered a very exceptional intersex morphology in humans. Or let's take barnacles. Elizabeth A. Wilson (2002) recounts how it took Darwin years to puzzle out the complex sexuality of these specimens. While usually hermaphroditic, Darwin discovered some separately sexed species but where the female animals also harboured tiny 'complementary males' living on their bodies – something Darwin initially thought were parasites, but comes instead to describe charmingly (if somewhat heteronormatively) as the female having 'little husbands' in her 'two little pockets' (Darwin, quoted in Wilson 2002: 284) – or carrier bags, we might say! This is just a snippet of the complicated story of barnacle sex and gender that Darwin, and Wilson drawing on his work, tell. Oysters? Eva Hayward (2012) points out that they change sex up to four times a year. Sea squirts? Similarly queer. In some colony-forming species, fertilization takes place inside an individual ascidian, but development takes place in the chamber the system shares. In other colonial ascidians, reproduction is asexual: buds develop and grow to full size on an adult, then break off as new individuals (Neimanis 2011). Starfish, in Hayward's (2008) moving tribute, exhibit a trans-speciation whereby we can understand regeneration as a kind of transsex.

In other words, all of these animals are fascinatingly and 'naturally' queer. It is not only this gender-and-sex queerness that I'm intrigued by, though – for the more we look, the more we find that queer is the new (and old) norm. The question that stands out for me is rather, *does it matter that these bodies are bodies of water, and in water too?* Roughgarden (2004: 30–31) expands this queer aquatic menagerie: she notes that many variations on hermaphrodism are found in the oceans, among fish, marine mammals, and other sea life. Most marine invertebrates are hermaphroditic, as are a large proportion of coral reef fish, including most species of wrasses, parrot fish, and large groupers, and some species of damselfish, angelfish, gobies, porgies, emperors, soapfishes, dottybacks, moray eels, and various deep-sea fish as well. Many of these fish oscillate between male and female, or they may be male and female simultaneously (31–35). For Roughgarden – and importantly for the story I'm telling here – this is not evidence of a more 'primitive' sexuality in 'less-developed' species. Going back to the dolphin, Roughgarden wonders if 'perhaps cetaceans are on their evolutionary way to the state that hermaphroditic fish have already attained' (41). Or, we could say: not evolution, but revolution! She also notes that examples of sex role complexity are often found in the sea: the female seahorse who places her eggs in the male seahorse's pouch; the male who then gestates and 'delivers' the young (45). Many other marine species display various forms of parental care of embryos, such as watching over and nourishing eggs on a sea floor or lake bottom, or even storing eggs in their cheeks (45). We can find such examples among terrestrial species too, but genderqueer lives are particularly abundant in the water. Might we then wonder, along with Roughgarden, what it is about *aquatic environments* that is so accommodating – and even facilitative of – diverse actualizations of sexual difference?

Roughgarden does not offer an answer to this question, and the connection that I'm picking up on here remains speculative. I'm brought back to the difference that Zimmer announces in claiming a fatal boundary between those bodies that are at home in water and those that are not, but I'm also reminded of Deleuze (1994a: 118) who remarks that 'evolution does not take place in the open air'. For the egg or the larva, water is facilitative not only as an intensive morphogenetic element within bodies but also as an extensive or external force that creates for bodies certain possibilities for life. In the case of the queer aquatic bestiary gathering above, perhaps the great diversity of sexual difference there indexes a gestational possibility, an unknowable not-yet, teeming below the surface. Again, there is great diversity of sexual difference on dry land, but the overwhelming examples of aquatic queerness make the question one worth pondering.

Or, we could wonder, again along with Roughgarden, about the ways in which these animals might give us an inkling of sexual difference still-unfolding and yet-to-come, or along with Hayward, about the ways in which these animals can teach us to understand sexuality and our embodiment thereof in less rigid ways – even, I would offer, as a testament to our own potentialities, folded within the actuality of our bodies as echoes of these aquatic kin. But the idea that sexual difference might *become differently* in the water suggests something else as well – bringing us back to Zimmer's underwater encounter with which this chapter began. 'Breathing' water is but one example of an impossible torsion that is marked by how a body is not only *of* water but *in* water. What a terrestrial, aquatic (or amphibian) body can do, and can withstand, also depends on one's relation to water as an enduring habitat, home, or environment.[18] Our being in water, we could say, is a specific, embodied, situated knowledge (Haraway 1988). The surface of the water and the water's edge are both membranes of differentiation, with their own kind of membrane logic. Thinking with this ecotone, we discover that water is also a limit at which a commonplace understanding of evolutionary temporality is torqued; progress is not a linear movement 'out of' the seas. As Roughgarden and Hayward suggest, and as we are about to explore in more detail, evolution can also be a past anticipated, a future remembered.

Waters remembered (moving below the surface)

Returning to the sea can also be an expression of untimely love. In Italo Calvino's story 'The Aquatic Uncle', N'ba N'ga is the paternal uncle of the protagonist Qfwfq (himself a time-and-space-travelling narrator, who has lived and seen it all – all the way back to when the Moon was only a climb-up-the-stepladder away). The story of N'ba N'ga comes up when 'it was clear that the water period was coming to end', and Qfwfq recounts what was gained and what was lost in this terrestrial transition. While the mass migration to dry land was excitedly underway, Qfwfq tells of his embarrassing uncle N'ba N'ga (a lobefish, from the extinct species of Coelacanthus), who refuses to let go of the ocean, or even contemplate that things might be better on dry land. He insists on staying mired in the ecotonal muck, has a penchant for nonsensical fishy proverbs, and can only measure the world through the logic of water columns and currents. Hypersea was clearly not on his radar. As Qfwfq puts it, 'it just wasn't possible to make him accept a reality different from his own'. The mortification Qfwfq experiences, though, is not only that his uncle is out of step with the terrestrial zeitgeist; worse than that, N'ba N'ga lures Qfwfq's fiancée, Lll, back into the water: they fall in love, and she relearns to swim.

We already noted that Ernst Haeckel got it wrong. Ontogeny, as a rule, does not recapitulate phylogeny, nor is the reverse true. Citing fish as a particularly telling example, phenomenologist Merleau-Ponty (2003: 260) reminds us that 'we do not find either less numerous or simpler types by going back in the history of the earth'. When Lll rejects Qfwfq in order to join N'ba N'ga in his aquatic life, this is not a 'regression' as in some kind of progress thwarted, or a reversal of evolutionary teleology. Just as water, in its multivalent hydrological cyclings of difference and repetition, thwarts easy geographies of local and global, so too do our watery evolution stories disturb a clean linearity of forward and back. Even if we often frame stories like Lll's as a 'return', Lll doesn't regress. She rather selects another possibility, reopened. The humble sea squirt (already noted above for its wild sex life) also provides a good disclaimer against phylogenetic 'progress' ostensibly mirrored in the unfolding of a single animal: while its newborns are vertebrate, this ascidian reabsorbs its rocky spine somewhere along the path to maturity. Like those rarest of rivers, repetition flows both ways. Here, 'progress' is like a strange kind of amnesiac repetition – repetition as the forgetting of a vertebrate future that for this creature quickly slips away as a morphogenetic past, the brain and the tail consumed, eaten by the developing self. Autotrophy? Perhaps. Chordate futurity digesting in the body, waiting to be selected. Past and future collide and switch.

Yet, despite Haeckel's technical missing-the-mark, I can understand where he's coming from. After all, what expectant human mother has not at some point imagined her foetus as tadpole, all fish eyes and fins, pre-amphibious, somersaulting its way through her amniotic seas? Her pasts literally well up inside her, time a crumpled up tissue, now responding to the swell. Something is remembered: a tail reabsorbed, an aorta hooked... Perhaps the watery bodies we gather in our carrier bags are also memories of a could-have-been and traces of futures not yet lived.

Lest these rememberings all sound a bit too precious, we could also call on the work of Sandor Ferenczi, erstwhile student and pen pal of Sigmund Freud. In a theory that he reluctantly published only late in life, Ferenczi suggested that dreams of water recall not only the trauma of birth, as we are expelled from our mothers' wombs, but also the phylogenetic 'catastrophe' of the drying up of the seas, a loss we tetrapods have shouldered for millennia. Countless tales from patients of fishy dreams, watery trauma, and briny passions[19] lead Ferenczi (2005: 45) to wonder:

> What if the entire intrauterine existence of higher mammals were only a replica of the type of existence which characterized that aboriginal piscine period, and birth itself nothing but a recapitulation on the part of the individual of the great catastrophe which at the time of the recession of the ocean forced so many animals, and certainly our own animal ancestors, to adapt themselves to a land existence, above all to renounce gill-breathing and provide themselves with organs for the respiration of air?

Our traumas are personal, says Ferenczi, but they are also phylogenetic – even geological, we could add. As Ferenczi aimed to clarify in his Thalassal proposition, our bodies harbour the memory of the terrestrial invasion, and a forsaking of the sea. The penis in the vagina,[20] the foetus in the uterus, the fish in the water – in these various watery embraces, Ferenczi postulates a shared symbolism that is more than semiotics. It is an embodied collective memory and a 'phylogenetic recognition of our descent from aquatic vertebrates' (1968: 45). Desire, loss, sociality, grief – these phenomena are biological as much as they are psychological or cultural. Ferenczi (perhaps also remembering a future still-to-come) called this a matter of the biological unconscious.[21]

Freud, apparently, was not impressed. And to add scientific insult to psychoanalytic injury, Ferenczi's theories were based in part on Haeckel's findings – which we know have been established as flawed. But just because evolution did not necessarily unfold from (less-developed) fish fry to the (more sophisticated) biped, the idea of watery return isn't fully washed away. The fossil record itself gives us another story of watery return in the forsaking of dry land by cetaceans. These marine mammals – whales, dolphins, porpoises – are certainly not fish, but this is the whole point of their story. Cetaceans both leave the sea and return there, queerly suturing fishy past and watery future together. Thinking about them as part of our own 'fishy beginnings' helps us imagine how our own bodies harbour not only watery traces of evolutionary pasts but also the latent watery potential of evolutionary futures not chosen.

When Darwin was writing his theories of evolution, the origin stories of whales were something of a mystery, although he did muse that a 'race of bears' could have conceivably evolved into whales. While his speculations were for the most part laughed right out of subsequent printings of *On the Origin of Species* (Zimmer 1998: 144–145), we now think that Darwin's suggestion was not as ludicrous as it once sounded. As one story tells it, whales are likely descended from a common terrestrial tetrapod ancestor known as the *Mesonychid*: a meat-eating wolf-like ungulate that lived about 65 million years ago. But as Zimmer notes, Mesonychids were slightly 'anatomically confused', given their environment, diet, and job in life. They had a taste for meat, but their stiff back did not let them run down prey. Instead they likely scavenged the bones of others' kills, or snapped with their snouts at turtles and the odd fish in the shallows near their homes. As a result, they soon developed rudimentary swimming abilities, and better teeth for hooking their aquatic prey.

A more recent story provides a slight variation: The closest known terrestrial relative to the whale was *Indohyus*, a fox-sized deer-like land mammal that did not like meat at all, and rather spent long amounts of time in the water in order to avoid becoming someone else's dinner. Eventually, with not a lot of other choice at hand, *Indohyus* developed a taste for fish, and for a more aquatic lifestyle all around (Briggs 2007). In either case, these land-dwellers eventually learned to swim deeper, their legs grew shorter, their feet grew webbing, and they became part of a genealogy of whales. Each of these earliest whales – *Pakicetus, Ambulocetus, Rodhocetus, Takracetus, Gaviocetus, Dalanistes* – honed its own specialities. Walking and swimming whales lived side by side. Some persevered in time, some did not, for reasons which are not altogether clear (recalling that descent is not teleological, or singly-purposed, and is interrupted by all sorts of unpredictabilities). The walkers died out, and by about 40 million years ago, whales were thriving without any terrestrial outcrop to cling to. They had officially changed their mailing address.

While commonplace evolution stories associate us hominids most closely with our primate kin, we also share considerable bodily connectivity to whales and other cetaceans. We both have lungs that breathe air, and giant brains wrinkled with neocortex. We both function best when our bodies are about 98 degrees Fahrenheit. We both survived infancy on a diet of our mothers' milk. Peel back the blubber of a cetacean's fin and you will see something not unlike our own human hands: five fingers, a wrist, an elbow, a shoulder. We are both social animals. We both gestate our babies within our own watery wombs, and then spend inordinate amounts of time training our young for life without us. In terms of what humans consider smarts, the Brazilian river dolphin leads the cetacean pod as our closest runner-up, with other primates an only somewhat distant second.[22]

As a partial explanation of these affinities, in the 1960s Sir Alister Hardy speculated about the existence of hydrophilic apes as an element of human evolution. This theory was subsequently picked up by Elaine Morgan (1972, 1982) and developed into the so-called 'Aquatic Ape theory'. As Morgan suggests, the siren song that beckoned the great whale's return to the sea could be understood as one of our evolutionary paths not taken. Most commonly accepted theories of human evolution revolve around something called the 'Savannah theory', whereby forest-dwelling apes literally came down from the trees due to major climatic changes that resulted in the dwindling of the massive African forests. On the propagating savannah, where a vegetarian diet was more difficult to accommodate, these apes become plains-dwelling hunters. They learned to run on two legs and use tools or weapons. They eventually became 'Man'. Morgan, however, was sceptical of this theory for more reasons than one. Not least by considering more carefully the place of females in the descent from ape to hominid, Morgan began to develop her own evolution story, suggesting that something else needed to explain the differences between humans and existing apes, which seemed strange, given our exceptionally close genetic alliances as primates. These differences include structural differences in our skeletons, muscles, skin, and brains; differences in posture and locomotion; differences in social organization; and differences in capacity for speech and intellect. Other not easily explained human departures from our primate kin include a naked foetus, a hairless human adult (who nonetheless maintains a strange wealth of head hair), large deposits of subcutaneous fat, and notably, innate diving reflexes and swimming infants. None of these traits is very ape-like.

So Morgan's story goes like this: during a gap in the human history fossil record, large swathes of the African continent were flooded by seas. During this time, some apes did indeed come down from the trees and became not hunters of the savannah, but semi-aquatic coastal dwellers. They spent their days diving and swimming, and living along the pebbly shores of these vast bodies of water. Later, when the seas receded, they returned to their former terrestrial address, but remarkably changed for the experience. Perhaps this ape lost its hair, because like the whale, she needed to stay warm in the water, and thus opted instead for a nice cushion of subcutaneous insulation. Perhaps she nonetheless held on to her abundant tresses (allowing her hair to grow thicker during pregnancy) so that her infant would have somewhere to cling while they paddled about together in the sea. Perhaps in water, where scent signals lose their usefulness and subtle visual cues are obscured, this ape needed to find her voice. Perhaps while navigating the seas she developed her fine sense of balance in an upright, bipedal position. Perhaps this predilection to stand on her own two feet came instinctively when she first waded, tentatively, into an increasing deep.

Because of the fossil record gap, neither the Aquatic Ape theory nor the Savannah theory can be irrefutably proven. Morgan maintains that the Aquatic Ape theory simply makes more sense. It requires fewer stretches of the imagination, fewer instances of convoluted logic. While her theories (not unlike Darwin's 'race of bears') were initially the subject of considerable scorn within the scientific community, more recently evolutionary biologists have returned to the Aquatic Ape theory with keen interest (while others, of course, remain fervent detractors).[23] But in many ways the *definitive truth* of the story is not really the point – we've already established that origin stories are necessarily a muddle, more or less. I'm interested instead in the Aquatic Ape's plausibility, and its allure. What is it about Morgan's version that calls to us, that asks the echoes in our salty tear ducts, or our watery wombs, to respond?

Ursula LeGuin responded to Elizabeth Fisher's carrier bag theory of evolution because she could see herself in it. We could say the same for Morgan's. It too is a feminist evolutionary tale, where gestating bodies and sexual difference are foregrounded. The lack of widespread uptake of her theories must be filtered through Morgan's (deemed inadequate) credentials as a journalist and housewife, rather than a lab-coated 'serious' scientist. If we take Donna Haraway's (1988) important claims for feminist objectivity seriously, then Morgan's situated knowledge makes her story most plausible, and certainly most interesting: it is a story that comes from somewhere, grounded in embodied knowledge of the world. In this framework, the

Descent of Woman (Morgan 1972) might reverberate through and transform our stories of the *Descent of Man* (Darwin 1988 [1871]).

There is also a more embodied empathy that we might feel with Morgan's story. Perhaps we experience our contemporary bulkiness and the cumbersome lumbering of dragging all this flesh around behind us, as a biological or phylogenetic memory, as Ferenczi would say. Our buoyancies constantly thwarted, dry land proved too unbearable for some, and not at all what it was cracked up to be. Some of us – whales, dolphins, porpoises – mutated into a cetaceous state. Even if it meant holding our breath for hours, for days, we would learn these tricks. Anything to return to our fishy beginnings. Our now-human bodies carry this echo of a watery return not chosen, a path back to the sea not taken. Isn't this what our human mammalian diving reflex, or a newborn infant's instinctual capacity to swim, in some ways demonstrates?

Put otherwise, even if becoming cetacean may not be ontogeny recapitulating phylogeny (or vice versa), I'm still intrigued by the power of a 'wrong theory'. The endurance of Haeckel's idea that our bodies are compelled to remember the sea suggests there is some plausibility to his postulations – and to Ferenczi's recapitulation of them. Like the mutual imbrication of psyche and soma that Ferenczi describes as 'amphimixis', our aquatic embodiment might be similarly amphimixic – an inextricable mutuality of organic memory, bodily capacity, and amplified imagination. When we start attuning to our own fishiness, our own cetacean almost-ancestry, and maybe amplify it through evolution stories like these, Ferenczi's suggestion that our organs remember, that our bodies are archives of deep times and tangled genealogies, does not seem that strange.

For aren't these ideas, at some level, 'verifiable' through a close attunement to the way we move, the way we love, the repetition of our animal and elemental others in us – gathered, and repeated differently? Our human bodies 'are coral reefs full of polyps, sponges, gorgonians, and free-swimming macrophages continually stirred by monsoon climates of moist air, blood, and biles', suggests Alphonso Lingis (2000: 28). Or in the words of feminist philosophers Hélène Cixous and Catherine Clément (1986: 88, see also Chapter 2) (remembering the gestational logic that connects the French homonyms 'mer' and 'mère'): 'we ourselves are sea, sands, corals, seaweeds, beaches, tides, swimmers, children, waves…seas and mothers'. While the language these philosophers use takes part of its power from metaphor – recall Suzuki's equation of our blood to seawater in one of the epigraphs to this chapter – neither description is *mere* metaphor. If it is a metaphor, this metaphor is only effective because it calls out a material resonance within us with that experience. We could say: *these are waters, remembered.* If we were not somehow materially in contact with these experiences, the metaphor would hold no sway. We verify this bodily empathy because our own embodiment soaks up and holds traces of our watery bodies' deep potentialities (their would-have-beens; their might-still-becomes) within us, tucked away in/as our carrier bags. This is evolution! We are materially connected to these watery pasts, even though these larvae differ from us in kind.

As with Irigaray above, Lingis does not imagine our animality as separate from our elementality. A transcorporeal connectedness between these realms insistently reverberates through Lingis's posthuman phenomenologies of embodiment. Our bodies as corals and polyps converge with our affective bodies and our motor bodies; in both cases we learn to feel and move by drawing on the echoes of other animals in our own flesh: 'It is when we see […] the mother elephant carrying her calf in grief for three days that we believe in the reality of maternal love' (Lingis 2000: 36); we ebb and flow with the rhythms and speeds of animal movements, which in turn initiate our own movements as 'our legs plod with elephantine torpor', or 'as our hands swing with penguin vivacity, our fingers drum with nuthatch insistence' (29). In sex, 'our muscular and vertebrate bodies transubstantiate into ooze, slime, mammalian sweat, and reptilian secretions, into minute tadpoles and releases of hot moist breath nourishing the floating microorganisms of the night air' (38). Our watery bodies can serve as the soupy gestational matter for our material passions and can invite a mingling of these passions in such a way that the discreteness of our individualized bodies begins to dissolve. While we can leak beyond the boundaries of our molar bodies, this transubstantiation of bodies into viscous ooze is also a marker of the mingling of our bodies with those potential bodies of water that we have incorporated – those fishy, watery beginnings that we carry with us as material, vestigial potentiality.

Our emotions and our movements are a response to the animal, vegetable, meteorological emotions and movements of which we are a part. In phenomenological terms, both human and other animal beings are variant 'folds within the world's flesh' (Toadvine 2007: 52), but these bodies are not affectively separate from the environmental and elemental milieus which they also gather and repeat, differently – for Lingis (2000: 28), 'the pulses of solar energy momentarily held and refracted in our crystalline cells' and 'the microorganic movements and intensities in the currents of our inner coral reefs'. These echoes are offered again not as metaphor, nor as scientific reduction, nor as 'mere' speculation, but rather as a modality of our lived embodiment. Lingis's phenomenology stresses that these echoes are the amplification of the potential we already hold, as elemental and animal bodies, gathering up and repeating their tangled pasts. Perhaps this is an extended kind of echolocation, across scrambled genealogies and symbiotic generations.

Unknowability as planetarity (or, becoming the water that we cannot become)

So what does it mean to remember our fishy beginnings? You might find yourself sinking, a bit breathless, in this undertow of affect and memory, of science and fable, of gut feelings and fossil records, motor-body archives, and a biological psyche. But isn't this what a posthuman feminist phenomenology of our watery bodies can do? In imagining ourselves as extended across space and time, but also suspended between ostensible fact and so-called fiction, this kind of phenomenology draws on all of our sensory apparatuses to find different kinds of stories to tell.

A posthuman feminist phenomenology, though, is also attuned to the limits of our stories, where stories dissolve beyond our capacities to tell them, even as we still gather them in our various carrier bags. I've suggested that being in water is a situated knowledge. Water in this sense has something to teach us about knowledge, and the incitement to know.

Let's go back to Lingis briefly, who, like Zimmer in the opening pages of this chapter, and like Ferenczi and Morgan and even old N'ba N'ga, is curious about what happens in our sloshy transition between water and air, or from land back to sea – over the span of millennia, or in the space of a single encounter. Contemplating the cetacean return to the sea, Lingis (2000: 32) notes 'the tedium of the bodies we had to evolve when we left the ocean':

> A hundred seventy pounds, of salty brine mostly, in an unshapely sack of skin: what a clumsy weight to have to transport out on bony legs! [...] When we return to the ocean, we have to pull a layer of rubber skin over our bodies, strap on a buoyancy compensator, an air tank with regulator and gauges, weight belt, eye mask, and flippers. And then how ludicrous we look when we lurch our bodies equipped with all these prosthetic organs out of the dive shop and wade with flippered feet across the beach till we reach deep water! In the deep, all these supplementary organs make our species-organs non-functional.

We find an empathy with our strange kin in and through our embodied difference – we can 'certainly understand the dolphins and the whales', writes Lingis (2000: 32), in their decision to forgo a terrestrial existence. Yet while our different capacities in relation to a watery topography do not impermeably contain us in discrete isolation from one another, they do inaugurate a border beyond which travelling proves fatal. We know that in becoming-animal, to destratify too far results only in annihilation (Deleuze and Guattari 1987: 270).

'A whale out of water', writes Jacques Cousteau (1972: 47), 'even though it is an air breather, dies very quickly. Despite its incredible power, it simply does not have sufficient strength to breathe in the open air'. The pioneering oceanographer further explains:

> A whale aground in the open air [...], is condemned to death. He has not the strength, nor the limbs, to regain the life-giving water. He smothers; and it is his very size and mass that kills him. All of his power, great though it is, is not sufficient to fill his lungs, to move the tons of blubber that cover his body. And he dies of asphyxiation. (44–45)

Or in the words of Rebecca Giggs (2015), witnessing the slow death of a stranded humpback on a beach in Western Australia, 'in the ocean its blubber fat insulates the whale and allows the animal to maintain a constant inner temperature. Out of the ocean, the blubber smothers it ... Though we were now shivering, the whale – only metres away – was boiling alive in the kettle of itself.'

Despite all of the ways in which we humans feel a deep affinity for water and our own cetaceous or fishy beginnings (and no less depend on water for life), for our terrestrial bodies the 'borders of the liveable', as Deleuze would say, begin at the water's edge. For our strange cetacean kin, this is also where they end – perhaps like this, on a beach, too large to euthanize in any kind of conventional manner, too expensive to blow up with dynamite (Giggs 2015). For our cetaceous kin, the open air means a demise of inevitable suffering.

Water, as a larger geographical body, situates animal bodies of water in different ways, calling out our specifically differentiated capacities and challenging our deficiencies. This membrane of differentiation does not cancel out our interpermeation in one another's bodies: we only experience the awkward inappropriateness of our human organs for the watery deep because enfolded in our own materiality is the remembered potential to breathe only intermittently, to dive to unimaginable depths, to communicate wordlessly through echoes with our kin, wandering as an 'overlapping network linked through a transparent ocean'.[24] Yet we also ultimately encounter the question of what is liveable. Different bodies (human, sunflower, toad, jellyfish) express varying abilities to live *in* water and *with* water. In other words, bodies are oriented in and towards water in species- or being-specific ways; humans, it follows, are situated in relation to water in a very human-specific way. This human specificity certainly differs from that of fish, but also from that of other mammals. For example, while our kinship with air-breathing whales is expressed in manifold ways, we eventually have to let go of the dorsal fin: the whale will always outswim us, while our own lungs inevitably give out. Our strange cetacean kin can dive to depths our own bodies could not fathom.

And our capacity to withstand life in the water involves more than morphology. As Zimmer notes, we still have hardly any idea of what cetacean intelligence means, or of what their brain-bodies are capable. Dolphins, for example, in their watery world, where everything touches everything, most likely experience themselves 'in' their bodies in a way altogether foreign to us. In their communication through echolocation visions, their interior and exterior worlds begin to blur, and 'our notion of self would be entirely meaningless to them' (Zimmer 1998: 134). We do not think that baleen whales can echolocate, but we have no idea what they might perceive or how they might engage their bodies in relations of intercorporeality (Zimmer 1998: 134). Cousteau (1972: 128), too, notes that there is so much about cetaceans' tactile sense about which we know almost nothing; their sensory life is undoubtedly complex, but we have barely scratched its surface. While ethological sciences continue to expand their knowledge base, we might consider the limits as well as the rewards of these pursuits.

The seas are teeming with events that humans will only ever glimpse. Any body's orientation to water as material substance, and as geographical location, serves as a *limit* that determines which milieus are habitable, withstand-able, and thus knowable. Water remains one step ahead of, and beyond, the limits of any body (regardless of their watery orientation). In this way (and in resonance with other feminist epistemological projects of situated knowledges), the grammar of water necessarily rejects total knowledge by *any* body. Because each body has a different relation to water *as a matter of survival*, no body can do what Donna Haraway calls 'the God Trick'. No body can ever fully know water. Even the most sophisticated deepwater submersibles and assisted breathing apparatuses will only ever take us so far, for so long. We humans can only be fully immersed in water as a temporary gesture – just as other species will never stand at the water's edge, contemplating its depths, nor experience the water's 10 degree fingers still crawling under warm-blooded skin after an early Spring dip off the dock clothed the lake's dawn breath. Our different embodied orientations to water tell us something about our varying capacities to *know* water. For me, this also underlines questions of incursion, hubris, and humility, as something water can teach us about difference, and knowledge.

It seems I have introduced a paradox. On the one hand, I passionately argue for a shared aqueous kinship between all bodies of water. It is this embodiment-in-common, I suggest, that can help us understand ourselves as bodies of water as meaningfully (ethically, politically) implicated in other bodies of water into and out of whom we flow. Within and as the hydrological cycles that animate this planet, our embodied watery debts are multiple and diffuse, as too are our gifts (poisonous or otherwise) to our watery others. At the same time, I've suggested that our situatedness as specific bodies means that there are depths that we cannot plumb. So, even if evolution stories amplify the ways in which our bodies of water are indebted to bodies that precede us, we must still give up the illusion of transparent filiation.

The paradox in mapping these chains of watery connections is thus also a risk. We return to the conundrum of difference in the hydrocommons, a key question that animates each of this book's chapters in its own way. In acknowledging our commonality, we risk succumbing to the idea that our embodied debts are fully knowable. Surely, if we are all bodies of water then your water is also, somehow, mine. So the logic would go: We are all part of the same big happy family tree, and we all know each others' secrets. Difference here is familiarized. It would become a problem that is 'solvable', something that can be assimilated. If the unknown creeps in at all, we get the feeling that our problem, if we have one, is simply lack of information: *we just don't know enough, or enough yet.* In other words, one could suggest that the only thing at stake here is the difference between ontological assertion (we are all connected…) and epistemological limit (…even if we can't humanly grasp, or know, the depth of those connections). But this is a false solution. It still holds out hope for mastery: *if only we could just know more deeply, more fully, more masterfully*… the problem would go away. All of the watery world would be at our fingertips – held tightly, securely, in our waterproof bags.

The danger doesn't stop there. While commonality risks the notion of subsumability, relegating the ocean to the zones of 'here be dragons' suggests another risk, too – one we might refer to as an oceanic Orientalism. As Stefan Helmreich (2009) describes, this is the kind of unknowability that was revived with the discovery of hyperthermophiles living (and thriving) in the dark abyss of deep sea vents. This is the unknowability of the 'Dark Continent' where the unknown swims within a colonial imaginary of the savage in the shadow realm. Helmreich quotes *New York Times* writer William Boyd, who speaks of the eerie wonder we must now feel, realizing that 'we and all the other light-eaters of Earth shared our planet with an alien horde that thrived in total darkness' (Broad, quoted in Helmreich 2009: 75). As Helmreich points out, this horde-speak harkens back to nineteenth-century descriptions of colonized peoples (in the words of social evolutionist Lewis Henry Morgan) as a 'promiscuous horde'. According to Helmreich, 'the alien of the alien ocean is sometimes figured as a primitive other, marked as such through the trope of darkness, a figure that both suggests an absence of enlightenment and calls up

the fearsome and fascinating dark bodies of racialist discourse' (76). Here we
see how racialized fear trades off with the maternal abyss, the feminine Other,
even the Vagina Dentata of fearful watery phantasy.

I am not interested in an unknowabilty that shadows knowledge of
a colonized other, or a dangerous feminine one either, but rather an
unknowability that we can learn from thinking with difference. Foucault has
written of the uncanniness of places as heterotopias; theorist of architectures
and watery places, Cecilia Chen (2013), has helpfully drawn on Foucault to
understand water as a non-place, as a place both comfortable and unfamiliar,
as a place that can become uncanny and transformed through upheavals
(Chen gives the example of a major oil spill). Chen here, too, talks about
waters as 'places at the thresholds of experience and comprehensibility'
(282) where the meaning of waters is neither steady, nor uniform, nor easily
mapped. Feminist cultural theorist Elspeth Probyn (2013: 10), too, has drawn
on Foucault's 'Other Spaces' to describe how we might map an oceanic world
of tuna: 'this is a heterotopic geography', she writes, produced from and
constitutive of a set of irreducible relations. These reminders of the unevenness
of a wet epistemology – its palimpsestic superimpositions; its scrambling of
simple coordination between the local and the global; its knowability quickly
caught up in an undertow of change – help us foreground the way in which
any definitive meaning of water cannot be held; water will not be captured
and contained in this way. While Foucault's heterotopias are helpful, I suggest
that turning to Spivak adds further depth to his insights. Parsing the relation
between water and knowledge specifically through a lens concerned with
coloniality emphasizes the ethics and politics at stake in any incitement to
know water, and to master it.

In the third chapter of her book *Death of a Discipline*, postcolonial feminist
Gayatri Spivak (2003) critiques the logic of globalization that tries to introduce
a knowable, plottable uniformity to the globe. She argues that instead of being
global, we should strive to be planetary: 'The globe is on our computers', she
writes. 'No one lives there. It ["the global"] allows us to think we can aim
to control it' (72). But, she continues, 'the planet is in the species of alterity,
belonging to another system; and yet we inhabit it, on loan' (72). To put it
otherwise, the language of 'globalization' for Spivak is strongly linked to a logic
of knowability and knowledge-control. It presumes a world that can be laid

out, grid-like, plotted on our GPSes and ultimately comprehended-conquered. Spivak counters the image of the globe ('even though it is not really amenable to a neat contrast with the globe') with planetarity: 'Planet-thought opens us up to embrace an inexhaustible taxonomy of the names [of radical alterity]' (73). Planetarity is '(im) possible' to represent because of this very inexhaustibility. It is always more than it is. But key for Spivak is the fact that this 'beyond' is also lived; it is also of us, with us, through us, alongside us (hence the 'im' of the possible is couched in a parenthetical signpost). 'To be human is to be intended toward the other' (Spivak 2003: 73), but this other-ness cannot be easily displaced onto a transcendental difference, derived from us as our not-I (mother, god, nature – or Water, as synecdoche of any of the above). Embracing 'planet-thought', she explains, can open up a different understanding of and relation to otherness:

> If we imagine ourselves as planetary subjects rather than global agents, planetary creatures rather than global entities, alterity remains underived from us; it is not our dialectical negation, it contains us as much as it flings us away. And thus to think of it is already to transgress, for, in spite of our forays into what we metaphorize, differently, as outer and inner space, what is above and beyond our reach is not continuous with us as it is not, indeed, specifically discontinuous. We must persistently educate ourselves into this peculiar mindset (Spivak 2003: 73).

In other words, we are riven through with this otherness, and it is enfolded in us and as us as well – but it *is underived from us*. We humans are not the origin of this relationality.

Planetarity is the species to which water belongs. This 'of me yet beyond me' is the unknowability to which water asks that I attend. Water as planetarity also suggests an epistemology that is engaged, embedded, embodied; a way of knowing that is somewhere, situated, implicated – in time, in space, in other bodies of other beings – but this is also a form of knowledge in which that location will always exceed my bounds (as even this 'my' leaks out of my watery body beyond the realm of any knowability). In an epistemological register, formulaic, codified, categorizable access to planetarity is not possible. We are its curious custodians rather than its masters. *Intimacy is not mastery.* We are always becoming water, but water is also always beyond us. We are becoming water that we cannot become – not in any full sense of finality, completion, or control.

In thinking knowledge with water, feminist concerns about power and responsibility swim to the surface.[25] Where knowledge and water collide, it seems crucial to know more about what we are doing to water, and to ourselves, as bodies of water, in light of water's ecological precarity. We *do* need more knowledge about the causes and effects of our plastinated oceans, about the catastrophic damage being done by the Tar Sands megaprojects to the Athabasca watershed and the many bodies nourished by it, about other extraction industries in the Amazon and the Niger Delta, about the effect of mining on the Great Barrier Reef in Australia, and about the even more shadowy shadow places (Plumwood 2008) of our fossil-fuelled loves. We *do* need more knowledge about the levels of heavy metals in our drinking water and about the levels of water in our aquifers that we are draining far too rapidly. And again, while these are ecological issues, they are also feminist and anti-colonial concerns. The harm that we do to water is never equally distributed across human bodies. The flows of biomatter also chart the flows of global power. In other words, a call to recognize water in the species of alterity, as unknowable, is not a call for an epistemology of ignorance (Tuana 2004). Unknowability is not about refusing to acknowledge water's many wounds and our different capacities to inflict and withstand those violences, but about recognizing that at the end of the day, water will still exceed us – our sovereign subject bodies, and our capacity to fully know.

How far should our quests for knowledge reach? A respect for water's unknowability is instead part of an epistemology that would seek a different relation to water – one in which we were not always bending it to a human will, or instrumentalizing aquatic life in the pursuit of human fantasies. The Census of Marine Life, for example, promises to document every single species of life in the seas; exploratory vessels are increasingly penetrating our oceans' benthic zones to document these mysterious ecosystems. The relationship between knowledge and water is not simple, but understanding this relationship seems also to be a question of distinguishing between kinds of knowledge – knowledge that commoditizes and colonizes, knowledge that generates necessary anger and action, knowledge that heals. Knowledge that builds communities, or knowledge that fractures them. Knowledge that responds, or knowledge that masters (see Code 2006; Smith 2012; Wilson 2008). Imagining ourselves as bodies of water, carrying each other across species, generations, and geographies – all audaciously heterotopic – might also demand learning something from water about our incitement to know.

Planetarity does not displace an ontological question with an epistemological solution: planetarity does not suggest that while some waters are knowable, others remain hidden or beyond our comprehension; planetarity rather insists that all water partakes in unknowability, as an ontological demand. Because all waters are gestational, always becoming different, always gathering existing and potential waters and recasting them, anew, no waters are fully knowable – not the water of the Other, nor the hypermarine channels burrowing through my own flesh. Despite all of the harm we do to it, in one sense water *is* inexhaustible – the things that it does and the bodies it proliferates cannot ultimately be predicted. Again, water is one step ahead of any body. As feminist theorist Karen Barad (2008a: 174) would say, water reminds us that the world is 'not a secret to be revealed' by us humans. It is rather in a constant process of emergence. As a gestational engine of life, growth, and change, water defies epistemological capture and containment – even, or especially, in our own bodies as carrier bags.

Aspiration, that oceanic feeling

Evolution stories help us think about water – both individual bodies of water and entire species as bodies of water – as a gestational milieu that connects us all. Gestation here is never a complete forsaking; its gifts are never entirely given, and the gestated body never leaves her gestational habitat entirely behind. We are always carrying these fishy beginnings. From an evolutionary perspective, not only is water a gestational habitat, but all of the life forms that evolution has experimented with along the way are gestational too – those first expressions of watery life themselves and their many proliferations that followed: marine invertebrates that still dwell in many ways unchanged in the deepest depths of the oceans; the multiplicities of fish that still populate the seas as well as those who ventured onto dry land; and those tetrapods who eventually returned to their watery habitats, temporarily or (so far) permanently. We are carrier bags in a constantly shifting network of potentialities in a temporality that anticipates the past and remembers the future.

In other words, evolution stories give us the means – openings and navigational charts – for amplifying our own watery indebtedness. These stories are the tales of scientists, but they are also fabulous and figurative. We carry them in our baggy imaginations, and they are written into our swampy humours. The geological echoes in our bones are literally the debris of worlds past. That 'oceanic feeling' we amplify might include: that all living beings require water for their gestation; that all living matter is composed primarily of water; that sexual difference is a particularly rich means for proliferating life, but that the actualization of this difference can and does take many forms; that with the terrestrial invasion of life this watery gestation and watery embodiment demanded various inventions, such as the amniotic egg, the tetrapod skin, big lungs, and Hypermarine physical imbrications; that even in the absence of reproductive gestation, symbiogenesis calls on water to facilitate its transfections. Evolution stories inaugurate ways of thinking about our watery human embodiment, in terms of both our own specifically human capacity as bodies to affect and be affected by other bodies and our historical and lateral continuities with other-than-human bodies of water. Stories like these pull us out of the limited and limiting comfort of our general human perspective and invite us to consider what we can learn when our perspective is stretched, shrunk, or dispersed. Evolution stories challenge the 'loose unity' of our human embodiment in order to see where and how we might drift, disperse, and dissolve into a new watery imaginary.

There are some aspects of our fishy beginnings that we will never be able to live. We can contact these beginnings, but only furtively, only on stolen time. To follow these resonances of past waters to the depths of their potentiality, we need superpowers, or borrowed organs, like Lingis suggests. And even still, in the dark, in our submersibles, everything could never be revealed. We will not master even that which makes up three-quarters of our sloshy selves. Yet our bodies can nonetheless hover, silent and suspended, below the surface, our lungs two inflated balloons that keep us from sinking.

Below the surface, at the borders of the liveable, perhaps we should not be surprised that, strangely, we have a kind of breath. Between inspiration and expiration, there is always a small gap – a pause really, where we are breathing neither in, nor out. We simply hover, with a suction lock in our lungs. The scientific name for this is *aspiration*. Below the surface, we still in some way breathe. We are suspended between our larvae and our actualizations as much as between water and air. No, our fishy beginnings are not altogether alien to us. They can be glimpsed, contacted… aspired to, but never fully captured.

We could also say that aspiration – this thoughtful suspension – is a kind of care, and an extension of care (attentive, in-between) for that which calls us to respond. If these aquatic creatures are our strange kin, echoing in us as both our pasts and potential futures, it is thus worth considering what we are also gifting to them, and to the watery milieu that becomes us all. When Irigaray (1991: 57) asks her interlocutor, 'did your idol not come from the bottom of the sea?', she suggests that amniotic waters are part of the greater element of water that continues to sustain us and protect us, after we emerge from these wombs. But she also asks: 'Did it not habitually return there at times of greatest peril?'; 'Did it not find its survival in the sea?' (57). While Irigaray – like Ferenczi, Calvino, and Morgan – might be invoking a cetaceous return, it is somewhat ironic, now, to imagine this return as a way to escape peril. It is a clear case of 'out of the frying pan, into the water', I'd say. After witnessing the humpback smother itself on that Western Australian beach, Giggs (2015: n.p.) sought out more information about beached whales:

> I learned that in the coastal currents some whales become entangled in abandoned fishing kit or ingest trash – bags, wrappers and mesh. Because they are so well insulated by that thick layer of blubber they attract fat-soluble toxins as well, absorbing heavy metals and inorganic compounds found in pesticides, fertilizers and the other pollutants that powder the modern sea. The body of a whale is a magnifier for these insidious agrochemicals because cetaceans live a long time and accrue a toxic load from their prey. Levels build up over many seasons, making some animals far more polluted than their surrounding environment.

In the context of increasingly plasticized oceans, carrier bags – those ubiquitous disposable progeny of late capitalism, providing literal rumination for earthbound cattle and floating through the seas as fancy-dress jellyfish – all of a sudden represent a different, more sinister kind of 'holding in relation' than LeGuin likely imagined. Knowing that the whale on the beach was destined for the municipal waste management facility, Giggs says she is also moved to think of the whale as landfill. 'It was a metaphor', she notes, 'and then it wasn't'. The same could be said about the whale, her insides harbouring stories of industrial debris, as dump.

When we consider the ways in which cetaceans and our other fishy beginnings echo through our own flesh, we might pause, and reflect on the ways in which we echo through them – literally whales-becoming-the-detritus-of-late-capitalism. Nor are these echoes metaphoric. Low-frequency active military sonar emits sound pressure of 120dB (a level that would damage our human ability to hear) for 3.9 million km², while mid-frequency sonar can emit continuous sound above 235 decibels, which is mostly like a rocket blast-off. High-intensity sonar and seismic waves snake along the ocean floor seeking oil and gas deposits. Meanwhile, background noise in the ocean doubles every decade mostly from commercial shipping traffic. Cetacean deaths sometimes surface as mass strandings, but necropsies show extensive internal bleeding in cranial regions (see Roburn 2013). Again, if we are always potentially becoming-cetacean, how are our strange aquatic kin becoming us?

Similarly, old N'ba N'ga, conjured from Calvino's pen in 1965, doesn't quite seem to predict the poisonous gifts that we humans will bestow upon our oceans in the coming decades. 'Down there', he explains to his nephew and his bride-to-be, Lll,

> changes would be very few, space and provender were unlimited, the temperature would always be steady; in short, life would be maintained as it had gone on till then, in its achieved perfect forms, without metamorphoses or additions with dubious outcome, and every individual would be able to develop his own nature, to arrive at the essence of himself and all things. (Calvino 1965: 79)

Even if N'ba N'ga's nephew insists that his aquatic uncle 'didn't conceal the problems, even serious ones', N'ba N'ga's version of the ocean world is hardly what we swim in today. Nor is this the ocean that swims in us.

Life began in the sea, and our bodies have been engaged in various retellings of this 'origin' story ever since. I'm not interested in narratives that put The Family back in place, but kinship in all of its queer and wondrous forms is still something I seek. This is the difficulty, of course: embracing queer stories of evolution as a ground of connection and responsibility without reinstating old myths of Dark Continents, Woman-as-Womb, and power plays of family ties. But no story is innocent, and this is the kind of trouble I'd like to – *that we need to* – stay with. We could say it is less about 'your inner fish' (to quote Neil Shubin's pop science title) than it is about remembering the water that keeps us all rather fishy in the first place.

4

Imagining Water in the Anthropocene

Prologue/*Kwe*¹

The beginning is blue. A rush of water, or wind, or static on the audio channel, or another kind of planetary breathing. Our eyes are drawn down from the sky to a beach, scattered driftwood. A fire combusts in one of the piles. In the water, now: a woman is weighted down by wet matter – her soaked sweatshirt, jeans, the sopping bedclothes that are the ocean's almost-waves. The water is deceptively strong, and persistent. Stumbling, struggling somewhat, she manages to stand. The woman is deceptively strong, and persistent. She drags a bucket, brimming, out of the dark sea.

She steps across the broken branches and beach debris and the sounds of these elemental labours fade. The bucket is heavy. Closer. Drawing on a deep well of power, with a grunt, she flings the contents of the bucket at you. You might expect murky seawater to meet you, but instead a ropy dark red runs down the screen. Her silhouette fixes you, as she faces back through the membrane that keeps you on this side, mostly dry. Maybe, you look at your hands. Are they clean?

Art, too, might be a body of water that we can attune our bodies to, and describe. Rebecca Belmore is an Anishinaabe performance artist, and *Fountain* (2005) is a single-channel video installation, that continuously loops for around two and a half minutes. You can watch it on your computer from Belmore's website, but in the gallery the video is projected upon a four by three meter screen that is a wall of running water. Originally shown in the Canadian pavilion at the 2005 Venice Art Biennale, it asks questions about bodies that are not separate from the water, where embodiment – here, an Indigenous woman's body – cannot be taken for granted. 'It goes without saying', writes Richard William Hill (2008: 69), 'that this blood will be read as a symbol of the violent history of colonial Canada flung in Canada's face'. But this waterblood is also a palimpsest: body, upon body, upon body, upon body. For Belmore, performance is about her body. She notes: 'With my body I can address history, I can address the immediate, I can address political issues.' For Belmore, although 'performance is deeply personal' (Nanibush 2014: n.p.), her body is also riven through with a past, and is a resting place and conduit for the politics of coloniality that both precedes her, and follows her, and gathers her up. Her embodiment is also something more. This (which?) waterblood as a body of water, incorporated, over and over again.

This is to say: in Belmore's *Fountain*, water erupts as lifeblood, kinship, wound, burden, accusation, question..

What is water?

Some years earlier in a converted cold storage warehouse on the northwestern shore of Lake Ontario, Belmore erects *Temple* (1996). Here, hundreds of litres of water spill over a monumental wedge construction, housed in what is now Toronto's Power Plant gallery on Queen's Quay. This temple is a quiet tidal wave, contained for the time being within rows, like shingles, of plastic milk bags. The water they hold suggests rust-brown and piss-yellow. The water is not quite clear but nonetheless iridescent in the gallery light. Bagged up like the units of lifeblood that it is, all of this water is also us. These samples are tapped and sourced from the city of Toronto's drinking water supply (faucets, pipes, and the lake itself). In a reminder of this transcorporeal flow, a working drinking fountain is placed under the crest of the wave. Beyond this, against the gallery's far wall, a staircase ascends to a small platform, where a telescope affords a view of the grey roll of Lake Ontario.

What is water?

If you were to leave the Power Plant gallery today, and walk a few blocks through downtown Toronto, you might turn into any number of corner convenience stores, and look for something to drink. Your choices would be many. In the section where bottled drinks are stacked, at least one third of the space is probably devoted to bottled water. There is little I can offer in this chapter that would add much to existing explanations of the absurdity of bottled water economics, particularly in places where one is lucky to have safe and clean drinking water flowing from a tap just steps away. Others have explained this (and more) in detail (see Hawkins, Potter, and Race 2015), and even suggested very reasonable ways of making sense of these plasticized pleas for 'frequent sipping'. What interests me here, however, is the way these little PET packages might offer an uncanny repetition of the aqueous imaginaries offered up in Belmore's artwork. There is an obvious repetition in play here, as the form we see in *Temple* – the milk bags lined up, row upon overlapping row, apportioning and transfiguring a dynamic flow into discrete, isomorphic units – is strangely reconfigured in the bottled waters lined up on the shop shelves.

I address the way that water has come to be dispensed as neat, exchangeable packages below. But I am also interested in another less obvious repetition at work across these plastic water bottles, and echoed in various kinds of advertising around them. One widely distributed brand of water by Nestle calls itself 'Pure Life', while another popular Canadian brand suggests we are 'Hungry for Life'. If we look across to the magazine rack, we might see these life-sustaining messages repeated again: in promotional campaigns by big corporations for World Water Day, in fundraising pleas for charitable 'development' organizations, in ads for office coolers and home water ionizers, and even one for a Giorgio Armani perfume – all of them telling us that 'water is life'. In this chapter I explore how certain aqueous imaginaries – those committed to an understanding of water as intimately, inseparably, tethered to *life;* those that course through the veins of Belmore's artwork, and are lit up, literally, as neon signs by activist of indigenous sovereignty movement *Idle No More* to proclaim that *Water Is Life* – are repeated by these plastic figurines and their discursive consorts. If we can reorient our relation to water, *as* bodies of water, by being attentive to artistic acts such as Belmore's, and even engaging actions of our own, what happens when this imaginary is repeated by these consumable units, and in popular discourses of water more broadly? What is the work of these repetitions?

What is water?

According to geographer Jamie Linton, water is what we make it. Belmore's art suggests certain understandings of how we've made water (to which we'll return shortly), but in his book *What Is Water* (2010), Linton unpacks a different story – perhaps even the 'backstory' of *Fountain* and *Temple,* and to an extent, of packaged water-life too. Linton's wet genealogy describes how once plural, emplaced, spirited, and storied waters are transformed into what Linton calls 'modern water'. In this chapter, I chart the emergence of modern water alongside colonial and 'global' water, specifically within the emergent context of Anthropocene discourse. While dominant rhetorics (within both science and cultural theory) figure the Anthropocene as a primarily lithic phenomenon, here I turn to what flows beneath this stony and terrestrial tale. On the one hand, I want to redress the Anthropocene narrative's own 'forgetting of water' by considering how Linton's diagnosis of our contemporary water imaginary might coalesce into something called 'Anthropocene water'. On the other hand, I don't want the story I am telling here to be dominated by an Anthropocenic narrative, aqueous or otherwise. My suggestion is that the figuration of bodies of water that I've developed in preceding chapters might potentially challenge these contemporary aqueous imaginaries of water as discrete, contained, and exchangeable, and tell a different kind of story. This challenge, however, is not a claim that Anthropocene water is 'false'; the challenge is rather an acknowledgement that all imaginaries are a congeries of matter and meaning – ideas entangled with material situations that offer various orientations towards thickly emergent worlds. Our decision can be to orient ourselves in one way, or another. We cannot dictate, once and for all, how to understand water. Phenomenologically crafted alter-imaginaries, however, can be a part of making other worlds possible.

Belmore's work is part of this imagining – an invitation to respond otherwise, specifically in the context of a call to decolonize water as part of a larger anticolonial imperative. Like all bodies of water, however, anticolonial waters, and their insistence that 'water is life', is an orientation that can be appropriated, and reoriented in yet another materialization of difference and repetition.[2] A sketch of some of the problematic ways in which anticolonial bodies of water get taken up and repeated in a neoliberal frame of individualism and commoditization reminds us that outcomes of figurations such as 'bodies of water' are never assured in advance. They are but 'moveable bridges' as Elizabeth Grosz (2011: xx) would say, for alternative orientations – that is, opportunities and openings, but never guarantees.

Swimming into the Anthropocene

We might begin by returning to Linton's primary quarry: what is water? As noted, Linton's answer (in an unwitting rejoinder to Irigaray[3]) is that water is 'not one'. Water, rather, is many, and according to Linton, what we make it. In other words, what water *is* is inextricable from how we imaginatively produce it. We can understand this claim in a number of ways, but Linton's emphasis is on the entanglement of social relations and discourses on the one hand, and environmental matters, on the other. The content of this word 'water', in other words, is neither neutral nor simply given. It corresponds to our values, behaviours, and orientations in regard to this wet substance that saturates our lifeworld. This doesn't mean we could include anything at all within this term; water has a materiality that places all kinds of limits on what can count as (what we now call) 'water'. We don't simply construct water *ex nihilo*. Linton's point is rather that what counts as water is changeable, and that water has a history. It is a substance, but it is also an idea. To ask what is water is thus to implicitly ask: what is water, in this place and at this time? Where does this idea come from and what does this idea *do*?

If water is what we make it, Linton argues, then what we've currently made – at this time, in this place that is the Western-dominated globalized world in an era of something we could call late capitalism – is 'modern water'. No longer the 'culturally impregnated waters of places and times' described by water historian Ivan Illich, water was transformed by the eighteenth-century chemistry of Antoine Lavoisie and his followers into stripped down, scienced-up chemical compound known as H_2O. In the modern era, water becomes a substance that is 'colourless transparent tasteless scentless' (Concise Oxford English Dictionary, quoted in Linton 2010: 78) – in other words, an 'abstract, isomorphic, measurable quantity' that is reducible to a fundamental unit of matter (Linton 2010: 14). In short, the name 'modern water' underlines both the location of that idea within a particular historical moment, but also the imaginative content of that place-time – namely, an Enlightenment scientistic postivitism of *knowability*.

These eighteenth-century modern chemistry abstractions of H_2O were then further 'modernized' by the animations of nineteenth-century hydrology, Linton argues, and the popularization of the modern hydrological cycle. Contrary to what we might imagine, this cyclical imaginary did not reanimate the wilful waters of premodern times. Within the new scientific and everyday imaginaries of water engendered by this schematic rendition, the hydrological cycle – diagrams for which you have no doubt seen in basic science textbooks

or popular environmental literature – made water even more amenable to
a new managerial discourse. 'Like the resources of the land', Linton (2010:
153) notes, 'water now becomes available to central planners [both in the US,
as well as in other nations] as a quantum'. Thus, not only is water rendered
abstract, measurable, and knowable as a chemical compound; in the guise of
modern water, water is also deterritorialized in a universalized and uniform
cyclical schema, becoming 'placeless'. One water is the same as any other
(18). We might understand Rebecca Belmore's *Temple* – a flow contained and
measured out into discrete units – as a perceptive rendition of this abstract
placelessness: when visitors to *Temple* looked through the telescope at the top
of the stairs adjacent to the milk-bag life-blood monolith, many reported that
they thought they were looking at a video, when what they were actually seeing
was Lake Ontario, just on the other side of the Power Plant wall (Burgess 1999:
n.p.). A distancing, indeed.

In Linton's (2010: 14) genealogy, modern water becomes 'the dominant, or
natural, way of knowing or relating to water, originating in Western Europe
and North America'. Importantly however, by the end of the twentieth
century, modern water is also 'operating on a global scale'. The culmination
of this instrumentalized abstraction is thus the morphing of 'modern water'
into 'global water' – that is 'the abstraction and representation of the world's
total hydrological stocks and flows' (22) and the entrenchment of 'global
hydrological discourse' (163). Following the First World War, hydrological
practice began to be deliberately coordinated on an international scale.
This intensified in the late 1960s and early 1970s with the proclamation of
the International Hydrological Decade by the International Association of
Scientific Hydrology (167–172).

While modern water initiated the abstraction and interchangeability of
water, global water scales this up, where we come to understand the world's
water crises as an overarching, global phenomenon. Linton (2010: 163)
argues that global water is directly conditioned by modern water's impetus
to quantification and measurement, such that the driving question of global
water is 'how much water is there in the world?' Moreover, the 'new global
water regime', which seeks integrated and coordinated means of managing
the (now rendered homogenous) water resources of the world, results in 'a
completely unworkable concept'. What human power would be practically

capable of managing the total amount of the world's water, or controlling it on a global scale? Citing global water critic Asit K Biswas, Linton underlines that 'a paradigm with such universal ambition suffers a critical breakdown when brought to bear on specific water issues' (217). When global water is understood as the amalgamation of millions of smaller units of an abstract substance called 'water', this gives us few resources with which to deal with issues as different and dispersed as contaminated tailings ponds in Canada's Athabascan watershed; drought enveloping farmland in California; arsenic contaminated groundwater in Bangladesh; floods in the modern urban core of Toronto; a melting polar ice cap; or privatization of water supplies in South Africa. In other words, treating water as quantifiable and instrumentalized not only risks its exploitation and deterioration; it also belies a management paradigm that is ultimately unworkable and unresponsive to specific water challenges, in specific places at specific times. Disembodied and displaced, global water – again, in a version of Donna Haraway's (1988) epistemological 'God trick' – is everywhere and nowhere, and thus difficult to respond to with attunement, or curiosity.

One of Linton's key points is that by evacuating water of its social content, even well-intentioned efforts to address the 'world's water crisis' become mired in global water's unworkability. When the terms of what water is are already set, any pleas to manage this water *better* become stymied in advance by these same terms. In other words, global water, like modern water, becomes naturalized through repetition of the same ideas, institutions, and mechanisms that gave rise to this particular idea of water in the first place. This reinforcement is perpetuated even by institutions that are aiming for more ecologically sound and socially just relations to water. Linton argues that 'global water governance' regimes of the 1980s and 1990s could be understood as participating in this naturalization. As I have argued elsewhere (see Neimanis 2009, 2014), calls to recognize water as a human right – within UN human rights apparatuses, as well as in the context of activist transnational organizing and justice-oriented legal scholarship – are in many ways laudable. Yet similarly, insofar as many of these well-meaning claims take a quantifiable, abstract substance as their starting point, they can also further naturalize an imaginary that bolsters the very problem they seek to address. Water is reinstated as something 'out there' that we can claim, and remains abstracted from our own implication in a hydrocommons with material contours and limits. Linton thus describes for us an aqueous imaginary – modern water and/as global water – that is not merely descriptively tied to contemporary water concerns and crises, but entangled in their very intractability.

Linton's analysis of what water is in our contemporary socio-historical moment spurs me to consider how his diagnosis of modern, global water might flow into emergent understandings of our current epoch as 'the Anthropocene'. The Anthropocene, as most of us are now aware, is the name for our new era of 'man-made' environmental and planetary disruption that experts are hailing from all corners (see Crutzen and Stoermer 2000; Steffen et al. 2011). While the International Commission of Stratigraphy has yet to officially proclaim its arrival, and while the 'golden spike' starting line of the Anthropocene is still hotly debated, the term is commonly used in both scholarly and generalist literature to denote our current time of anthropogenic ecological disruption.

My suggestion is that the modern/global water imaginary described by Linton might also closely connect to what I'm calling 'Anthropocene water'. Exploring this connection does two things. First, it disturbs the dominant framing of the Anthropocene in geological terms. For certain, the lithosphere is the key slate onto which accounts of the Anthropocene are written – deciphered by present-day stratigraphers and to be read, presumably, by some distant future decoder of our fossilized remains (although if we humans are anthropocening ourselves out of existence, it does beg the question of who these future readers might be). Such geological thinking has, moreover, opened up rich and productive thinking about humans and how we might rethink our own human being and becoming in post-anthropocentric, and specifically geontological, terms (see Povinelli 2014; Yusoff 2015). But the dominance of the Earth's stony archive-in-the-making belies the water that flows through and beneath these accounts. My invitation in thinking about Anthropocene water is thus, in the first place, a suggestion to pay more attention to the hydrosphere as the (again, oft-overlooked) fascia that lubricates and connects the Earth's lithosphere to its biosphere and atmosphere, those more popular players in this Anthropocene drama. Rising sea levels, melting ice caps, parched interiors, rogue storm surges and strange weather, rapid aquifer depletion and massive-scale water rechoreographies through irrigation, dam-building, and riparian 'straightening' all remind us that our current epoch's radical terraforming is often explicitly the work of water – and that these are labours in which we humans are variously entangled.

Water has certainly always been an intense site and agent of planetary terraforming, but in an Anthropocene narrative, this shapeshifting is figured either as a result of our attempts to control water (damming, irrigation) or as an out of control response by water to these attempts at control (storms, sea levels). Put otherwise, adopting an aqueous orientation to the Anthropocene reminds us that the keyword of this epoch is control – where, unsurprisingly, the perverse antidote to waters out-of-control is *more* control and managerialism (see Crist 2013) – such as Linton describes in terms of modern and global water regimes.

To connect Linton's modern, global water to an idea of Anthropocene water thus allows us, secondly, to map the overlaps between the 'makings' that Linton discusses and the more general claims and imaginaries that are taking hold as an Anthropocene worldview. One place where Anthropocene research is specifically connected to water is in a short video called 'Water in the Anthropocene' (2013) – part of the online presence of *Welcome to the Anthropocene* (www.anthropocene.info). This film details some of the anthropogenically induced changes to the hydrosphere about which we should be concerned. It notes, for instance, that as of the time of the film's making, 800 million people live without safe drink water, 2.4 billion people lack adequate sanitation, and 1.7 billion live in areas where groundwater extraction is happening at a faster rate than recharge. In earth-moving efforts of monumental proportions, we've erected 48,000 large dams worldwide and moved more sediment than natural erosion and rivers. Two thirds of all major river deltas are sinking, exacerbated by massive extraction and mining industries. Half of all of the wetlands in the world have been drained by us. And, as warmer temperatures result in higher amounts of water vapour into the atmosphere, the water cycle is intensifying – meaning that what is wet becomes wetter, while the dry turns to dust.

This video's account of water in the Anthropocene flows neatly into the picture of global water that Linton has already sketched for us. We see modern/ global water memes of depersonalized control, placelessness, and isomorphic abstraction not only represented but also amplified in the video's computer-generated graphics. Beginning as a dark circle, slowly illuminated by a beam of light that arises behind it, the globe begins to spin. We zoom in and out of its displays, circling and surveying the water crises that dot the orb's surface: large dams illuminated with shards of light; animated weather patterns announced in colour codes familiar to us from satellite weather maps; fractures of blue veins that retract and disappear. The blue, green, and brown planet rotates at a scale and speed mostly impossible to grasp, as though we might be holding it between our fingers, like a golf ball, or a ripening plum, checking it out from this angle, then from that. This is a perspective that our living, breathing, wet bodies (entirely absent from this show) could never inhabit. Modern water (exchangeable and isomorphic) and global water (undifferentiated in an amorphous blue – everywhere and nowhere in Haraway's 'God trick') are here rendered clear. Linton points out that within a global context of hydrology, quantities and flows become so abstract as to become meaningless. 'Water in the Anthropocene' – tellingly produced for the 'Global Systems Water Project' – uncannily visualizes this distancing and placelessness. Even if, as I argued in earlier chapters, becoming a body of water depends on stretching and torquing the bounds of our comfortable human perspective, 'Water in the Anthropocene' pulls out too far; we lose our embodied grip altogether; we are situated nowhere.

But Anthropocene water also adds something new to the imaginary of global water described by Linton. Importantly, the phenomena enumerated by the Global Water Systems Project are not just descriptions of a morphing planetary hydrosphere: they specifically underline changes to that hydrosphere that are anthropogenically induced. In short, this is a story of man-made water. 'We are altering the global water system', the video's narrator tells us. A persistent – but undifferentiated – 'we' begins most of the video's sentences. *We* have done this; Anthropocene water is *our* accomplishment. In other words, Anthropocene water not only confirms that water is 'made'; it puts particular emphasis on the fact that this making is done *by us*. One important question begged by these formulations is thus *who is this 'we'*? The video does not provide an answer to this question, or even suggest that it might be one worth asking. 'In a single lifetime *we* have become a phenomenal geological force', the Global Water Systems Project tells us. In an era of our collective making, in a lifetime indexed to the timescale of our own, this statement firmly tethers global, modern water to the imaginary of the Anthropocene. According to an Anthropocene water imaginary – and this is my second point – *we humans are (uncritically) all in this together.*

This homogenization and levelling of human difference – what Kathryn Yusoff (2015: 4) names 'the supposed unity of the "Anthropos" as it is gathered into the geologic' – is characteristic of a more general Anthropocene imaginary (see Neimanis, Åsberg, and Hayes 2015), and neatly mirrors the homogenization of water as abstract, exchangeable, and isomorphic, as described by Linton. Humans, in the Anthropocene, are apparently no different. Geographer Lesley Head (2014: 2) refers to this characteristic of Anthropocene discourse as the 'species error'. She writes, 'we have conceptualized the Anthropocene with an undifferentiated human, again contrary to the abundant evidence of spatial and temporal differences in influences below the species level'. For Head, this homogenization of humans is in the first place simply false – what she calls 'a category mistake in conceptualization of the Anthropocene' (4). Head reminds us that the most common Anthropocene chronology dates this era to the Industrial Revolution and the rise of fossil fuels. Thus, 'despite widespread recognition of human influences on fire and fauna in the Pleistocene, there is not a serious suggestion that the Anthropocene is a Late Pleistocene phenomenon' (4) – underlining the point that an era named for human incursion only really means to implicate *some* humans, in an evolutionary and temporal sense.[4] And, probably more significantly, even post-Industrial Revolution, our 'togetherness' in this mess is clearly a problematic claim. As Malm and Hornborg (2014: 3) note, and as Head underlines, 'uneven distribution is a condition for *the very existence* of modern, fossil-fuel technology'. In other words, Anthropocene homogenization of humans is ironically lodged at a moment when differences among them become in one way notably amplified.

The issue of human difference in terms of anthropogenically induced change is of course both one of responsibility (which processes and modes of being, anchored in which situated communities, are exacerbating these changes?) and one of vulnerability and resistance (who is incited to forge new ways of being and becoming? who is bearing the brunt?). While social location (class, gender, age) is clearly salient here, global flows of colonial power are equally relevant. Indeed, the Anthropocene may also index an important mutation in forms of colonial power, where colonizers need not physically occupy a place with their discrete bodies for the environmental effects of (neo)colonial power to be felt. This is underlined, for example, by returning to the case of ice thaw and climate change (two key actors in an Anthropocene imaginary that again bring the 'aqueous Anthropocene' into relief). Due to permafrost degradation among other factors, levels of mercury in the Arctic food chain are intensifying (MacDonald, Harner, and Fyfe 2005). Given the Arctic's low population and little industrial activity, this phenomenon begs questions of which bodies shoulder the heaviest burden of polar warming, and which bodies are most implicated in stoking those planetary fires. A related example I described in Chapter 1 concerns the bioaccumulation of various anthropogenic contaminants, making their way north from warmer regions. Hitchhiking upon atmospheric transport vectors, pollutants from the more temperate regions condense and concentrate in colder Arctic climes (Bard 1999; Hansen 2000). One result is a gendered, raced, and multispecies entanglement, biomagnified within a breastfeeding body. The breast milk of Inuit women, nourished by a staple diet of sea mammal fat, serves literally as what Foucault would have called a 'dense transfer point' of power – in this case materialized in the toxic waste matters that move slowly and stealthily from watery body to watery body, beginning in the industrialized and industrializing zones of the globe's temperate regions: human-machine assemblage, to waterway, to ocean and atmospheric current, to plankton, to whale, to breastfeeding body – only then to be downloaded to the infant body many times magnified (Hansen 2000; Trainor et al. 2010: 146–147). Indeed, at one point in the recent past, 'the greatest body burden known to occur from environmental exposure [was] found in Inuit mothers' (Dewailly quoted in Trainor et al. 2010: 147).

Within this example of toxic breast milk, a whole slurry of concerns swirl: biomagnification reminds us that not only is water itself a vector of contamination, but so too are the bodies of non-human animals. Toxic breast milk is also a clearly gendered issue, where sexual difference is indeed biologically marked (through lactation) but always within sociocultural valences of power. 'Body burden' is both a biochemical descriptor, but also a way of naming social, cultural, gendered, and species-related inheritances of response and responsibility. These examples foreground questions of environmental justice, for sure, but to frame them as coloniality also marks the longer histories of human incursion in the 'New World' whose effects still condition this present. While the Arctic is 'generally considered to be one of the last pristine regions on Earth', its populations (human and more-than-human) again bear the brunt of global human imperialism. This kind of incursion 'at a distance', precipitated by massive fossil fuel burning, consumption, and toxic release into planetary waters and weathers (out of sight, out of mind), traces new vectors of coloniality, and emerging markers of vulnerability and survivance (Vizenor 1999) across difference. The more general point again is: in cases such as these, any human 'togetherness' is acutely riven with differences that matter. If we are all in the same boat, why do some of us seem to be (to quote poet Stevie Smith) not waving, but drowning?

None of these questions – coloniality, race, gender, species, class, culture, taste – is separable from the others, and importantly, none of them is separate from us, who may be reading this at distances thousands of kilometres from the source. As I explored more thoroughly in Chapter 1, the problem of the 'we' has long been acknowledged by some feminist theories as the most difficult, but also urgent ethical and political question. This is all the more salient once we understand that identity and difference, or commonality and separation, exist in exasperatingly incommensurable ways, right up inside of one another. As black feminist Audre Lorde championed, we may share many things as women, but we are also striated by our differences – differences that are vital strengths. These cross-cutting tangles of mutual implication and ineluctable alterity demand, among other things, that we acknowledge how oppressions or vulnerabilities that affect others also affect us, *and are affected by us.* Black feminism and the idea of a politics of location (Rich 1986) gave us tools for thinking through the tricky business of interconnection but also the specificity of social justice movements. It now behoves us to bring this theoretical agility to Anthropocene thinking, where difference and connection are also material, and connected to hydrological, geological, and other kinds of environmental movements. Lorde reminded us that 'there is no such thing as a single-issue struggle because we do not live single-issue lives' (1984: 138). The intersecting axes that she refers to must now also be thought across species and elemental lines, across timescales both vast and molecular, across generations and geographies. We are both intimately situated bodies, but also transcorporeally inserted into the lives of all others. Living this kind of multiscalar and multivalent ontology is one of the key challenges of the Anthropocene.

Toxic breast milk also illuminates how incursions into the 'earth' and other (always different) human bodies are not discrete questions, in either their inter- or intra-relations. Too often, Anthropocene thinking lacks attention to the ways in which circuits of matter and differentiated flows of human power are entangled. A notable exception is a recent proposal by geographers Simon Lewis and Mark Maslin (2015), who explain the Orbis hypothesis – that is, that the Anthropocene's 'golden spike' might in fact be the arrival of Europeans in the 'New World' and the advent of the modern 'world-system' of globalization, trade, and colonialism. As Audra Mitchell (2015: n.p.) notes, the crucial point of the Orbis hypothesis is its linking of 'forms of agency, power, and violence that have contributed to the Anthropocene'. She further underlines two key points about Lewis and Maslin's argument. First, it 'draws a direct link between the constitutive violence of colonialism' and the idea of earthly Anthropocenic changes – in other words, that interhuman violence is a question that must be considered when thinking about any kind of golden spike. As Mitchell points out, this opens up an important new register for critique. Her second key point is closely connected, namely that 'the wounds inflicted by colonization' upon humans also remain 'engrained in, and integral to, very lively Earth systems that persist today and will continue far into the future'. The violent legacy of colonialism persists and rebounds not only (following Aime Cesaire and Frantz Fanon) on the colonizers, 'but on the global, interspecies populations of generations' that follow. Mitchell also sounds a cautious note: we shouldn't take this to mean that the colonization of the New World 'caused' the Anthropocene – the entanglement of worldly forces is too complex for such direct causal proposals. This founding violence, however, needs to be braided into any necessarily pluralistic account of Anthropocene onset.

Mitchell does not suggest that we name the Anthropocene after this colonial game-changer, but her analysis echoes other propositions to do just that, as a way of marking these important interhuman faultlines. Head points to other such nominations of our contemporary era – the Capitalocene (Huber 2008; Malm 2013; Moore 2013) or the Econocene (Norgaard 2013), for instance – as additional attempts to implicate more specific social and economic drivers of Anthropocenic change. Here, it is a specific mode of being human (not only colonialism, but also late capitalism and the biopolitical 'resourcing' of any lively matter that capitalism can get its hands on, including water) that most deserve our critical focus. Donna Haraway (2015) reminds us that the 'Plantationocene',[5] with its indictment of slavery-dependent plantation enclosures, has also been suggested as another way of naming this era (which, she hopes, may be a boundary event that with any luck will be as short and thin as possible). These terminological challenges all signal a growing call to acknowledge that not all humans are in this together, in exactly the same way.

For Head (2014: 4), moreover, the conceptual error of the collective 'we' is not the only concern. In the second place, she notes that this indiscriminate implication of humans is a political question that can result in 'political paralysis', insofar as papering over important differences among humans as drivers of anthropogenic planetary change limits the 'potential to mobilize the kinds of political action that its constituent evidence demands' (3). If all humans everywhere are both the cause of the problem *and* the problem's undifferentiated receiving end, one likely response, notes Head, is a paralytic fatalism. Other critical and cautious takes on an Anthropocene imaginary buttress this position. Connecting again to Linton's claims regarding the distancing effect of global hydrological calculus, the abstraction and scale of climate data as a key trait of the Anthropocenic view results in similar political disconnection (see Duxbury 2010; Neimanis and Walker 2014; Neimanis, Åsberg, and Hayes 2015). While one orientation of such responses can be a kind of Anthropocene denialism (where environmental change is too big, or too distant, or too abstract to be 'real'), a second orientation is the easy consumption of apocalyptic doom. Claire Colebrook (2011: 53) for instance discusses a growing cinematic imaginary of the world's end in terms of an orientation where 'there is neither panic nor any apparent affective comportment that would indicate that anyone really feels or fears [this threat]' – what she refers to as 'hyper-hypo-affective disorder' (45). (Moreover, this helps us to see how these 'no future' scenarios are precisely invested in the future – a future that the hailing of the Anthropocene seeks to guarantee by proselytizing its End. In ostensibly affirming that we're all doomed, an Anthropocene imaginary actually seeks to ignite the belief that we're not. Not unlike watching those same Hollywood blockbusters, proclaiming the 'Anthopocen-ocalypse' acts as a kind of inoculation to that same reality. The horror of it all paradoxically comforts us: it's not really going to happen.) A key point in these scenes of 'paralytic doom' is their lack of specificity. If Anthropocene water is a giant tsunami that washes equally over us all, what is left to be done?

In short, just as Linton argues that a homogenized global water cannot result in workable solutions to problems of water management, Head and others suggest that addressing the problems of the Anthropocene to a homogenized humanity are just as likely to result in political entropy, ineffectuality, or plain old missing-the-mark. Yet, Linton suggests that global/ modern water is the dominant kind of water that we've made. We might add to his proposal the idea of Anthropocene water – a dominant imaginary that is flooding how we orient ourselves towards our planetary hydro-commons. The question again is not whether this imaginary is 'right' – it just *is*. More helpful is asking: what kind of alter-imaginaries might gestate other kinds of worlds?

Learning from anticolonial waters

If concepts and figures help us make sense of the world, they do so by selecting, foregrounding and allowing us to appreciate certain aspects of a phenomenon, while necessarily backgrounding or de-privileging others. Elizabeth Grosz (2012: 14) suggests that 'concepts do not solve problems that events generate for us', but 'they enable us to surround ourselves with possibilities for being otherwise'. Concepts – including feminist figurations as embodied concepts – open for us ways of ethically and justly living with the paradoxes and knots of the problems that are the very air we breathe, and the water that buoys us. Concepts, in Grosz's words, are 'modes of address, modes of connection: they are "movable bridges" between those forces that relentlessly impinge on us from the outside to form a problem and those that we can muster within ourselves to address such problems'. But as I also argue, this force we muster is also a lived materiality that too is of this world, even as we have to torque these materialities through new imaginative mangles.

Somewhat unlike Grosz (and her Deleuzian inspiration), I suggest that concepts are always also material.

This does not mean that concepts are simply given; their materiality is as lively and multiple as any other. In staking out the contours of a specific imaginary, concepts give us a handhold for engaging with the world, in certain ways, on certain terms. While Linton describes modern, global water as 'the' way we currently relate to matter, he also makes clear that other competing imaginaries precede it. Less central to his account, but crucial here, is the recognition that many alter-imaginaries still flow in modern/Anthropocene water's undercurrents – other material-semiotic configurations that might orient us otherwise. Similarly, while the Anthropocene discourse is beginning to solidify a certain way of responding to a set of ecological crises that are increasingly colliding in an image of planetary distress, this hegemonic view is contested by other conceptual apparatuses. For example, Donna Haraway (2015: 160), suggests that an alternative to the kinds of Anthropocene thinking outlined above might be something she calls Chthulucene. Against the homogenization and anthropo-centring of the Anthropocene, and even the pessimism, resignation and/or regret of the Plantationocene or Capitalocene, Haraway's Chthulucene invites multiple stories of worlds that will allow us to 'make kin' with and as 'something other/more than entities tied by ancestry or genealogy' (161). This making means the remembering, acknowledging, and further fostering of relationships between humans and non-humans. It seeks to rebuild real and imagined places of refuge for weathering this storm and nurturing multispecies ecojustice with whatever grace we can muster. It is not only attentive to, but is impossible without, the differentiations that so much Anthropocene thinking elides.

My own proposition is less *cene*-ic. Bodies of water, as figuration, invite us to amplify a relational aqueous embodiment that we already incorporate, and trans-corporate. Bodies of water ask us to imagine these corporeal waters as part of a hydrocommons that we make, and that makes us in turn. This conceptual, yet embodied commons that I've developed through a feminist posthuman phenomenology in the preceding chapters, seeks to get us out of the discrete individualism that underpins dominant Western theories of body-subjects as discrete and autonomous. At the same time, it attends to the anthropocentrism of a nature/culture split, and offers a different kind of environmental imaginary that draws on a feminist lineage of relational ethics and distributed bodies. In a feminist tradition of a politics of location and assemblage (Haraway 1988; Lorde 1984; Puar 2012; Rich 1986), it seeks a version of embodiment that acknowledges both common matters and unknowable alterity. Bodies of water recognize the need to understand waters as emplaced, specific, and contingent on relations, but they reject the binary of 'local' and 'global' as well. Resonant with Sandilands's (2001) understanding of queer ecologies, bodies of water as figuration asks us to respond to wounds of other bodily waters in which we are implicated, even at a distance. Rather than responding to the alarm clock ring of the Anthropocene with a quick insistence that we are all in this together, this figuration seeks to acknowledge the unsettled terms in which we live as bodies of water, with other watery bodies that materialize in temporal and spatial tangles. The figuration of bodies of water, as I've described in earlier chapters, is mobilized through the intra-corporeal logics of posthuman gestationality and difference.

Bodies of water, I suggest, can be an alternative to the dominant imaginary of the Anthropocene. While I do not dispute the 'facts' of the aqueous Anthropocene, and agree that we are currently exacerbating many kinds of water crises that urgently need to be addressed, I am reminded by Haraway that it matters what kinds of stories we tell. There is a fine line between critiquing a problem and reinstalling the terms that inevitably sustain it, and recapitulate it anew. To call for more attention to the 'aqueous Anthropocene', as I do above, is thus a fraught endeavour. Kathryn Yusoff (2015) saliently reminds us that whatever our critiques of Anthropocene-talk might be, this term is also a 'password' for rethinking what it means to be human in distinctly posthuman, geontological terms. Similarly, I think the aqueous Anthropocene can be a 'door' or a 'threshold', as Deleuze and Guattari (1987) would have it, for reimagining our embodiment as aqueous all the way down, across times, bodies, and places. In some ways, the Anthropocene forces us to consider how our differences as bodies are crucial to any kind of planetary future, yet simultaneously to reflect on our commonality as planetary species (see also Chakrabarty 2012). Yet at the same time I want to step back from Anthropocene talk to allow different kinds of stories to do their work – perhaps to begin to dissolve the hegemony of the Anthropocene, even if this can only be a slight blurring of its edges.

'Bodies of water' is thus one alternative, but it supports and flows into others. Although my understanding of bodies of water, as an antidote to Anthropocene water, emerges primarily through philosophical and phenomenological explorations that I detail in earlier chapters, and charts a path through feminist theories of relational embodiment, my advocacy of this figuration is sustained by the conversations and commitments it shares with those other imaginaries that disturb the Anthropocene narrative. One example of this is the *Kwe* worldview offered by Rebecca Belmore.[6] I don't claim to speak *for* this imaginary, but as anthropologist Margaret Somerville (2014: 407) reminds us (also in relation to water and indigenous imaginaries), artworks are gifts, or transitional objects, and 'a way of bridging different cultural understandings, relationships and knowledges'. Artworks such as *Fountain* and *Temple* are thus for me sites of collaborative inquiry that can introduce me to Anishnaabe understandings of water without any pretense of full knowledge or subsumption.[7] In a posthuman phenomenological orientation, I can engage these artworks and allow my own bodily uptake of them to open glimpses into other kinds of imaginaries that might resonate with my own. I don't engage them in order to distil some kind of grand proclamation about indigenous cosmologies of water, but to read them as concrete exercises in ways of being in the world (to paraphrase Stephen Muecke 2004: 11), that can give me insight into the context they emerge from – a context that also imbricates me.[8]

For, I also flow through the water that fills the plastic bags of *Temple*. This water is certainly, at one level, a comment on drinking water quality that has been a hot-button question of indigenous environmental justice in Canada for years. In the same year as Belmore produced *Fountain*, over 800 members of the Kashechewan First Nations community of Northern Ontario (Canada) were evacuated when *E. coli* bacteria was discovered in the water supply. Along with around 100 other First Nations communities, Kashechewan had been under a long-term boil-water advisory due to inadequate treatment facilities and/ or training of those people in charge of maintaining them. In 2013, the local paper of the city (in prosperous, cosmopolitan Southern Ontario) in which I mostly grew up reported that most of the people living on the Six Nations reserve, just a thirty-minute drive down the road from me, lived without access to clean water. In Southern Ontario, nestled between the world's largest reservoirs of freshwater and intersecting gridlines of the some of the world's most modern hydrological infrastructure, this lack is certainly not an issue of geographic remoteness. Again, coloniality courses through the flows of water justice, but its spatiotemporal logics don't fit any simple map.

Belmore's art joins numerous forms of protest from indigenous people and their supporters against these settler colonial double standards. Her bags of water contain these current events, but they also gather up more than questions of infrastructure. 'Contamination' is not just a biophysical question, but pertains to other kinds of survival as well. As Anishinabe scholar Deborah McGregor (2009: 39) notes, 'from an Aboriginal perspective … Water is a living, spiritual being with its own responsibilities to fulfil'. Water, in an Anishinabe context, 'is not just an environmental concern; it is a matter of cultural survival' (37). Survival here unfolds in many guises – cultural, which is also economic, political, individual, as well as straightforward biophysical endurance. In the understanding recounted by McGregor, water is an integral part of spiritual life, but these questions are not separable from quotidian experiences of boil-water advisories. McGregor explains how her own formal involvement in First Nations water issues came in the wake of the Walkerton Inquiry in 2000, after *E. coli* (again) in the municipal drinking water supply of that Ontario town resulted in the deaths of seven people and illness of thousands more (damage to non-human water bodies was not enumerated). Yet again, the terms of this inquiry underscore the sense in which 'water is, and always has been, viewed as precious by Indigenous communities' (McGregor 2009: 37); *E. coli* is one face of a much more multifaceted relation to water. Belmore's *Temple* evokes the intricate weave of these questions. What is it, she asks, that we have come to worship at this 'temple'? Water's holism as contiguous with Creation? Massive hydrological infrastructure as the 'temples of modernism'? The 'fit and healthy body' of the late capitalist consumer, needing regular 'hydration'? Something else? Maybe each of us – indigenous or not – is interpellated by all of these questions, but in different ways and to different effect.

As we noted earlier, water in the Anthropocene is focused on questions of control, and can be emblemized in terms of a 'drinking water' – the PET bottle of water a fitting symbol for the aqueous Anthropocene where the key concerns are: How will we humans remain hydrated? What provisions will we humans need to weather this storm? Belmore's *Temple* doesn't dismiss the importance of clean drinking water and the technologies needed to ensure it;

rather she places these questions in the context of other nested questions from which they can't be extracted.

As McGregor makes clear, water is not a static 'thing' about which First Nations communities (also far from static) are concerned. Water is also multiple. Even as one of its aspects comes into focus in a specific situation (say, water as a storied ancestor, or water as a problem in the tainted contents of a plugged chlorine injector), all of its aspects are latent in water's depths. Moreover, water isn't something that we simply act on (or act for, or against). McGregor stresses that water has its own responsibilities to fulfil to other beings of Creation. Water is not, in this sense, a passive backdrop or 'resource'. 'Water is a relation', writes McGregor (2009: 37). The double entendre (whether deliberate or not) of this phrase is telling: water is both what connects different kinds of bodies and water is also kin or one of our 'relatives', a body in its own right. These multilayered logics and orientations of water are evoked in Belmore's *Fountain*. Here, blood turns to water (water is our literal kin), but water also turns to blood: an indictment, a wound, a violence, a colonial incursion. In both McGregor's Anishinabe account and in Belmore's art, watery relations are also gendered. There is a specific responsibility here that is borne by sexually different bodies (recalling the gender-specific 'body burden' of toxic contamination evoked earlier). Josesphine Mandamin and other First Nations grandmothers who have undertaken arduous walks around the Great Lakes in order to heal those water-relations again materialize this responsibility as differently moving with differently gendered bodies. In the past years, many other water walks, river walks, and healing walks have been organized, primarily by indigenous women, as a reminder of our human responsibilities to water.

While the language of gendered responsibility can jar against contemporary Western feminist theories (particularly in a posthuman vein) of gendered relations to the environment, I am equally wary of a view that would categorize these responsibilities as signifying an 'essentialist' indigenous view of either sexual difference *or* water. I am instead interested in how this *Kwe* engagement with water nonetheless resonates with my own understanding of bodies of water, as also situated in the context of sexual difference. When Mandamin asserts that 'as women, we are carriers of water', she means something different than I do when I talk about water, gestationality, and sexual difference in previous chapters of this book. But we are both responding to the connection between gestationality and water, enacted in different ways across sexually different bodies. Essentialism, like gender, and women, and difference, and water, is a floating signifier, constantly realigning and resignifying in context. Nor should these descriptions be misinterpreted as just another romanticized view of the 'ecological Indian' (Krech 1999). Belmore's work is fiercely contemporary and decidedly unromantic. (There is nothing 'authentically Indian' about the putrefaction of water contained in plastic bags on a wave-shaped concrete plinth – but nor is this 'un-Indian'.) Belmore (quoted in Hill 2008: 69) herself has said that her relationship to traditional Anishinabe culture 'is marked as much by rupture and dislocation as it is by continuity'. In our current situation of planetarity, this is the likely situation of us all in relation to the cultures we 'come from', although to different degrees. A refusal of the ecological Indian doesn't make Belmore's work 'less indigenous', whatever that might mean, but rather reminds us that these indigenous engagements with water respond to a context that is very much *now*, even as it also holds deep pasts. 'Ancient' and 'modern' are false binaries that serve certain ends, usually colonial ones (Muecke 2004), and the alignment of these terms with those of 'ecological' and 'destructive' are similarly untenuous.[9]

I will have to leave the troubling question of whether First Nations and other indigenous people are closer to Nature or better custodians of the Earth to others more willing to engage with those terms of debate. My intention here is rather to underline that the imaginary of water that imbues the accounts offered by Belmore and further elaborated by McGregor is markedly different from Anthropocene water. In these various indigenous understandings, water is understood as alive, rather than as mute matter; it is a relation, rather than a thing. It is emplaced, rather than substitutable. Water 'manifests a relational ethic that connects human and non-human realms' (Strang 2013: 190); it is part of 'all our relations' (La Duke 1999). While McGregor directly affirms these commitments, and *Temple* and *Fountain* more complexly question the ways in which these commitments are variously under occupation, Anishinabe and other indigenous understandings of water render palpable a sense that *water is life*.

I sketch out some of these contours of a water imaginary from a *Kwe* perspective for two reasons. In the first place, I have to acknowledge that my elaboration of 'bodies of water' as a figuration has a long a line of debts, both direct and indirect. As I've noted, my thinking in this book does not emerge from indigenous traditions, and looks instead to primarily Western feminist and other philosophical resources to articulate a certain kind of alter-imaginary to global/modern water and its Anthropocene counterpart. At the same time, the continued insistence that there is another kind of relation to water that informs other ways of being in the watery world by artists such as Belmore and scholars and activists like McGregor, Grandmother Mandamin, and many, many others clears space for thinking differently with water. I am interested in how a posthuman feminist phenomenology of water, as lively, as gestational, and as relational might intersect with (and learn from) indigenous understandings of water. Secondly, I describe this 'water is life' imaginary in order to think further about the work of aqueous imaginaries in the entanglements of Anthropocene waters. 'Water is life' has become a refrain for many different kinds of protest spearheaded by *Idle No More*, a grass-roots indigenous sovereignty movement that began in Canada in 2012 with a series of teach-ins in the province of Saskatchewan, but has since grown into one of the largest mass indigenous movements in Canadian history. Along with its allies, *Idle No More* seeks a resurgence of indigenous nationhood specifically in the context of protecting the lands and waters from corporate, government, and other forms of environmental exploitation and degradation. Protecting waterways has been one main area of focus. 'Water is Life' is an alternative to modern/global and Anthropocene water. In the repetition of 'water is life' across texts, bodies, and other media, *Idle No More* is an explicit 'doing' of an imaginary that might take greater hold in the traces of these repetitions: *Water is life, water is life, water is life.*

Water is life? Commodity, charity and other repetitions

As Haiven and Khasnabish remind us, radical imagination (i.e. those imaginaries that seek transformation) is something we *do*; it is not a possession to be 'had', but a process that must be continually engaged and reengaged, negotiated and renegotiated. The cultivation of a shared imagination is 'an active process, not a steady state' (Haiven and Khasnabish 2014: 7), and always exists in tension with competing imaginaries. To facilitate its transformative potential requires active sustenance.

I like Haiven and Khasnabish's description of the radical imagination because it tempers a phenomenological reading of my 'bodies of water' figuration as primarily descriptive. As I stressed in Chapter 1, 'bodies of water' is both something we already are and a certain embodied orientation and potential we can amplify. Convoking this embodied figuration with Haiven and Khasnabish's 'radical imagination', we can think harder about how we might enact the kinds of embodied ethics that 'bodies of water' articulates; we can think about the work, or politics, required to sustain the aqueous imaginary it incites. By politics, I quite simply mean those actions we take and decisions we make that are always inadequate to the problems and issues they confront – but which need to be made and taken nonetheless. If ethics are always aspirational and incomplete, politics is what we have to do to 'stay with the trouble', as Haraway would say (2015), with whatever kind of grace and concern and curiosity that we can summon. This work can be – and most often is – partial, strategic, and compromising (in both senses). These actions, or tasks, or materializations, are never in themselves a perfect metonym of an imaginary (i.e. a part that faithfully and felicitously condenses the whole) because this would imply that the imaginary comes first, before the work required to enact it. The work of politics here might be better understood as a trace (a mark, an impression) that signals the imaginary that one hopes to build and sustain. This 'doing' of an imaginary can't present an imaginary wholesale, but engages the work required to keep negotiating it, and proposing it anew.

To think about politics as a trace that marks or impresses also reminds us that these traces work on bodies, situations, and worlds (Ahmed 2004). We might understand this in the terms of the Deleuzian difference and repetition that I outlined in Chapter 2, where every repetition necessarily recasts that which materially conditions it and writes it anew. This understanding of difference and repetition is helpful in thinking through the figuration that 'we are all bodies of water' – yet bodies who are not the same. It might also help us think through how aqueous imaginaries are emergent – coalescing through the work of these bodies, but as Haraway alerts us, with no guarantees. Repetitions have no teleology, no set course, and are always worlded in relation to other repetitions. Repetitions can go askew. New possibilities for materializing bodies emerge, and co-emerge. In short, while the dominant effect of repeated traces is the reinforcing of a norm, the necessary underbelly of the repetition is its potential unmooring. Bodies of water as an imaginary must swim into being, but the 'doing' of this figuration can also be done 'badly' – that is, reoriented otherwise, again. *That* we repeat and world other bodies and imaginaries is not in question; the question is rather *how*. Not: *will* I repeat as a body of water, but: *how*.

Rebecca Belmore's *Fountain* is one response to this question of 'how'. Her artwork, like the *Idle No More* activism that in part fills out her work's context,[10] engages in the 'doing' of an imaginary that avers that 'water is life'. As noted earlier, this refrain aims to strengthen an alternative to modern/ global water, and Anthropocene water, where water is abstracted as nothing more than a resource for human use and human control. On billboards, in tweets, on posters and flyers, on T-shirts, in speeches and teach-ins, in flash-mob performances and round dances, in poetry and in academic scholarship, *Idle No More* participants and supporters *as* bodies of water enact the angry, hopeful, contagious power of this refrain. These bodies repeat this imaginary – 'water is life' – as one way of orienting ourselves to and as bodies of water, in thoughtful relations of care and concern. But Belmore's artwork also does something else: in *Temple*, for example, she provides an uncanny repetition of Anthropocene water as well. All of those little plastic sacs of life, abstracted and contained, displaced from the lake just on the other side of the wall, also repeat the PET bottles that are the metonyms of Anthropocene water – abstracted, controlled, and contained, for human consumption and 'survival'. In the space of *Temple*, Belmore thus opens another space to think again about the work of repetitions.

For, if we look beyond the invocations of *Idle No More*, we see that 'water is life' as an imaginary – or a concept for living otherwise – is indeed being amply repeated. As I noted in the introduction to this chapter, Nestle, a leading multinational bottled beverage company is also selling us 'Pure Life', while filtration systems and ionizers remind us that 'water is life', too (so buy me!). One way of approaching this phenomenon is through the analytic of lively commodities, where, if water is indeed 'life', we might consider what we are doing in the appropriation, buying and selling of this lifeblood. The crucial and timely debates about the commodification of life have been engaged with care elsewhere.[11] Here, I am rather interested in the repetition of 'water is life' as an imaginary. What possibilities are affirmed in this commoditized repetition, and which ones are foreclosed?

Before turning to this analysis, let's consider a few of the other ways in which this repetition happens. While the PET water bottle is one popular canvas for turning 'water is life' into a commodity, we should note that not all bottled water is solely geared towards the bottom line of corporate profit. A new wave of 'ethically branded bottled water' (Hawkins, Potter, and Race 2015) has arisen in the past decade, where consumers are implored to buy specific brands whose profits will be directed towards water-related charitable causes. Choosing a specific brand 'is presented as an act of generosity and connection' (Hawkins, Potter, and Race 2015: 191). While the tagline 'water is life' is not used directly, one of the world's leading purveyors of 'ethical water' is One Water: 'When you drink One, the world drinks too'. The imaginary on offer draws explicitly on the 'water is life' ethos, reminding us: water sustains us all; *we are all in this together*.

I'll return to the implications of this idea, but for now I want to use ethically branded water to make a link to other kinds of philanthropic work that addresses water-related crises in part through promoting the idea that 'water is life'. For example, as water crises mount and access to drinking water around the globe comes increasingly under pressure, 'water is life' has become a campaign slogan for various development organizations and charities focused on Africa and Asia. 'WATERisLIFE' is in fact the name of one large US-based charity whose mission is 'to provide clean water, sanitation and hygiene programs' through 'community-driven' and 'community-engaged' activities in Africa (http://waterislife.com/about/why-wil). My aim is not to pass judgement on the efficacy of some of this organization's individual programs – distribution of water filtration drinking straws, pump repair, and water source fencing, just like the donation of bottled water profits, may seem like good enough ideas, and may very well bring some reprieve to parched bodies in dry lands. I am interested rather in how 'water is life' is not just a statement, but like other repetitions, it is the gathering of those that came before, but put forth anew. I am interested in how difference and repetition here are once again shown to be not the autopoietic reworking of a bounded matter simply recapitulating itself in different ways, but always, in feminist terms, made and remade in context, and oriented by various valences of power. In one notable promotional video of its work, for instance, WATERisLIFE (2014) presents 'The Girl Who Couldn't Cry'.[12] This 1:20 minute video depicts a 'first person' account of a girl 'born into the [unnamed] slums of India' who doesn't cry – not when she finds out 'what [her] mother's job really was' (i.e. a physically abused sex worker), nor when her brother dies a violent death on the slum streets (we're not exactly sure from what; we see only his face-down bloodied corpse as spectacle for the gathering slum-dwellers), nor when she is forced into child marriage to a man with a greying beard (him grinning, her terrified), nor when she, as a young teen, holds her own baby child. The punchline of the video? The lack of crying was 'not because [she] didn't want to, but because [she] couldn't'. The screen then shifts to text that tells us: 'Extreme Dehydration prevents the body from producing tears.' While the work of WATERisLIFE may at first appear to be on same page as *Idle No More* in protesting lack of water infrastructure for communities that have borne the brunt of coloniality and its accompanying gender, class, and racial oppressions, the details of this promo reel show how the repetition of this imaginary goes considerably astray. Rather than *Idle No More's* call for nation-to-nation sovereignty, we have a repetition of racist discourses of white saviourism and of a gendered, brown body. 'White men saving brown women from brown men', indeed (Spivak 1988).

Or, we might also look at 'The Future We Want: Drop by Drop' campaign (2012) organized by the UN Conference on Sustainable Development as part of its Rio+20 activities. This action featured a Europe-wide competition to design a print advertisement that 'inspires the European public in a positive way'…'to preserve water, now and for future generations' (http://www.dropbydrop.eu/en). Among hundreds of entries (by both amateur and professional designers), many offer renditions of the pervasive 'blue planet', or remind us that 'water is precious', and entreat us to 'save water'. Teardrop shapes are plentiful. Unsurprisingly, one of the key messages of the campaigns is that 'water is life' – a phrase that repeats over and over again in the Drop by Drop images. Of interest to me here is the way that the sheer volume of entries enables us to catch the mobility of this concept in action: single frames of the message are transformed into a moving image, animating the ways in which this phrase becomes variously storied, when scrolled through at speed.

First, while blue is a popular theme colour, the more entries we look at, the more we notice that blue is soon outpaced by white, and even the absence of colour altogether – a crystal clear transparency. At once reminding us of the 'modern' water described by Linton (tasteless, odourless, colourless, placeless, meaningless), we also see how this abstraction of water connects to an imagined sense of purity. Where other colours (brown, black) are used, the deployment is mostly predictable: a black-lipped black mouth is filled with parched and cracked dirt; brown children scrounging the last drops of water from broken earthen vessels. One print titled 'the global unconscious' features an unclothed black child sipping directly from a dream-like pool. Here, a blue imaginary lines up with and serves as a point of confluence for greenwashing, whitewashing, and other projects of capitalist and colonial cleanliness. We might contemplate, then, the stakes of claiming that 'water is life' in the context of a highly racialized imaginary, or in the context of its corollary – the purported negation of race and its dematerialization surfing across an undertow of transparency and purity.

As repetition continues to do its work, we also note how 'Water is life' morphs, in more than a few cases, into the slogan 'choose life'. Teardrop shapes transmutate into wombs, holding small blue bodies. Water replaces amniotic fluid, or is infused into watery blue babies through a hydrological umbilicus. In other words, a 'water is life' imaginary is not all that repeats. We also get a repetition of decades-old anti-abortion imagery that sacralizes the (usually floating, non-contextual) foetus. Here we could ask: what are the stakes of claiming water is life on a terrain where 'life' has already been dangerously co-opted?

And again: it is impossible not to note that while some designs feature brown children, these are primarily as parched and dehydrated symbols of loss, misery, and death, yet beacons for the future are blue/white. We can better understand the tethered logic of a white 'pro-life' storyline with a brown 'no future' message if we consider them in the context of reproductive futurism. One poster featuring a foetus curled up in a blue drop/womb makes this clear: 'Don't touch my future', it insists. Lee Edelman (2004) has argued that we should be suspicious of political agendas that make pleas for the 'social good' through the mobilization of a naturalized child-figure. While environmentalism may not have been Edelman's main target, Nicole Seymour (2013: 7) points out that Edelman's theory 'certainly has the potential to spark objections to environmental agendas grounded in heterosexist, pro-reproduction rhetoric'.

Referring to environmental campaigns that often feature 'children of the future', Seymour notes that in images such as these 'concern for the future qua the planet can only emerge, or emerges most effectively, from white, heterosexual, familial reproductivity' (7). While the children featured in the Drop by Drop campaign are not explicit products of heteronormative unions, the very reliance on the child calls compulsory hetero- and reprosexuality into service. In this use of children, environmental problems are moreover 'domesticated', rather than being linked to larger structures such as sexism, racism, and classism (Seymour 2013: 7; see also Sheldon 2013). In the context of these arguments, the campaign's parched brown bodies on the brink of death, alongside its white foetuses floating in pure amniotic waters, are clearly more than statements of fact. Instead, they shore up an imaginary of reproductive futurism that implies whom the future should be for.

A racialized reproductive futurism also helps us make sense of the Drop by Drop winning entry, whose copy reads: 'Wasting water will kill the future / Change begins at home'. The image features a hand (body out of view) holding a blue (water?) gun, pointed at the head of a white, cherubic baby. The nonsensical deployment of a water gun pointed at a baby in order to signify 'wasting water' aside, the fact that this image was chosen as the best hope to 'inspire' us to change our orientations to water is troubling in the gendered and raced messages it distils. So, what are the stakes of claiming 'water is life' where life-fulfilment is drenched in heteronormativity and family values, saturated by straight time and a progress narrative of messianic future orientation? We might also note that 'a jury of experts led by France's advertising guru, Mr. Jacques Séguéla chose the ad from more than 3,500 ads submitted to the competition from 45 European countries', and the winner took home 5,000 Euros. Not only in the pixels of this picture, but also in the context of its reproduction, questions of for whom and in the name of what this 'inspiration' is intended are amplified.

My main point here, though, is that when the repetition of 'water is life' is in the service of a racist, colonial, and heteronormatively domesticated reproductive futurism, we start to see how the imaginary offered by *Idle No More*, or explicitly articulated in an Anishinabe worldview, holds no guarantees. The invocation of a reproductive futurism itself alerts us that the future is never simply given, but like water, is made and unmade, and can be oriented through the kinds of imaginaries we support and the conceptual contexts (indigenous sovereignty, or development messianism?) that they buttress. Similarly 'water is life' can be repeated, but to very different ends. As Hawkins, Potter, and Race (2015: 192) argue, the success of ethically branded bottled water (ironically) relies on the contagion of affect and information that have been generated by anti-bottled water activists. Selling water depends on a 'misrepetition' or a repetition, redirected. As with bottled water, so too with the Drop by Drop campaign: repetition of 'water is life' is both an alibi, and a diversion.

And finally, when we think about the messages propagated by these diversions – 'when you drink One Water, the whole world drinks too' – we might be struck to find that in exploring alternatives to an Anthropocene water imaginary, we have uncannily wound up back at that very same place. As the founder and CEO of the ethically branded One Water has argued, 'people have recognized that water is water; why wouldn't you opt to buy a brand that changes people's lives?' (Fry, quoted in Hawkins, Potter, and Race 2015: 189). Water is water, one water is same as the next – isomorphic, exchangeable, displaced, abstracted. In a queer way, 'water is life' comes to support the very idea it hopes to challenge. At its heart, all repetition harbours the potential not only for productively differing, but also for unimaginable mutation – joyful or otherwise. As with all repetitions of 'life', germ-lines are not easily contained.

We may start to wonder about the possibilities for reimagining water, when imaginaries and figurations are as vulnerable to redirection as the flows of the river themselves. Yet, with the drums of a round dance echoing in our ears, or the remnants of the ropy red liquid flung from Belmore's *Fountain* still almost-running down our hands, we might also ask: what are the stakes of giving up on reimagining, and just walking away? Even though imaginaries hold no guarantees, part of my argument in this book is that they are one of the best lifeboats we've got. So, perhaps we turn into the rapids, and hold on.

Material imaginaries and other aqueous questions

My wager in this book has been that the figuration of 'bodies of water' might enable us to create a more capacious aqueous imaginary for being responsive to other human and non-human bodies with whom we share a planetary existence. 'Bodies of water' can be an alternative to the idea of Anthropocene water, and can resonate with other alternative imaginaries, such as 'water is life', despite the risks of co-optation that this involves. But this raises a question: how can figurations – concepts or theories – bring us any closer to the matter of water? Isn't 'bodies of water' just another concept amongst those others – modern water, global water, Anthropocene water – that it seeks to upset? Given the vulnerability of figurations and imaginaries that we've just outlined, it may seem a strange place to pin our watery hopes.

My reason for nonetheless pushing the idea of this figuration and the imaginary that 'bodies of water' offers is related to the idea that concepts are shot through with materiality. They are inextricable from the matters they ostensibly only 'theoretically' describe. Karen Barad's (2007) theory of intra-action has been widely taken up as a way to think through the entanglement of matters – how, for example, fish are not 'in' rivers, but how fish and rivers *world* each other. Rejecting the *a priori* atomism of things, Barad insists that relata do not precede relations; things are rather perpetually worlding – that is materializing from the intra-actions of always emergent things-in-phenomena (136). Intra-actionism, in short, is a helpful framework for getting a grip on the co-extensiveness of worldly matters. Equally helpful, though, is an application of intra-action to conceptual worlds, where figures or concepts also follow from co-emergent entanglement. On this account, we need to consider that concepts do not invent the world *ex nihilo*, nor do they merely describe it. They too are co-emergent with the materialities they grapple with.

As Barad (2008b: 140) argues, 'discursive practices are not speech acts, linguistic representations, or even linguistic performances'. Importantly, '[d]iscursive practices and material phenomena do not stand in a relationship of externality to one another'; they are 'mutually implicated in the dynamics of intra-activity' (140). Which is to say: Water does not precede the concepts we use to engage it, any more than the words we use to fabricate material reality. Discourses are, in Haraway's (1988) and Barad's (2007) terms, boundary-making projects and practices through which the contours of a phenomenon become meaningful, intelligible, and sensible. Concepts and figurations co-habit our world as various companion species, fulfilling various needs and offering different orientations.

Imaginaries, concepts, discourses, and figures all function as invitations to imagine otherwise. They are all moveable bridges; they are normative forces.

If I deploy these terms somewhat loosely, it is specifically because I wish to stress that all of these notions – so often relegated to the side of culture, the immaterial, the representational, and so on – are material-discursive phenomena, tethered to materialities they might purportedly only describe. Throughout this book I have stressed that concepts are embodied – but this doesn't mean that they are simply given. Words too – a theory, a concept, a poem – are multivalent intra-actions of matter and meaning. In this sense, I feel compelled to pull back slightly from Linton's key claim that 'water is what we make of it'. This is of course true, in a number of senses (we imagine water in ways that affect what it is and can be; we make it through our anthropogenic material incursions from megadams to toxic spills to wetlands restorations projects; we also make water in the sense that our own bodies give it shape and form – we are bodies as which it can live). But perhaps Linton does not sufficiently stress that water also makes the 'it', whatever that be. If water is an idea, it is a material, embodied idea. As such, it expresses limits and capacities and potentialities that in part determine which discourses, ideas, concepts, or figures can emerge.

Imaginaries expressed through discourse and concepts – such as 'modern, global water' or 'Anthropocene water', or even 'bodies of water' and 'water is life' – are not mere words to be placed upon the external reality of water, in yet another version of culture framing nature. Imaginaries are made through the entanglements of matters – both wet and wordy. The point here is that Anthropocene thinking and (modern, global) Anthropocene water are not 'false'. Importantly, these are concepts or figures that are entangled in the specific matters of the world to which they respond. 'Water is life' responds to the lively and essential qualities that water holds; but it also responds to a survivalism that is entirely congruent with Anthropocene thinking. We have to acknowledge that Anthropocene water has taken hold because, as of yet, the materiality of water also accommodates this imaginary: water's ontological specificity – its fluidity, gestational capacity, and ability to respond to what and how we make it – is also what makes it a good tool for Anthropocene imaginings. Water *can* be bottled and sold, evidently. Mighty rivers *can* be dammed, for a certain amount of time anyways, and rivers *can* be rerouted to make deserts bloom. Water *can* take an unbelievable amount of our shit – literally and figuratively – and life *can* also mean neoliberal survival in a colonial world. This material potentiality is what Anthropocene water – with its attention to malleability and control – selects and foregrounds.

Although we may disagree with or challenge many aspects of this worldview, Anthropocene water *does* exist. It is not 'just' an idea, fabricated solely by human brains, in an abstract laboratory of thought; it is no less genuine than bodies of water, or Kwe, or *Fountain*. These all emerge from various intersecting material practicalities and possibilities. Material, worldly waters intra-act with human apparatuses of framing, agency, and knowledge (also material) in an articulation that becomes Anthropocene water – or something else. Anthropocene water is not an imposter that must be pushed aside so that the 'real' water can stand up. But there is much about water's materialities to which Anthropocene water as a figure responds rather poorly. In its focus on guaranteeing (non-specific, exchangeable and quantifiable) water as a resource to mostly individual and non-differentiated humans, Anthropocene water dams other aspects of a more robust aqueous imaginary: water's transcorporeality, its posthuman gestationality, its unknowability, and necessary tracing of difference. In troubling the abstraction and homogenization of Anthropocene water, a posthumanist feminist figuration – bodies of water – can suggest different orientations; different selections of water's materialities and logics, and an amplification of those.

All of this to say: an imaginary and its figurations hold no guarantees. No imaginary can be installed simply with a triumphant flourish. The answer will always be a question.

What is water?
  here/not here/and mine/not mine/and
  (it belongs to itself, Lee Maracle reminds us)[13] *and*

What is water?
  (KWE)

What is water?
  tiny ocean, and sweat, and pipe, and urine, and PET bottle, and stream, and

What is water?
  an alibi, a lover, a debt, a promise,

What is water –

Notes

Introduction

1   Jackson (2013) provocatively wonders whether contemporary posthumanism might look very different, and open to different possibilities, if its genealogy were traced not through Foucault, but instead through postcolonial theorist Aime Cesaire, or even more radically, through black feminist writer and theorist Sylvia Wynter.

2   Many if not most of these debates are happening in conference rooms (and their corridors) and on blogs; it is difficult to therefore cite them using rigorous academic practice, but it does not make these debates less real. The key ways in which Object-Oriented Ontology departs from feminist new materialism is also convincingly argued in Rebekah Sheldon's (2015) chapter 'Form/Matter/Chora'.

3   Justifying study of the non-human as both proper to and important for gender and feminist studies has been taken up in Grosz (2012) and Colebrook (2012), among other places. (See also my argument in 'Natural Others?' (2014).) Rather than rehearsing those arguments at length, I hope this book as a whole will contribute to this debate and press the issue that Robyn Wiegman (2012: 39) tags as 'humanism's colonization of the province and practice of both politics and knowledge production within Women's and Gender Studies as we have known them'.

4   Having researched water primarily within feminist circles for over a decade, it is difficult to articulate this internal critique. It is often expressed in casual comments but far less often recorded and published. As I make clear, the value of feminist posthumanism versus some other nonfeminist versions is its explicit articulation of human and non-human oppressions, and their mutual conditioning of one another. This is probably the most valuable lesson of ecofeminism – which has also been heartily attacked within some corners of feminism. It is far easier to substantiate feminist critiques of ecofeminism than it is internal critiques of feminist posthumanism. While some of these critiques

(to my mind, helpfully) question a certain gender normativity and tricky essentialism that some very circumscribed ecofeminist arguments espouse, most ecofeminist work rejects this essentialism. It is therefore interesting to think about where critiques of ecofeminism are rooted. My suspicion is that it is at least in part connected to a profound dis-ease with a perforation of the species boundary, but also in part connected to our 'object desires'. As Wiegman (2012) unpacks, feminist scholarship has disidentified with 'woman' as its proper object, taking 'gender' as the replacement. But is 'gender' capacious enough to encompass the non-human? As Wiegman notes, the 'turn from *women* to *gender*' will have to keep turning, 'soon, no doubt, from *gender* to whatever will come to signify the ways in which it will have failed' (40). Will posthuman feminism have to engage this next disidentification, too, if it is to 'realize its full potential', as Wiegman suggests?

5   Importantly, the specific content of these claims has varied between feminisms. In the case of reproductive rights, black feminisms and indigenous feminisms have had very different stakes in fighting for bodily autonomy than have white, middle-class feminisms. The liberal language of autonomy has also been treated with suspicion among feminists of colour – which is also why these feminisms are a crucial part of the genealogy of posthuman feminism.

6   Jackson (2013: 672) points out that this does not mean that black or colonized subjects do, or must, remain humanists. Black critics such as Gordon did not seek uncritical admittance into the hallowed halls of humanism; they rather attempted to transform the category from within.

7   This is not to say that there aren't other historic and contemporary understandings of water that counter this hegemonic notion – the Syilx Okanagan indigenous cosmology poetically enacted by Jeanette Armstrong (2006), or the social natures of water described by Vandana Shiva in regards to Rajasthan's communal water tanks (2002), or the cultures around acequias in New Mexico and southern Colorado in the United States that enact as a form of irrigation facilitative of multispecies life (Garcia 2007) are just a few examples. But for certain, these do not represent dominant imaginaries of water in our contemporary world. The existence of such alternatives, however, is precisely what proves Linton's point, and shows up the *naturalization* of modern water as a social nature.

8   Recent examples include Fluid States-Fluid Sounds: http://www.soundstudieslab. org/wp-content/uploads/2014/11/FLUIDSTATES_FLUIDSOUNDS_call.pdf and Fluid Identities and Continuities: http://catracrt.ca/2014/09/21/412/

9   On multispecies ethnography, see Kirksey and Helmreich (2010). However, with its attention to animal species as the most salient earth others in these investigations, this method does not quite capture my focus on water.

Chapter 1

1   The phenomenological notion of the 'natural attitude' needs to be critically and cautiously approached by feminist and intersectional scholars, as it assumes a neutral 'everyday' or 'ordinary' way of being-in-the-world according to which these things appear as simple facts of existence, and that this appearance would be common to human experience. While this view may hold generally at the species level, it is too dismissive of how intersectionality and assemblages of power and belonging (Puar 2012) shape our experience of the material world. An uncritical natural attitude also belies the humanist error (with its attendant androcentricism, ablism, and racism) in accordance with which many phenomenological projects need to be critically scrutinized. At the same time, the bracketing of one's habitual relations to things can nonetheless bring to light both how the natural attitude invisibilizes marginalized and queer orientations towards things-in-the-world (see Ahmed 2006) and how even these queer experiences can require further de-sedimentation of their own habitual assumptions. In other words, identifying dominant orientations to things in the world is a useful practice. Moreover, one's own natural attitude need not be common to all knowing bodies.

2   I discuss the relationship between flat ethics and flat ontologies in 'No Representation without Colonisation?' (2015).

3   Both Florence Williams's (2012) book on *Breasts: An Unnatural History* and Eva-Maria Simms's article on toxic incorporeality 'Eating One's Mother' (2009) briefly describe the transit of toxins into Arctic waters and up the food chain to lactating Inuit mothers, but in ways that need to be questioned. The racism of Williams's imperative 'don't picture Eskimo Man in sealskin on the top of the food chain. Picture his suckling baby' (239) is troubling, to say the least. Her story focuses primarily on her own circumstances, and one of her key messages is her relief that regulations around certain toxins are better in the United States than elsewhere. While Simms expresses a more genuine concern for bodies beyond her own milieu, she also unwittingly juxtaposes activist-writers such as Sandra Steingraber who heroically seek out knowledge about their contaminated

bodily waters, with Inuit mothers who 'go about the business of caring for their pregnant selves in the traditional ways, and do not know that they have been contaminated and invaded' (273). The knowledge-crusader versus the naïf is a colonialist trope that ignores other research (Trainor et al. 2010) that underlines high levels of knowledge and concern within indigenous communities. Simms's claim also suggests that if these mothers only knew more or better, they would act differently – but when the toxins permeate the air, water, and food around you, real choice is a false promise, and shifts the responsibility for toxic contamination away from its systemic sources.

4   There may be an additional objection: that the poisons travelling in breast milk are not *technically* part of our 'bodies of water' as most of these toxins (and others I discuss in this chapter) are lipophilic and contained in breast milk's fatty content. My point, however, is that both our watery corporeal flows and planetary rivers and seas are nonetheless the vectors and highways for these pollutants.

5   As Merleau-Ponty (1962: vii) notes, phenomenology is at its most basic 'the study of essence'. For Merleau-Ponty, however, this is not the biologically reductive or deterministic essentialism that feminism mostly abhors. Merleau-Ponty's essences are not incompatible with bodies as changing, becoming: 'It is true neither that my existence is in full possession of itself, nor that it is entirely estranged from itself, because it is an action or doing, and because action is, by definition, the violent transition from what I have to what I aim to have, from what I am to what I intend to be'; I 'accomplish my own existence' (382). Moreover, 'it is impossible to superimpose on man a lower layer of behaviour which one chooses to call "natural", followed by a manufactured or cultural or spiritual world. Everything is both manufactured and natural in man' (189). See also Helen Fielding (2000) on Merleau-Ponty's essences.

6   See also Eric Alliez (2004), in particular Chapter 3, and Brian Massumi (2002), in particular Chapter 8, both of whom agree that phenomenology cannot escape the paradigm of solipsistic subjective humanism. Graham Harman (2005: 52–53) has also lamented the fact that Merleau-Ponty ultimately 'steps back' from the innovative potential of his philosophy; the phenomenologist 'artificially limits the scope of the cosmos to that of human awareness' and in the end is no more than 'a product of his age'. Deleuze (1994a: 51–52) moreover criticizes what he assesses as phenomenology's inability to admit difference *as difference* into its philosophy. Despite his quarrels with certain aspects of phenomenology, Deleuze also acknowledges its potential in various ways. In his essay on Sartre entitled

'He Was My Teacher', Deleuze (2004: 77) notes that the work of Merleau-Ponty is 'brilliant and profound', even if (unfortunately, in Deleuze's estimation) 'tender and reserved'. Deleuze (1994a: 64–66) also acknowledges Heidegger and Merleau-Ponty's contributions to the development of an ontology of difference.

7   Other commentators who think the chasm between Deleuze and phenomenology need not be that wide include Leonard Lawlor (1998), Ted Toadvine (e.g. 2004), Henry Somers-Hall (2006), William Connolly (2011), and Renaud Barbaras (2004: xxii, 2001, and 2006). Feminist phenomenologist Gail Weiss (1999: see chapter 6 'Écart') is one of the few philosophers who emphasizes the debt that Deleuze owes to Merleau-Ponty in the context of rethinking difference through intercorporeality, although she does not pursue this connection in great depth. See also Tamsin Lorraine (2011: 4).

8   Deleuze's theory on bodies has an acknowledged debt to Spinoza and the question Spinoza poses: What can a body do? (see Deleuze and Guattari 1987: 153; 253–265). For a deeper discussion on Deleuze's debt to Spinoza in terms of a theory of bodies, see Ian Buchanan (1997).

9   'Is it not necessary', ask Deleuze and Guattari (1987: 270) 'to retain a minimum of strata, a minimum of forms and functions, a minimal subject from which to extract materials, affects and assemblages?'; after all, 'you have to keep small supplies of significance and subjectification, if only to turn them against their own systems when the circumstances demand it' (160).

10 For deeper descriptions of the actual and virtual see 'The Actual and the Virtual' (Deleuze and Parnet 2002) and *Difference and Repetition* (1994: 208–214).

11 See Samuel Mallin's (1979) work *Merleau-Ponty's Philosophy*.

12 It is important to insist that this 'rightness' is always in the context of a body's specific capacities, and not in terms of an idealized body. All human bodies are differently abled; the loose unity of cohesion and 'rightness' will look different for different bodies. While it is possible to read a problematic ablism into Merleau-Ponty (particularly in his discussions of pathological embodiment), it is also possible to deploy his insights for understanding bodies in more inclusive terms. See also Note 1 above on the natural attitude.

13 Vicki Kirby (2006: 132) argues that Merleau-Ponty's ontology of the flesh is a 'major assault on our most routine notions of subjectivity'.

14 This understanding is already foreshadowed in *Phenomenology of Perception*, where Merleau-Ponty (1962: 250) discusses the body in space as a 'system of possible actions, a virtual body with its phenomenal "place" defined by its task and situation'; in other words, the body I live is only ever a 'provisional sketch'

(1962: 198) of what it might be. Similarly, the world is for Merleau-Ponty (1962: 219) an 'open totality, the synthesis of which is exhaustible'; there is a 'depth' of objects 'that no progressive sensory deduction will ever exhaust' (216).

15 See Toadvine (2014) for a compelling discussion of how Merleau-Ponty's phenomenology also accommodates an 'asubjective time' – that is, the time of elementality, the time of worlds that precede and outlive us – at the heart of lived time. In this way, Toadvine convincingly defends Merleau-Ponty against charges of what Object-Oriented Ontologists call correlationism.

16 My knowledge of Mallin's practice of body hermeneutics is primarily first hand, as a student of his from 2001 until around 2005. Mallin never published work on this methodology which he robustly worked up over decades of practice. The lineaments for it, however, can be traced in his reading of Merleau-Ponty's phenomenology (see Mallin 1979). My own understanding of phenomenology is immensely indebted to Mallin, even in our moments of disagreement.

17 Felix Gonzalez Torres, *Untitled* (Water), 1997. Shown at the Koffler Gallery in Toronto, 2002.

18 See Karen Barad (2007) on onto-epistemology.

19 For example, a nineteenth-century understanding of embodiment in the West was 'ecological', as documented by environmental historian Linda Nash. This contrasts with the dominant twentieth-century experience of ourselves as discretely bounded individuals, which emerged in tandem with Western allopathic medicine that saw disease as intrinsic to an individual body and isolatable body parts (Alaimo 2010: 90). Rosi Braidotti (2011) invokes the concept of 'organs without bodies' to describe the liminal space of the late twentieth century where bodies stopped being more than the sum of their parts, and instead those parts (a womb, a kidney, a heart) were rendered increasingly detachable, fragmentable, and alienable through biotechnology.

20 An alternative view is offered by Drew Leder (1990), who also points to biotechnological interventions such as sphygmomanometers that allow us to 'access' blood pressure, x-rays that allow us to see our lungs, or colonoscopy that makes the lumen visible. For Leder, however, 'the absences that haunt my bodily depths are not effaced by these reflective maneuvers' (44). In other words, Leder argues, while such apparatus give us data, we still do not experience our insides; the absences persist. Leder does suggest that other systems of knowledge, such as Taoism and Buddhism, may be better equipped at bringing the subtle (rather than completely absent) workings of our molecular selves into perception, and he hints that such Eastern knowledge would also be a matter of training. I take

this as in part a challenge to his own assertion of the ontological invisibility/ inaccessibility of our recessive bodies. This also clears the way for my own wager, namely that we can hone or train our phenomenological attunement (paradoxically) by using the knowledge of the very systems that also obfuscate the appearance of visceral embodiment to us.

21 Donna Haraway (1988), 'Situated Knowledges'.

22 See Haraway (1988) 'Situated Knowledges' and Code (2012), 'Taking Subjectivity into Account'.

23 Deleuze also draws heavily on science to describe bodies. As John Protevi (2001: 2–3) writes, 'we are [...] confronted in Deleuze's works with a radically materialist philosophy that engages all the powers of contemporary physics and biology to analyze and intervene in those sectors of the contemporary global system which gleefully embrace difference and flow'. Deleuze not only tolerates a scientific perspective, but in fact demands that our philosophy of bodies include it – yet is careful not to slip into science as mere symbol or metaphor. Deleuze (quoted in Smith 1997: xxiv) suggests that 'perhaps these dangers are averted ... if we restrict ourselves to extracting from scientific operators a particular conceptualizable character which itself refers to non-scientific domains, and converges with science without applying it or making it a metaphor'.

24 As Protevi (2005: 195) has written in regards to Deleuze's position on the organizing tendency towards subjectification, 'this utility is primarily [...] a resting point for further experimentation'.

Chapter 2

1 The term 'sexuate' is a neologism used by English translations of Irigaray's work, as well as by Irigaray herself when communicating in English. As Rachel Jones (2011: 4) explains, ' "sexuate" refers neither to a mode of being determined by biological sex nor to a cultural overlay of gendered meanings inscribed on a "tabula rasa" of passively receptive matter. [...]. Rather it signals the way that sexual difference is articulated through our different modes of being and becoming, that is, in bodily, social, linguistic, aesthetic, erotic, and political forms'; sexuate difference, as understood by Jones is the 'irreducible difference which inflects every aspect of our being'. In Emily Parker's (2015: 91) helpful parsing, 'sexuate difference' is a term 'for the incalculable non-procreative alterity of bodies, without dimorphism'. In keeping with these interpretations, I use

the term 'sexuate difference' in this chapter if I am discussing it in ways that correspond to the above, but in context, the more general term 'sexual difference' is still sometimes called for.

2　This particular way of formulating this ethical demand was worked out by Mielle Chandler and me in our co-authored chapter 'Water and Gestationality: What Flows Beneath Ethics' (2013). My thinking in this chapter picks up on and extends this collaborative work.

3　To my knowledge, Irigaray does not use the precise term 'gestationality', although the concepts of the maternal, the placental, and the intrauterine are all prominent in her work. The appropriateness of this specific term, 'gestationality', was suggested to me by Mielle Chandler during her review of a very early draft of this project. Chandler expounds the notion of gestationality in reference to the work of Emmanuel Levinas (2008).

4　For good examples of this refutation that span decades of Irigarayan commentary, see Shildrick (1997), Braidotti (2003), and Jones (2011).

5　For example, Braidotti (2000, 2002, 2003, 2006), Grosz (2004, 2005), Lorraine (1999), and Olkowski (2000) all suggest an understanding of the feminine body in Irigaray's thought as at least in part 'virtual', enfolding both a history and an unknowability. The notion of 'becoming woman' as tied to a material metaphor of fluidity is also charted in Canters and Jantzen's *Forever Fluid* (2005).

6　Irigaray (1985b: 140–141) does not explicitly confront Deleuze by name in her writings, but she invokes his work in her expressed scepticism about 'multiplicities', 'desiring machines', and 'the body without organs' that, in her view, threaten effacement and appropriation of feminine pleasure and desire. Irigaray's criticisms of Deleuze are echoed by Jardine (1984) and Grosz (1994), although more recent work by Grosz (e.g. 2005) is more interested in the resonances between Irigaray and Deleuze. Indeed, a certain body of feminist scholarship has devoted itself to examining the relation between Irigaray and Deleuze. See Grosz (2004, 2005, 2011), Braidotti (2000, 2002, 2003, 2006b, inter alia), Lorraine (1999), Colebrook (2000), Olkowski (2000), Haynes (2012).

7　There is little indication in Irigaray's own texts that she would understand 'woman' as inclusive of trans-women or other non-binary genders. While this aspect of her work should rightfully be critiqued, I believe we can still find usefulness in her theory of elemental embodiment, and I argue it is possible to read Irigaray's understanding of sexuate bodies against some of her own statements. As Emily Parker (2015: 91) helpfully notes, by focusing on Irigaray's most recent claim that there are no 'neuter individuals', we could expand this to include alterities and differences beyond binarisms. *My* use of the term 'woman' does not indicate an endorsement of binary gender.

8   These commentaries not only point out the challenge that Irigaray presents to feminist theory (particularly when the stakes of biological essentialism are not only philosophical but also ethical and decidedly material) but also reveal some of the ways in which bodily and environmental matters have been a grappling ground for feminist theory for decades. As Elizabeth Stephens (2014: 191) helpfully remarks: 'That debates about the status of the biological in Irigaray's work were so central to its initial reception is thus important – not because they represent a misreading of her work, but because they are indicative of the complex and contentious role the biological has played within the history of feminist theory'.

9   Such claims are difficult because 'new materialism' is not exactly new. See Ahmed (2008), Sullivan (2012), and van der Tuin and Dolphijn (2010). To suggest that Irigaray is an early (even anachronistic) feminist posthuman thinker or new materialist, as I do in this chapter, underlines that feminist new materialism is not amenable to linear narratives, but rather gathers possible pasts and potential futures in an ongoing unfolding.

10 See van der Tuin and Dolphijn (2010) on transversal genealogies within new materialisms and also Clare Hemmings (2011). I provide a more detailed exploration of Irigaray's relationship to feminist new materialisms in 'Thinking with Matter, Rethinking Irigaray: A "Liquid Ground" for Planetary Feminism' (2016).

11 See Note 7 above regarding Irigaray and trans* embodiment.

12 *Marine Lover* is her most watery text, although other essays also take up fluidity and waters. Breath is dealt with in many texts (Irigaray 1999, 2002a, 2002b), and is arguably the element on which she has most explicitly focused. Fire has not been extensively examined by Irigaray, although she notes that in an unpublished study she examines fire in relation to the work of Karl Marx (A. Martin 2000: 165 n34).

13 While Irigaray would say 'both sexes' I would say 'all sexes'.

14 Kelly Oliver (1995) and Tasmin Lorraine (1999) provide helpful comments on Irigaray's *Marine Lover*, both suggesting that Irigaray does not adequately consider how Nietzsche's philosophy of the eternal return might also admit the return of difference. Both Oliver and Lorraine nonetheless find Irigaray's critical attention to Nietzsche's elision of the maternal and sexual difference compelling.

15 A similar association is made in Hélène Cixous's text 'Sorties: Out and Out: Attacks/Ways Out/Forays' (Cixous and Clément 1986), where she discusses the feminine body/of writing as diffuse, never fully knowable, fecund and overabundant, thus comparing it to a sea. In Cixous's text, like Irigaray's, the relation between the feminine, the maternal body, and the sea is invoked as ambiguous slippage and overlap, facilitated in part by the French language, where 'mer' and 'mère' (sea and mother) are homonyms. Cixous describes how men cannot separate themselves from 'seas and mothers' (88). She continues: 'But that's it – our seas are what we make them, fishy or not, impenetrable or muddled, red or black, high and rough or flat and smooth, narrow straits or shoreless, and we ourselves are sea, sands, corals, seaweeds, beaches, tides, swimmers, children, waves … seas and mothers' (88–89).
    In a move similar to Irigaray's, Cixous invokes a complex relationship between the feminine and the fluid that is hardly a direct, complete, or exclusive relation. In her descriptions, the relation of the feminine body to the sea is on some level metaphorical, but it is also materially constitutive and topographical, that is, the feminine is not only like water but also of water and in water in a variety of ways. A closer comparison of the relation between the feminine and the 'mer/mère' figurations in Cixous and Irigaray's work warrants further study.

16 It serves also to recall here that water, as a chemical entity, is not bound to a fluid form, and Irigaray certainly picks up and plays on these ambiguous actualizations in her work. However, when Irigaray refers to ice, vapour or other manifestations of water, they are referred to by those other names.

17 See Alphonso Lingis (1994), in particular Chapter 8 'Fluid Economy' and Chapter 11 'Elemental Bodies'.

18 Men are in fact usually even more watery than women, since women generally have a higher percentage of body fat than men.

19 Hence another connection is also introduced here – to our evolutionary watery beginnings – but this discussion will be explicitly taken up in Chapter 3.

20 See Irigaray's (1993a) essay on Merleau-Ponty, 'The Invisible of the Flesh', where she criticizes Merleau-Ponty for his failure to acknowledge the dispersed relation of tactility between mother and foetus in the intrauterine environment.

21 In posthuman feminist theorist Karen Barad's (2007) terms (see Chapter 1), such ontological cuts that separate out entangled phenomena are an enactment of 'agential separability' – that is, a mode of worlding and making knowable that belies the on-going intra-action of matters. These cuts are enacted by all kinds of apparatuses of knowledge.

22 See Shildrick's (1997: 25) critique of representations of women's bodies and
    reproduction that show 'the status of the foetus or embryo, even the pre-
    conceptus at times, [as] characterized as free-floating, independent, radically
    other than the mother herself'. Shildrick, like Irigaray, reminds us that the
    foetus has a necessary relationship to and a dependence on a specific gestational
    medium that, I am stressing, is also a body of water itself.

23 Irigaray bases this on her reading of Nietzsche's *Thus Spoke Zarathustra* (1982),
    to which *Marine Lover* explicitly alludes. Irigaray finds Nietzsche's replication of
    the self-same in Zarathustra's penchant for heights, love of birds and disavowal of
    fish, and his crossing of bridges that keeps him from acknowledging the sea (see
    Nietzsche 1982, particularly Part One). Interestingly, however, Zarathustra also
    makes several references to his relation to the sea. For example, the Overman
    is referred to as a sea (125), and Zarathustra also talks of himself as a river in
    relation to the sea: 'I want to plunge my speech down into the valleys. Let the
    river of my love plunge where there is no way! How could a river fail to find its
    way to the sea? Indeed, a lake is within me, solitary and self-sufficient; but the
    river of my love carries it along, down to the sea' (198). Passages such as these,
    alongside Zarathustra's additional frequent comments on his need to 'go down'
    and 'go under' in fact suggest that Nietzsche indeed acknowledges his connection
    to and reliance on the fluvial feminine more than Irigaray would allow. I return
    to the evolutionary connections in Irigaray's love letter to Nietzsche in Chapter 3.

24 Note the significance of the term 'differenciation' (internal force of differing)
    alongside the more common English-language term 'differentiation' (differing
    from something external). Deleuze (1994a) makes extensive use of this
    conceptual slippage and deploys as well the concept of 'differenc/tiation' to
    underline the force of difference as simultaneously at work both internally and
    in relation. In this chapter, I mostly opt for the simpler 'differentiation', but hope
    that it will be read with this Deleuzian inflection.

25 Here again we see the inhospitability of Deleuze's philosophy to binary
    oppositional conceptual systems. Reading bodies of water through a Deleuzian
    framework that would understand this watery system as both open and closed
    also challenges Olkowski's (2000) reading of Irigaray and Deleuze, where she
    argues that Deleuze characterizes the world as an 'open whole' while Irigaray
    stops short of this, instead insisting on a 'totalizing framework' (Olkowski 2000:
    103–104). Reading the work of Deleuze and Irigaray together, and particularly
    through our bodies of water, I suggest, shows that both would reject such
    binaristic options. (Olkowski does get at a key point here, however, when she

notes the burden put on fluidity in Irigaray's work: within a totalized framework the fluid must always 'be in excess with respect to form as well as permanently unstable by nature [104]'. Olkowski's observation here opens towards my own proposal, that is, that bodies of water are both finite *and* always still yet-to-come).

26 To insist on this specificity is certainly not to make any claims about 'motherhood' or to privilege breeding over other kinds of gestation and facilitation – a point to which I come back at the end of the chapter. It is possible to note the necessity of feminine waters for the proliferation of human life without tying it to an argument for the elevation of female reprosexuality. At the same time, while the possibility of ectogenesis (out-of-body gestation) looms imminent on our horizon, we have not yet accomplished it. Shall science deliver to us this possibility in any viable or sustainable way, the very real elision of the maternal-gestational waters will no doubt bring with it questions and consequences we are only beginning to contemplate. See, for example, Olkowski (2006) on the intersubjective significance of the maternal-embryonic relation. On the feminist philosophical implications of ectogenesis see, for example, Gelfand, ed. (2006), Aristarkhova (2005), and Murphy (1989). Or, as Irigaray (2015: 103) herself writes:

> The sexuation of the living is thus an essential key to an ecological ethics. It is also a crucial aspect of such an ethics, as it allows the species to survive through natural generation for which no fabrication can be substituted. Besides, whatever the technical mediations, the sex hormones must intervene to produce a new embryo. And it would be a pity if technical mediation would become substituted for an amorous union in the reproduction of living, as, alas!, it is already the case for a part of the animals.

27 Taking such claims at simplistic face value can be difficult, though, as Irigaray is simultaneously critiquing the phallogocentric symbolic economy in which woman, and sexual difference, as we currently know them, exist. In this same passage, she insists that the source of the ethical relation between two is cultivating the question 'who are you?' In leaving identity open, and by refusing the reduction of one to similarity or comparison with the other, Irigaray may give us room to radically renegotiate the identities of the bodies who hold this question between them.

28 For discussions, see Parker (2015), Jones (2011), Deutscher (2004), Stone (2003, 2006, 2015), and Braidotti (2002, 2003, 2006b).

29 Again: it is crucial that attention to the different social realities of the genders also consider how trans* bodies experience these violences, both materially and

discursively. I attempt to pry open Irigaray's theory of sexual difference enough to admit a discussion of non-binary sexuate difference, but Irigaray herself offers little direct or explicit assistance in this endeavour.

30   This is in spite of overt pleas for reproductive futurisms and off-putting trends of 'yummy mummies' and the Hollywoodification of pregnancy. Of course, these trends cover over the racism, classism, and homophobia in which maternity is still mired, where only some pregnant bodies and mothers are valued. In short: while critiques of cultures of maternity and pregnancy are certainly necessary, these can't be at the expense of maternal labours *tout court*.

31   While some readings focus on teasing out the nuanced differences between Deleuze and Irigaray (see Haynes 2012), I am more interested in how an amplification of their resonances can bring out certain tendencies and propositions in Irigaray's work that are otherwise washed away under the force of her dominant proclamations on sexuate difference.

32   My argument for sexual difference itself as a force of differentiation, and as applicable beyond human bodies, has strong resonances with Rebecca Hill's (2015) argument for the same, where she draws on Elizabeth Grosz, Gilles Deleuze, Henri Bergson, and Jakob von Uexkull, although she arrives at this through a different pathway in Irigaray. My position here is also strongly resonant with Elizabeth Grosz's (2011) argument in *Becoming Undone*.

33   As Lorraine (1999: 164) notes, 'it may be that Deleuze takes such mutual implication of lines of flight for granted'.

34   Here, we could also add Maurice Merleau-Ponty's ontology of the flesh – discussed in Chapter 1 – as deepening the notion of gestationality even further. While Irigaray has indeed criticized Merleau-Ponty's notion of the flesh as presuming a symmetrical reversibility that would subsume the relation of two under the logic of the one, a careful reading of Merleau-Ponty shows that this is not the case. For Merleau-Ponty the 'flesh' is indeed a virtuality in the way we have just described above in relation to Deleuze's egg. See Vicki Kirby (2006) for a reading of Merleau-Ponty's ontology of the flesh (against Irigaray) as a fecund theory of gestationality.

35   Similarly, Rachel Jones (2011: see chapters 6 and 7) finds that Irigaray's own statements that privilege the heterosexual couple are 'at odds' with the ways in which Irigaray herself describes sexuate difference more expansively.

36   See also Penelope Deutscher's (2002) helpful reading of Irigaray's later work. As Deutscher claims, Irigaray's contributions to understanding sexual difference are best when she leaves the content of that term unspecified, as a pair of 'empty brackets' (2002: 49).

37 I am indebted to David Morris's (2007) accounts of the 'onto-logics' of faces and animals for my own suggestion that amniotics can be understood as an 'onto-logic'. From Morris, I have gleaned an understanding of how an onto-logic can be helpful for understanding human embodiment in terms of an underlying kinship that this embodiment shares with other expressions of being. In other words, this kinship reveals itself not in terms of *what* these bodies are, but rather in terms of *how* they are. Morris is keen to stress that 'logic' in this sense is not a formulaic theory used after the fact to explain something, but rather is more closely related to the Greek notion of 'logos' whereby logic is a being's inherent accounting for itself.

38 Importantly, 'we' do not make these cuts in the form of intentional decisions, although this can also be the case. In Barad's theory (2007) of agential separability, it is the ongoing intra-actions of matters of all kinds (things, ideas, words, apparatuses of knowledge, times, places, other phenomena) that 'world' these cuts; these cuts are the ways in which agency is an ongoing 'doing', rather than something we have or are given.

39 As Chandler and I (2013) argue: 'Within the binary logic of these frameworks, facilitation denotes "means" rather than "ends," passivity in contrast to activity; and it lacks the bounded self-determination essential for sovereignty. Water gives us material evidence of an alternative mode of being that seeks to problematize this hierarchical binary logic. We term this mode of being "gestationality"'.

40 I've written about this elsewhere in 'Speculative Reproductions' (Neimanis 2014).

41 In Chapter 4, I discuss the commodification of the notion that 'water is life', particularly in terms of bottled water and charitable campaigning.

Chapter 3

1 'You have made your way from worm to man, and much in you is still worm. Once you were apes, and even now, too, man is more ape than any ape./ Whoever is the wisest among you is also a mere conflict between plant and ghost' (Nietzsche 1982: 124).

2 In *Je, Tu, Nous*, Irigaray (1993c: 37) criticizes a 'Darwinian model' of behaviour that she characterizes as life's struggle against both the external environment and other living beings. We should bear in mind that this common understanding of Darwinian thought as a 'survival of the fittest' also known as social Darwinism ignores the much more nuanced position of both Darwin and other evolutionary models, as I briefly explore below.

3   Most convincingly, Sheets-Johnstone (2007: 328) argues that both
     phenomenology and evolutionary science are grounded in descriptive
     foundations. She suggests that as a remedy to the former's ignorance of the latter,
     phenomenologists need to 'practice philosophy close-up' (334), which would
     mean 'consulting primary sources in invertebrate biology, ethology, and more,
     i.e. learning of animals in their natural habitats' (334). Yet, Sheets-Johnstone
     assumes too facilely that evolutionary biological research has produced a
     cohesive body of knowledge with no controversy or contradiction between
     reputable scholars. Sheets-Johnstone speaks of the biological literature as if it
     were a transparent map of the 'truth'. Such assumptions ignore evolutionary
     biology as a continuously evolving body of knowledge itself. Evolutionary
     theories need to rely heavily on speculation and conjecture, not least due to the
     fact that the fossil record has many important gaps and deficiencies. For example,
     not even seventy years ago the scientific consensus was that life on Earth
     began 600 million years ago. That figure has since been considerably revised
     to at least 3.9 billion years (Margulis 1982; Margulis and Sagan 1986). Sheets-
     Johnstone might exemplify what Elizabeth A. Wilson (2015; see Introduction
     and Chapter 1, in particular) describes as feminist engagements with science that
     aren't critical enough. Wilson calls for mutually interrogating dialogues that leave
     both 'sides' (feminist theory and biological sciences) transformed.
4   See *Creative Evolution* (2005), which seeks a philosophy that could accommodate
     both the continuity of all living beings and their differences implied by
     evolutionary change. Bergson suggests that the only way to do so would be to
     start from an examination of real life and the evolution of species.
5   Merleau-Ponty (2003) directly addresses Darwinian thought, as well as the
     interpretations of evolution that were being propagated at the time he was
     writing, in *Nature: Course Notes from the College de France*.
6   See both *A Thousand Plateaus* (Deleuze and Guattari 1987) and Deleuze's (1994)
     references to evolutionary thought and embryology in *Difference and Repetition*.
7   Elizabeth Grosz's (2004, 2005) work, to which I will return below, provides a
     strong argument for revisiting evolutionary theory and Darwinian thought
     specifically as a way to bridge the unproductive interdisciplinary divide between
     the life sciences and continental philosophy, as well as the persistent dichotomy
     of 'nature' and 'culture'. Grosz, similar to Sheets-Johnstone, muses about
     philosophy's amnesia regarding humanity's embodied evolutionary debts, but
     in the context of how it might enrich feminist and anti-oppression politics and
     theory. Braidotti (2002, 2006) more subtly folds an evolutionary perspective

into her recent work, as she argues for the ways in which evolutionary theory (if cautiously used, in an embedded manner) can contribute to a revitalization of attention to *zoe* in philosophy. Donna Haraway makes an explicit case for attending to our evolutionary histories. Despite her novel rereading of our 'naturecultural' evolution stories, Haraway (2003: 15) nonetheless refers to herself as a 'dutiful daughter of Darwin'. For feminist critiques of the so-called 'facts' of evolution, see Fox Keller (1996), Gowaty, (1997, 2003), E. Lloyd (1996), Griet Vandermassen (2004), Emily Martin (1996), and Anne Fausto-Sterling (1997, 2003). Other significant continental philosophical treatments of evolution include the works of Keith Ansell Pearson (1997, 1999), Robert O'Toole (1997), and Manuel DeLanda (1997).

8   Drawing on Bergson, Ansell Pearson (1997: 183) notes that 'on a certain model one could legitimately claim that the "success" of a species is to be measured by the speed at which it evolves itself out of existence'. Hardly the 'fitness' that commonly comes to mind in contemporary sociobiological notions of evolution!

9   Evolution is where 'a semiotic fragment rubs shoulders with a chemical interaction, an electron crashes into a language, a black hole captures a genetic message, a crystallization produces a passion, the wasp and the orchid cross a letter' (Deleuze and Guattari 1987: 69).

10   Nor does Grosz specifically reference Irigaray or *Marine Lover* in this passage. Irigaray is elsewhere acknowledged in this text though, as one of Grosz's (2004: 13–4) '(ghostly) guides'.

11   I am quite taken with the idea of evolutionary bodies citing one another as another kind of feminist politics of citation – in line with Gloria Wekker (2007) and Sara Ahmed's (2008) varying takes on these citational politics that keeps alive marginalized genealogies of ideas. Both are about acknowledging debts and cultivating connections. And if, as Vicki Kirby (2013) insists, there is no culture separate from nature, but only ever 'nature writing itself', over and over, then this overlap of bodily and textual citation is more than mere simile, or analogy.

12   Deleuze repeats the example of a tortoise whose anterior member and neck can contort in ways that would kill us (Deleuze 1994a: 215; Deleuze and Guattari 1987: 47).

13   Not all amphibians lay their eggs in water: some eggs are buried in the flesh of their mother's back, while some grow inside their father's throat, or cling to his thighs (Zimmer 1998: 108). But in all cases, the point is that these eggs require a watery environment to carry nourishment and allow waste to pass in and out of the egg throughout the gestational period.

14 The Hypersea theory complements microbiologist Lynn Margulis's theories
    of endosymbiosis, which argue that the driving force of evolution is in fact
    symbiotic relationships between organisms of often different phyla or kingdoms.
    See Margulis (1971) and Margulis and Sagan (1986); also Protevi (2007),
    Olkowski (2006). The Hypersea theory foregrounds the role and necessity of
    watery habitats and conduits in these symbiotic relations.

15 See also Michel Serres (2007) on parasites.

16 While Grosz (2004: 67) does indeed make references to sexual difference
    as incalculable, she also insists on sexual difference as 'two nonreducible
    forms … which have their own interests, needs, organic body parts, and ways of
    negotiating the world through them'. This for Grosz is an 'irreducible binarism'.
    In the end, she claims that

    > The Darwinian model of sexual selection comes to a strange anticipation of the
    > resonances of sexual difference in terms of contemporary feminist theory! It provides
    > the outline of a nonessentialist understanding of the (historical) necessity of sexual
    > dimorphism (67)

    This quote exemplifies the trouble with Grosz's claims here; on the one hand, it
    insists on sexual difference as nonessentialist (virtual?), but on the other already
    invokes its actualized form in sexual dimorphism. Here, Grosz (and a reading of
    her work) encounters the same challenges as we find in Irigaray (particularly in
    its 'forgetting' of trans bodies). Grosz hints towards a mitigation of this point by
    suggesting that sexual dimorphism is a '(historical) necessity', and thus perhaps
    a feature of our own specific space-time. But she is not adequately clear on this.
    Even if we feel confident that sexual difference 'will not pass', can we make the
    same claims – as Grosz seems to – for masculine/feminine dimorphism?

17 Despite her focus on sexual dimorphism, Grosz (2004: 69) also acknowledges
    that this is not the only mechanism by which life proliferates; she notes that
    even self-fertilization of hermaphrodites usually involves 'a crossing interchange
    between two hermaphroditic individuals' – which suggests a reading of sexual
    difference closer to what I am suggesting, where the bodies of what is different
    and what gets crossed are not determined in advance.

18 At the same time, our human capacity to hold our breath below the surface for
    several minutes underlines vestigial traces of these possibilities swimming in
    our swampy flesh. The most accomplished 'free-divers' (divers who dive without
    the aid of breathing and pressure-regulating apparatuses) can hold their breath
    for almost three minutes while descending to depths of over 100 metres and
    then returning to the surface (Ferraras, 'The Deep Deep Blue'). The same could

be said about the ability for infants to survive the first few moments of life in water without 'breath'. *Waterbirth International* explains this in terms of (a) the placental prostaglandin levels that inhibit a newborn's breathing reflex, (b) the fact that babies are born experiencing oxygen deprivation (apnea), which does not induce breathing or gasping, (c) the physiological barrier that prevents hypotonic water from mingling with the hypertonic lung fluids of the foetus, and (d) by the mammalian diving reflex that closes the glottis and ensures water would not be swallowed, or inhaled.

19 I cannot resist mention of Ferenczi's (2005: 57) most audacious observation: 'the peculiar fact that the genital secretion of the female among the higher mammals' which has an 'erotically stimulating effect' ... 'possesses a distinctly fishy odor (odor of herring brine)'.

20 While Ferenczi's notes hold a heteronormative tone, it is not a stretch to imagine any number of sexual practices invoking a similar Thalassal imaginary and the yearning for an aqueous home.

21 For a more extended discussion of our phylogenetic memories in relation to tears, see Gibbs and Hawke (2008) 'Sandor Ferenczi's Thalassal Trend'. See also Hawke, 'Evolutionary Water' (2011) for a discussion of Ferenczi, also in relation to Elaine Morgan's theory of the Aquatic Ape.

22 An encephalization quotient (EQ) measures how big a mammal brain should be according to the weight of an average-brained mammal of a given weight and then factors in how far above or below this average a particular mammal's brain actually is (Zimmer 1998: 220). While Homo Sapiens have an EQ of about 7, various dolphins come in at the low to mid '4' range. A killer whale's EQ is 2.57, while the nearest primate's EQ is the chimpanzee's, at 2.34 (221).

23 Morgan's theories are developed extensively in *The Descent of Woman* (1972) and *The Aquatic Ape* (1982). Support for her theories can be found in Verhaegen, Puech and Munro (2002) and other articles by Verhaegen. See also the collection of papers presented in 1999 at the 'Symposium on Water and Human Evolution'.

24 Zimmer notes that dolphin sociality may be far more sophisticated than human intersubjectivity, but that we may not appreciate this because 'our anthropomorphism inevitably makes it hard to understand an intelligence other than our own' (131). As a result, we may use the criterion of 'self-awareness' as a mark of intelligence, without realizing that 'a choice between self-awareness and the lack of it may be one that dolphins don't have to make' (133). Dolphins have hierarchies and conflicts and may even be able to name each other, but dolphin 'society may nevertheless be one of an overlapping network of minds, wandering

linked through a transparent ocean'; 'If dolphins are in fact continually sharing and exchanging interior and exterior worlds with one another, our notion of self would be meaningless to them' (134).

25   These questions are equally important where knowledge – and knowledge of waters – is caught in a weir of late capitalism, where knowledge-making is funded by corporate interests. The general assumption prevails that knowledge is unquestionably a good thing. Where knowledge is commodified, where knowledge is seen as a means to an end (i.e. profit), and where *more* knowledge is actively promoted, we might choose to be more vigilant about the conditions and uses of knowledge production.

Chapter 4

1   *Kwe* is the Anishinaabemowin word for woman, or life-giver (Anishinaabe are a First Nation whose traditional territories are around the Great Lakes of Turtle Island, or Canada). KWE was also the title of a solo exhibition by Rebecca Belmore at the Justine Barnicke Gallery (Toronto) in 2014. Belmore has referred to herself as an Anishinaabe (kwe) artist. This word is not my language, but it offers a syntax I am trying to understand, with respect.

2   In Chapter 2, I explore Deleuze's concept of 'difference and repetition' in relation to the posthuman gestationality of water. I suggest that water is a powerful enactment of this Deleuzian idea: water is always 'the same', yet in its constant transformation as/in/through bodies across time and space, it reminds us that matter is always becoming different. The idea of posthuman gestationality allows us to think of water both as a commons and a facilitation of life-in-the-plural, and life becoming different. I return to the concept of difference and repetition below.

3   Irigaray's essay 'This Sex which is not one' argues for an understanding of the feminine as always plural and becoming. This idea is explored in relation to water in Chapter 2.

4   Since Head's paper, increasing numbers of theories have been forwarded to establish the Anthropocene era's 'golden spike'. While the Industrial Revolution may be the most common one, others include vague notions such as the beginnings of agriculture, or very precisely dated spikes such as the Trinity detonation of 1945. Lewis and Maslin (2015) provide a compelling review of the various proposals – concluding, interestingly, that the Industrial Revolution

likely does not fulfil the criterion of providing 'a globally synchronous marker'. Lewis and Maslin also offer the colonization of the 'New World' as a serious proposition, which I return to below. Despite these interesting debates, however, my interest is not in precisely 'marking the Anthropocene', but in considering the work that the idea of the Anthropocene does more generally.

5   Haraway attributes this term to the participants of a conversation at Aarhus University in 2014. See Haraway (2015: 162 n 5).

6   I suggest the designation 'Kwe' with some hopeful trepidation (or trepidatious hope). As noted above, Kwe is the Anishinaabemowin word for woman, or life-giver, and Belmore has referred to herself as an Anishinabe (kwe) artist. She has also suggested that she is 'native/woman/artist' but also 'woman/native/ artist', but at the same time expresses frustration as an artist that 'people can't see beyond the "Indian-ness"' (Nanibush 2014: 216). By using 'Kwe' to name an orientation to the world that her work offers, I seek a word that captures all three of these things in their complex relation, while also trying to avoid a suggestion that Belmore's work is 'the' representation of Anishinabe cosmology, or that *she* is. At the same time, I also want to hold on to the alternative concepts that she offers as necessarily linked to Anishinabe philosophy and culture, and thus I turn to other Anishinabe scholars to help flesh out the ideas that circulate in her work. Beneath this all, I recognize that my use of this word 'Kwe' here is suspect. I nonetheless want to accept the consequences of taking this risk.

7   Artworks are not the only way, of course. My own learning must come from various kinds of respectful listening to other words and activisms, too.

8   It is a difficult task, as a white settler once in Canada, now in Australia, to invoke indigenous 'philosophies' or 'ways of life'. At the same time, I think working in the sweaty and impossible space of the cultural interface is necessary despite its inevitable failure. Here I call on important lessons taught to me by Dorothy Christian and Rita Wong in our collaborative endeavours in making *Thinking with Water* (eds. Chen, MacLeod, and Neimanis 2013). I am also inspired by the work (among many others) of Stephen Muecke (2004: 10), who writes, 'if I ask what distinguishes indigenous and non-indigenous orientations to the world, it is not to keep them apart, it is to ask what modes of relatedness between them are possible'. To transpose Muecke's careful modes and methods of scholarship into my own project, I look to Belmore's work not to assert that it is the same as my work on 'bodies of water', nor to suggest it is inalienably separate, but rather to think about the productive nature of their resonances.

9   In discussing human-water kinships in coastal Northern Territory of Australia, Elizabeth Povinelli (2015) makes clear that the indigenous worldviews of water here also include negotiations around green dollars, mining companies, and iPods. Human relationships with water are always determined within complex contexts – whether those humans are indigenous or aboriginal, or not.

10   Rebecca Belmore is not aligned with *Idle No More* in any 'official' capacity, but has expressed her support for its mission, noting in a response to an interview about politics: 'I want more Idle No More' (Nanibush 2014: 217).

11   See for example, Rajan (2012).

12   See https://www.youtube.com/watch?v=rPNAG8Q_0V4. Last accessed 10 February 2015.

13   Maracle in *Downstream* (2016).

References

Ahmed, S. (2000), *Strange Encounters: Embodied Others in Postcoloniality*, London: Routledge.

Ahmed, S. (2004), *The Cultural Politics of Emotion*, Edinburgh: Edinburgh University Press.

Ahmed, S. (2006), *Queer Phenomenology: Orientations, Objects, Others*, Durham: Duke University Press.

Ahmed, S. (2008), 'Imaginary Prohibitions', *European Journal of Women's Studies*, 15(1): 23–39.

Ahmed, S. (2014), 'White Men', *Feminist Killjoys*, 4 November 2014. Available online: http://feministkilljoys.com/2014/11/04/white-men/ (accessed 10 February 2016).

Alaimo, S. (2009), 'Insurgent Vulnerability and the Carbon Footprint of Gender', *Kvinder, Køn & Forskning*, 3–4: 22–33.

Alaimo, S. (2010), *Bodily Natures: Science, Environment, and the Material Self*, Bloomington: Indiana University Press.

Alliez, E. (2004), *The Signature of the World: What is Deleuze and Guattari's Philosophy?*, trans. E.R. Albert and A. Toscano, New York: Continuum.

Ansell Pearson, K. (1999), *Germinal Life: On Difference and Repetition in Deleuze*, Routledge: New York.

Ansell Pearson, K. (1999), 'Viroid Life: On Machines, Technics and Evolution', in K. Ansell Pearson (ed.), *Deleuze and Philosophy: The Difference Engineer*, 180–210, Routledge: New York.

Anzaldua, G. (1987), *Borderlands/La Frontera: The New Mestiza*, San Francisco, IL: Aunt Lute Books.

Aristarkhova, I. (2005), 'Ectogenesis and Mother as Machine', *Body and Society*, 11(3): 43–59.

Armstrong, J. (2006), 'Water is Siwlkw', in *Water and Indigenous Peoples*, Paris: UNESCO.

Åsberg, C. (2013), 'The Timely Ethics of Posthumanist Gender Studies', *Feministische Studien*, 31(1): 7–12.

Barad, K. (2007), *Meeting the Universe Halfway: Quantum Physics and the Entanglement of Matter and Meaning*, Durham: Duke University Press.

Barad, K. (2008a), 'Living in a Posthumanist Materialist World: Lessons from Schroedinger's Cat', in A. Smelik and N. Lykke (eds), *Bits of Life: Feminism at the Intersections of Media, Bioscience and Technology*, 165-176, Seattle: University of Washington Press.

Barad, K. (2008b), 'Posthumanist Performativity: Toward an Understanding of How Matter Comes to Matter', in S. Alaimo and S. Hekman (eds), *Material Feminisms*, Bloomington: Indiana University Press.

Barbaras, R. (2001), 'Merleau-Ponty and Nature', *Research in Phenomenology*, 31: 22–38.

Barbaras, R. (2004), *The Being of the Phenomenon: Merleau-Ponty's Ontology*, trans. T. Toadvine and L. Lawlor, Bloomington: Indiana University Press.

Barbaras, R. (2006), *Desire and Distance. Introduction to a Phenomenology of Perception*, trans. P.B. Milan, Stanford, CA: Stanford University Press.

Bard, S. M. (1999), 'Global Transport of Anthropogenic Contaminants and the Consequences for the Arctic Marine Ecosystem', *Marine Pollution Bulletin*, 38(5): 356–379.

Bartlett, A. (2004), 'Black Breasts, White Milk? Ways of Constructing Breastfeeding in Australia', *Australian Feminist Studies*, 19(45): 341–355.

Beauvoir, S. (2010), *The Second Sex,* trans. C. Borde and S. Malhovany-Chevallier, New York: Knopff.

Belmore, R. (1996), *Temple*, Installation – Water, plastic, fountain, telescope, wood.

Belmore, R. (2005), *Fountain*, Video installation – Video projected onto a water screen.

Bennett, J. (2010), *Vibrant Matter: A Political Ecology of Things*, Durham: Duke University Press.

Bergson, H. (2005), *Creative Evolution*, New York: Cosimo Classics.

Blackman, L. (2010), 'Bodily Integrity', *Body & Society*, 16(3): 1–9.

Braidotti, R. (2000), 'Teratologies', in C. Colebrook and I. Buchanan (eds), *Deleuze and Feminist Theory*, 156–172, Edinburgh: Edinburgh University Press.

Braidotti, R. (2002), *Metamorphoses*, Cambridge: Polity Press.

Braidotti, R. (2003), 'Becoming-Woman: Or Sexual Difference Revisited', *Theory, Culture and Society*, 20(3): 43–64.

Braidotti, R. (2006a), *Transpositions*, Cambridge: Polity.

Braidotti, R. (2006b), 'The Ethics of Becoming-Imperceptible', in C. Boundas (ed.), *Deleuze and Philosophy*, 133–159, Edinburgh: Edinburgh University Press.

Braidotti, R. (2011), *Nomadic Subjects*, New York: Columbia.

Braidotti, R. (2013), *The Posthuman*, Cambridge: Polity Press.

Briggs, H. (2007), 'Whale "Missing Link" Discovered', *BBC News*, 17 December 2007. Available online: http://news.bbc.co.uk/2/hi/science/nature/7150627.stm (accessed 10 February 2016).

Buchanan, I. (1997), 'The Problem of the Body in Deleuze and Guattari, Or, What Can a Body Do?' *Body and Society*, 3(3): 73–91.

Burgess, M. (1999), 'Imagined Geographies of Rebecca Belmore', *Parachute*, 93: 12–20.

Butler, J. (1993), *Bodies that Matter*, New York: Routledge.

Caldwell, A. (2002), 'Transforming Sacrifice: Irigaray and the Politics of Sexual Difference', *Hypatia*, 4: 16–38.

Calvino, I. (1965), *Cosmicomics*, California: Harcourt Press.

Canters, H. and G. Jantzen (2005), *Forever Fluid: A Reading of Luce Irigaray's Elemental Passions*, Manchester: Manchester University Press.

Chakrabarty, D. (2012), 'Postcolonial Studies and the Challenge of Climate Change', *New Literary History*, 43(1): 1–18.

Chandler, Mielle (2008), *Gestational Matters: Sovereignty, Ethics and the Lifeworld*. PhD Dissertation. York University.

Chandler, M. and A. Neimanis (2013), 'Water and Gestationality: What Flows Beneath Ethics', in C. Chen, J. MacLeod, and A. Neimanis (eds), *Thinking with Water*, 61–83, Montreal and Kingston: McGill-Queen's University Press.

Chen, C. (2013), ' "Mapping Waters": Thinking With Watery Places', in C. Chen, J. MacLeod, and A. Neimanis (eds), *Thinking with Water*, 274–298, Montreal and Kingston: McGill-Queen's University Press.

Chen, M. (2012), *Animacies: Biopolitics, Racial Mattering and Queer Affect*, Durham: Duke University Press.

Christian, D. and R. Wong (2013), 'Untapping Watershed Mind', in C. Chen, J. MacLeod, and A. Neimanis (eds), *Thinking with Water*, 232–253, Montreal and Kingston: McGill-Queen's University Press.

Cixous, H. (1976), 'The Laugh of the Medusa', *Signs*, 1(4): 875–893.

Cixous, H. (1986), 'Sorties: Out and Out: Attacks/Ways Out/Forays', in H. Cixous and C. Clément (eds), *The Newly Born Woman*, 63-129, trans. B. Wing, Minneapolis: University of Minnesota Press.

Code, L. (2006), *Ecological Thinking: The Politics of Epistemic Location*, Oxford: Oxford University Press.

Code, L. (2012), 'Taking Subjectivity into Account', *Education, Culture and Epistemological Diversity*, 2: 85–100.

Colebrook, C. (2000), 'Is Sexual Difference a Problem?' in I. Buchanan and C. Colebrook (eds), *Deleuze and Feminism,* 110-127, Edinburgh: Edinburgh University Press.

Colebrook, C. (2011), 'Earth Felt the Wound: the Affective Divide', *Journal for Politics, Gender and Culture*, 8(1): 45–58.

Colebrook, C. (2012), 'Feminist Extinction', in H. Gunkel, C. Nigianni, and F. Soderbacl (eds), *Undutiful Daughters: New Directions in Feminist Thought and Practice*, 71–84, New York: Palgrave MacMillan.

Connolly, W. (2011), *A World of Becoming*, Durham: Duke University Press.

Cousteau, J. (1972), *The Whale: Mighty Monarch of the Sea*, Garden City: Doubleday.

Crist, E. (2013), 'On the Poverty of Our Nomenclature', *Environmental Humanities*, 3: 129–147.

Crutzen, P. J. and E. F. Stoermer (2000), 'The Anthropocene', *IGBP Newsletter*, 41(17): 17–18.

Darwin, C. (1998 [1871]), *The Descent of Man*, Amherst: Prometheus Books.

De Landa, M. (1997), *A Thousand Years of Non Linear History*, New York: Zone Books.

De Lauretis, T. (1987), *Technologies of Gender: Essays on Theory, Film, and Fiction*, Bloomington: Indiana University Press.

Deleuze, G. (1994), *Difference and Repetition*, trans. P. Patton, New York: Columbia University Press.

Deleuze, G. (2002), *Nietzsche and Philosophy*, New York: Columbia University Press.

Deleuze, G. (2004), *Desert Islands and Other Texts 1953–1974*, in D. Lapoujade (ed.), trans. M. Taormina, Paris: Semiotexte.

Deleuze, G. and F. Guattari (1987), *A Thousand Plateaus*, trans. B. Massumi, Minneapolis: Minnesota University Press.

Deleuze, G. and F. Guattari (1994), *What Is Philosophy?*, trans. H. Tomlinson and G. Burchell, New York: Columbia University Press.

Deleuze, G. and C. Parnet (2002), *Dialogues II*, trans. E.A. Ross, New York: Columbia University Press.

Deutscher, P. (2002), *The Politics of Impossible Difference: The Later Work of Luce Irigaray*, New York: Cornell University Press.

Deutscher, P. (2004), 'The Descent of Man and the Evolution of Woman', *Hypatia*, 19(2): 35–55.

Deutscher, P. (2011), 'Animality and Descent: Irigaray's Nietzsche, on Leaving the Sea', in M. Rawlinson, S. Hom, and S. Khader (eds), *Thinking with Irigaray*, 55–76, Albany, GA: State University of New York Press.

Di Chiro, G. (2010), 'Sex Panic', in C. Mortimer-Sandilands and B. Erickson (eds), *Queer Ecologies: Sex, Nature, Politics, Desire*, 199–230, Bloomington: University of Indiana Press.

Diprose, R. (2002), *Corporeal Generosity: On Giving with Nietzsche, Merleau-Ponty and Levinas*, New York: SUNY Press.

Duxbury, L. (2010), 'A Change in the Climate: New Interpretations and Perceptions of Climate Change through Artistic Interventions and Representations', *Weather, Climate and Society*, 2(4): 294–299.

Edelman, Lee (2004), *No Future: Queer Theory and the Death Drive*, Durham: Duke University Press.

Emoto, M. (2005), *The True Power of Water: Healing and Discovering Ourselves*, Oregon: Beyond Words Publishing.

Fanon, F. (1986), *Black Skin, White Masks*, London: Pluto Press.

Fausto-Sterling, A. (1997), 'Beyond Difference: A Biologist's Perspective', *Journal of Social Issues*, 53: 233–258.

Fausto-Sterling, A. (2003), 'Science Matters, Culture Matters', *Perspectives in Biology and Medicine*, 46(1): 109–124.

Ferenczi, S. (2005), *Thalassa: A Theory of Genitality*, London: Karnac Books.

Fielding, H. (2000), ' "The Sum of What She Is Saying": Bringing Essentials Back to the Body', in D. Olkowski (ed.), *Resistance, Flight, Creation: Feminist Enactments of French Philosophy*, 124–137, Ithaca, NY: Cornell University Press.

Fox Keller, E. and H. E. Longino (1996), 'Language and Ideology in Evolutionary Theory: Reading cultural Norms into Natural Law', in E. Fox Keller and H.E. Longino (eds), *Feminism and Science*, 154–172, Oxford: Oxford University Press.

Fukuyama, F. (2002), *Our Posthuman Future*, New York: Farrar, Straus and Giroux.

Gaard, G., ed. (1993), *Ecofeminism: Women, Animals, Nature*, Philadelphia, PA: Temple University Press.

Gaard, G. (1997), 'Towards a Queer Ecofeminism', *Hypatia*, 12(1): 114–137.

Gaard, G. (2001), 'Women, water and energy', *Organization and Environment*, 14(2): 157–172.

Gaard, G. (2003), 'Explosion', *Ethics and the Environment*, 8(2): 71–79.

Gallop, J. (1988), *Thinking Through the Body*, New York: Columbia University Press.

Garcia, P. (2007), 'Acequias: Cultural Legacy and Grassroots Movements', *Sustainable Santa Fe*, 12 October 2007. Available online: http://www.lasacequias.org/news/ (accessed 10 February 2016).

Gatens, M. (1996), *Imaginary Bodies: Ethics, Corporeality and Power*, London: Routledge.

Gelfand, S. (2006), *Artificial Womb Technology and the Future of Human Reproduction*, Rodopi: New York.

Gibbs, A. and S. Hawke (2008), 'Sandor Ferenczi's Thalassal Trend and the Role of Affect in Psychosomatic Relations', *Thalassa: Hungarian Journal of Psychoanalysis*, 19(1): 37–57.

Giggs, R. (2015), 'Whale Fall', *Granta Magazine*, 133, 18 November 2015. Available online: http://granta.com/whale-fall/ (accessed 10 February 2016).

The Girl Who Couldn't Cry [film], WATERisLIFE, 5 May 2014. Available online: https://www.youtube.com/watch?v=rPNAG8Q_0V4 (accessed 10 February 2016).

Gowaty, P. A. (1997), 'Darwinian Feminists and Feminist Evolutionists', in P. A. Gowaty (ed.), *Feminism and Evolutionary Biology*, 1–18, New York: Chapman Hall.

Gowaty, P. A. (2003), 'Sexual Natures: How Feminism Changed Evolutionary Biology', *Signs: A Journal of Women in Culture*, 28(3): 901–921.

Grosz, E. (1994), *Volatile Bodies: Toward a Corporeal Feminism*, Bloomington: Indiana University Press.

Grosz, E. (2004), *The Nick of Time*, Durham: Duke University Press.

Grosz, E. (2005), *Time Travels*, Durham: Duke University Press.

Grosz, E. (2011), *Becoming Undone: Darwinian Reflections on Life, Politics and Art*, Durham: Duke University Press.

Grosz, E. (2012), 'The Future of Feminist Theory: Dreams for New Knowledges?', in H. Gunkel, C. Nigianni, and F. Soderback (eds), *Undutiful Daughters: New Directions in Feminist Thought and Practice*, 13–22, New York: Palgrave Macmillan.

Guenther, L. (2006), *The Gift of the Other: Levinas and the Politics of Reproduction*, Albany, NY: SUNY Press.

Haiven, M. and A. Khasnabish (2014), *The Radical Imagination*, London: Zed Books.

Hansen, J. (2000), 'Environmental Contaminants and Human Health in the Arctic', *Toxicology Letters*, 112–113: 119–125.

Haraway, D. (1985), 'A Manifesto for Cyborgs: Science, Technology and Socialist Feminism in the Late Twentieth Century', *Socialist Review*, 80: 65–108.

Haraway, D. (1988), 'Situated Knowledges: The Science Question in Feminism and the Privilege of Partial Perspective', *Feminist Studies*, 14(3): 575–599.

Haraway, D. (1992), 'Ecce Homo, Ain't (Ar'n't) I a Woman, and Inappropriate/d Others: The Human in a Post-Humanist Landscape', in J. Butler and J.W. Scott (eds), *Feminists Theorise the Political*, 86–100, London: Routledge.

Haraway, D. (2003), *The Companion Species Manifesto*, Chicago: Prickly Paradigm Press.

Haraway, D. (2004), *The Haraway Reader*, London: Routledge.

Haraway, D. (2007), *When Species Meet*, Minneapolis: Minnesota University Press.

Haraway, D. (2008), 'Otherworldly Conversations, Terran Topics, Local Terms', in S. Alaimo and S. Hekman (eds), *Material Feminisms*, 157–185, Bloomington: Indiana University Press.

Haraway, D. (2015), 'Anthropocene, Capitalocene, Plantationocene, Chthulucene: Making Kin', *Environmental Humanities*, 6: 159–165.

Harman, G. (2005), *Guerilla Metaphysics: Phenomenology and the Carpentry of Things*, Chicago, IL: Open Court.

Hawke, S. (2011), 'Evolutionary Water: Wombs, Seas, Tears and their Utraquistic Relation', *Altitude: An e - Journal of Emerging Humanities Work*, 9: 1–25. Available online: www.thealtitudejournal.com (accessed 10 February 2016).

Hawkins, G., E. Potter, and K. Race (2015), *Plastic Water: The Social and Material Life of Bottled Water*, Cambridge, MA: MIT Press.

Haynes, P. (2012), *Immanent Transcendence: Reconfiguring Materialism in Continental Philosophy*, London, New York: Bloomsbury.

Hayward, E. (2008), 'More Lessons From a Starfish: Prefixial Flesh and Transspeciated Selves', *WSQ: Women's Studies Quarterly*, 36(3/4): 64–85.

Hayward, E. (2012), 'The Sexual and Ethical Ambiguity of the Beloved Bivalve', *Indyweek*, 26 December 2012, Available online: http://www.indyweek. com/indyweek/the-sexual-and-ethical-ambiguity-of-the-beloved-bivalve/ Content?oid=3223332 (accessed 10 February 2016).

Head, L. (2014), 'Contingencies of the Anthropocene: Lessons from the "Neolithic"', *The Anthropocene Review*, 1(2): 113–125.

Helmreich, S. (2009), *Alien Ocean: Anthropological Voyages in Microbial Seas*, Berkeley: University of California Press.

Hemmings, C. (2011), *Stories That Matter*, Durham: Duke University Press.

Hill, R. (2015), 'Milieus and Sexual Difference', *Journal for the British Society of Phenomenology*, 46(2): 1–10.

Hill, R.W. (2008), 'Fountain', in R. Houle, et al. (eds), *Rebecca Belmore: Rising to the Occasion*, 69–75, Vancouver, BC: Vancouver Art Gallery.

Hird, M. (2004), *Sex, Gender and Science*, New York: Palgrave Macmillan.

hooks, b. (2000), *Feminist Theory: From Margin to Centre*, Cambridge, MA: South End Press.

Huber, M.T. (2008), 'Energizing Historical Materialism: Fossil Fuels, Space and the Capitalist Mode of Production', *Geoforum*, 40: 105–115.

Husserl, E. (2001), *Logical Investigations*, London: Routledge.

Irigaray, L. (1985a), *Speculum of the Other Woman*, trans. G. Gill, Ithaca, NY: Cornell University Press.

Irigaray, L. (1985b), *This Sex Which Is Not One*, trans. C. Porter, Ithaca, NY: Cornell University Press.

Irigaray, L. (1991), *Marine Lover of Friedrich Nietzsche*, trans G.C. Gill, New York: Columbia University Press.

Irigaray, L. (1992), *Elemental Passions*, trans J. Collie and J. Still, New York: Routledge.

Irigaray, L. (1993a), *An Ethics of Sexual Difference*, C. Burke and G. Gill, Ithaca, NY: Cornell University Press.

Irigaray, L. (1993b), *Sexes and Genealogies*, trans. G. Gill, New York: Columbia University Press.

Irigaray, L. (1993c), *Je, Tu, Nous: Toward a Culture of Difference*, trans. A Martin, New York, London: Routledge.

Irigaray, L. (1994), *Thinking the Difference*, trans. K. Montin, New York: Routledge.

Irigaray, L. (1996), *I Love to You*, trans. A. Martin, New York: Routledge.

Irigaray, L. (1999), *The Forgetting of Air in Martin Heidegger*, trans. M. B. Nader, Austin: University of Texas Press.

Irigaray, L. (2000), *Why Different? A Culture of Two Subjects: Interviews with Luce Irigaray*, S. Lotringer (ed.), trans. C. Collins, New York: Semiotext(e).

Irigaray, L. (2002a), *Between East and West*, trans. S. Pluhacek, New York: Columbia University Press.

Irigaray, L. (2002b), *The Way of Love*, trans. H. Bostic and S. Pluhacek, London, New York: Continuum.

Irigaray, L. (2015), 'Starting from Ourselves as Living Beings', *Journal of the British Society for Phenomenology*, 46(2): 101–108.

Irigaray, L. and E. Parker (2015), 'Interview: Cultivating a Living Belonging', *Journal of the British Society for Phenomenology*, 42(2): 109–116.

Jackson, Z. I. (2013), 'Animal: New Directions in the Theorization of Race and Posthumanism', *Feminist Studies*, 39(3): 669–685.

Jackson, Z. I. (2015), 'Outer Worlds: The Persistence of Race in Movement "Beyond the Human"', *GLQ: A Journal of Lesbian and Gay Studies*, 21(2–3): 215–218.

Jardine, A. (1984), 'Women in Limbo: Deleuze and His Br(others)', *SubStance*. 13(3/4/5): 44–60.

Jones, R. (2011), *Irigaray: Towards a Sexuate Philosophy*, Cambridge: Polity Press.

Jones, R. (2015), 'Vital Matters and Generative Materiality: Between Bennett and Irigaray', *Journal of the British Society for Phenomenology*, 42(2): 146–172.

Kheel, M. (1993), 'From Heroic to Holistic Ethics: The Ecofeminist Challenge', in G. Gaard (ed.), *Ecofeminism: Women, Animals, Nature*, 243–271, Philadelphia, PA: Temple University Press.

Kingsolver, B. (2010), 'Water Is Life', *National Geographic*, April 2010. Available online: http://ngm.nationalgeographic.com/2010/04/water-is-life/kingsolver-text/1) (accessed 5 February 2016).

Kirby, V. (1997), *Telling Flesh: The Substance of the Corporeal*, New York: Routledge.

Kirby, V. (2006), 'Culpability and the Double Cross: Irigaray with Merleau-Ponty', in D. Olkowski and G. Weiss (eds), *Feminist Interpretations of Merleau-Ponty*, 127–146, University Park: Pennsylvania State University Press.

Kirby, V. (2013), *Quantum Anthropologies: Life at Large*, Durham: Duke University Press.

Kirksey, E. and S. Helmreich (2010), 'The Emergence of Multispecies Ethnography', *Fieldsights*, 14 June 2010. Available online: http://www.culanth.org/fieldsights/277-the-emergence-of-multispecies-ethnography (accessed 10 February 2016).

Krech, S. (1999), *The Ecological Indian: Myth and History*, New York, London: W.W. Norton.

La Duke, W. (1999), *All Our Relations: Native Struggles for Land and Life*, Cambridge: South End Press.

Lawlor, L. (1998), 'The End of Phenomenology: Expression in Deleuze and Merleau-Ponty', *Continental Philosophy Review*, 31: 15–34.

Leder, D. (1990), *The Absent Body*, Chicago, IL: University of Chicago Press.

Lee, R. (2012), 'That Oceanic Feeling', in R. Lee, A. Patrizzio, and K. Yusoff (eds), *Rona Lee: That Oceanic Feeling*, 12-18, Southampton, UK: John Hanson Gallery.

LeGuin, U. (1989), *Dancing at the Edge of the World: Thoughts on Words, Women, Places*, New York: Grove Press.

Lewis, S. and M. Maslin (2015), 'Defining the Anthropocene', *Nature*, 519: 171–180.

Lingis, A. (1994), *Foreign Bodies*, New York: Routledge.

Lingis, A. (2000), *Dangerous Emotions*, Berkeley: University of California Press.

Linton, J. (2010), *What Is Water?: The History of a Modern Abstraction*, Vancouver: UBC Press.

Little, C. (1990), *The Terrestrial Invasion: An Ecophysiological Approach to the Origins of Land Animals*, Cambridge: Cambridge University Press.

Lloyd, E. (1996), 'Science and Anti-Science: Objectivity and Its Real Enemies', in L. H. Nelson and J. Nelson (eds), *Feminism, Science and the Philosophy of Science*, 217–259, Boston, MA: Kluwer Academic Publishers.

Lorde, A. (1984), *Sister Outsider*, California: Crossing Press.

Lorraine, T. (1999), *Irigaray and Deleuze: Experiments in Visceral Philosophy*, Ithaca, NY: Cornell University Press.

Lorraine, T. (2011), *Deleuze and Guattari's Immanent Ethics: Theory, Subjectivity and Duration*, Albany, NY: SUNY Press.

Macdonald, R., T. Harner, and J. Fyfe (2005), 'Recent Climate Change in the Arctic and Its Impact on Contaminant Pathways and Interpretation of Temporal Trend Data', *Science of the Total Environment*, 342: 5–86.

MacLeod, J. (2013), 'Water and the Material Imagination: Reading the Sea of Memory against the Flows of Capital', in C. Chen, J. MacLeod, and A. Neimanis (eds),

Thinking with Water, 40–60, Montreal and Kingston: McGill-Queen's University Press.

Mallin, S. (1996), *Art Line Thought*, Dordrecht: Kluwer Academic Publishers.

Mallin, S. (1979), *Merleau-Ponty's Philosophy*, New Haven: Yale University Press.

Malm, A. (2013), 'Steaming into the Capitalocene', Paper presented to the Institute of British Geographers Conference, London, August 2013.

Malm, A. and A. Hornborg (2014), 'The Geology of Mankind? A Critique of the Anthropocene Narrative', *The Anthropocene Review*, 1(1): 62–66.

Maracle, L. (2016), 'Water', in Dorothy Christian and Rita Wong (eds), *Downstream*, 41–48, Waterloo, ON: Wilfred Laurier University Press.

Margulis, L. (1971), 'Symbiosis and Evolution', *Scientific American*, 224: 48–57.

Margulis, L. (1982), *Early Life*, Boston: Science Books International.

Margulis, L. and D. Sagan (1986), *Origins of Sex*. New Haven: Yale University Press.

Martin, A. (2000), *Luce Irigaray and the Question of the Divine*, London: Maney Publishing for the Modern Humanities Research Association.

Martin, E. (1996), *Flexible Bodies: The Role of Immunity in American Culture-From the Days of Polio to the Age of AIDS*, Boston, MA: Beacon Press.

Massumi, B. (2002), *Parables for the Virtual*, Durham: Duke University Press.

McGregor, D. (2009), 'Honouring Our Relations: An Anishnaabe Perspective on Environmental Justice', in J. Agyeman, P. Cole, R. Haluza-Delay, and P. O'Riley, *Speaking for Ourselves: Environmental Justice in Canada*, 27–41, Vancouver: UBC Press, 2009.

McMenamin, M. and D. McMenamin (1994), *Hypersea*, New York: Columbia University Press.

Merleau-Ponty, M. (1962), *Phenomenology of Perception*, trans. C. Smith, New York: Routledge.

Merleau-Ponty, M. (1968), *The Visible and the Invisible*, trans. A. Lingis and C. Lefort (eds), Evanston: Northwestern University Press.

Merleau-Ponty, M. (2003), *Nature: Course Notes from the College de France*, trans. R. Vallier, Evanston: Northwestern University Press.

Midgely, M. (1992), *Science as Salvation: A Modern Myth and Its Meaning*, London: Routledge.

Minteer, B. (2012), 'Geoengineering and Ecological Ethics in the Anthropocene'. *BioScience*, 62(10): 857–858.

Mitchell, A. (2015), 'Decolonising the Anthropocene', *Worldly IR*, Available online: https://worldlyir.wordpress.com/2015/03/17/decolonising-the-anthropocene/comment-page-1/#comment-148 (accessed 21 April 2015).

Mitchell, L. M. (2001), *Baby's First Picture: Ultrasound and the Politics of Fetal Subjects*, Toronto, ON: University of Toronto Press.

Moore, J. (2013), *Anthropocene, Capitalocene and the Myth of Industrialization II*. Available online: http://jasonwmoore.wordpress.com/ (accessed 17 January 2014).

Morgan, E. (1972), *The Descent of Woman*, London: Souvenir Press.

Morgan, E. (1982), *The Aquatic Ape*, London: Souvenir Press.

Morgensen, U. B., et al. (2015), 'Breastfeeding as an Exposure Pathway for Perfluorinated Alkyates', *Environmental Science and Technology*, 49(17): 10466–10473.

Morris, D. (2007), 'Faces as the Visible of the Invisible: Toward an Animal Ontology', *PhaenEx*, 2(2): 124–169.

Morrison, T. (1987), *Beloved*, London: Vintage.

Muecke, S. (2004), *Ancient and Modern: Time, Culture and Indigenous Philosophy*, Sydney: UNSW Press.

Murphy, J. (1989), 'Is Pregnancy Necessary?', *Hypatia*, 4: 66–84.

Murphy, M. (2013), 'Distributed Reproduction, Chemical Violence, and Latency', *S&F Online*, 11(3). Available online: http://sfonline.barnard.edu/life-un-ltd-feminism-bioscience-race/distributed-reproduction-chemical-violence-and-latency/ (accessed 10 February 2016).

Nanibush, W. (2014), 'An Interview with Rebecca Belmore', *Decolonization: Indigineity, Education & Society*, 3(1): 213–217.

Neimanis, A. (2009), 'Bodies of Water, Human Rights and the Hydrocommons', *Topia: Canadian Journal of Cultural Studies*, 21: 161–182.

Neimanis, A. (2011), 'Strange Kinship and Ascidian Life: 13 Repetitions', *Journal of Critical Animal Studies*, 9(1): 117–143.

Neimanis, A. (2014), 'Speculative Reproduction: Biotechnologies and Ecologies in Thick Time', *PhiloSOPHIA*, 4(1): 108–128.

Neimanis, A. (2015), 'No Representation without Colonisation? (Or, Nature Represents Itself)', *Somatechnics*, 5(2): 135–153.

Neimanis, A. (2016), 'Thinking with Matter Rethinking Irigaray: A "Liquid Ground" for a Planetary Feminism', in Hasana Sharp and Chloe Taylor (eds), *Feminist Philosophies of Life*, 42-66, Montreal: McGill-Queens University Press.

Neimanis, A. and R. L. Walker (2014), 'Weathering: Climate Change and the "Thick Time" of Transcorporeality', *Hypatia*, 29(3): 558–575.

Neimanis, A., C. Åsberg, and S. Hayes (2015), 'Posthumanist Imaginaries', in K. Backstrand and E. Lovbrand (eds), *Research Handbook on Climate Governance*, 480–490, UK: Edward Elgar Publishing.

Nietzsche, F. (1982), 'Thus Spoke Zarathustra', in W. Kauffman (ed. and trans.), *The Portable Nietzsche*, 103–439, New York: Penguin Books.

Nixon, R. (2011), *Slow Violence and the Environmentalism of the Poor*, Cambridge: Harvard University Press.

Norgaard, R. B. (2013), 'The Econocene and the Delta', *San Francisco Estuary and Watershed Science*, 11: 1–5.

Oliver, K. (1995), *Womanizing Nietzsche: Philosophy's Relation to the 'Feminine'*, New York: Routledge.

Olkowski, D. (2000), 'Body, Knowledge and Becoming-Woman: Morpho-Logic in Deleuze and Irigaray', in C. Colebrook and I. Buchanan (eds), *Deleuze and Feminist Theory*, 86–109. Edinburgh: University of Edinburgh Press.

Olkowski, D. (2006), 'Merleau-Ponty: Intertwining and Objectification', *PhaenEx*, 1(1): 113–139.

O'Toole, R. (1997), 'Contagium Vivum Philosophia: Schizophrenic Philosophy, Viral Empiricism and Deleuze', in K. Ansell Pearson (ed.), *Deleuze and Philosophy: The Difference Engineer*, 163–179, Routledge: New York.

Oyama, S., P. E. Griffiths, and R. D. Gray (2001), *Cycles of Contingency: Developmental Systems and Evolution*, Cambridge: MIT Press.

Parker, E. (2015), 'Introduction: From Ecology to Elemental Difference', *Journal of the British Society for Phenomenology*, 46(2): 89–100.

Phillips, A. (2015), *The Politics of the Human*, Cambridge: Cambridge University Press.

Plumwood, V. (1993), *Feminism and the Mastery of Nature*, London: Routledge.

Plumwood, V. (2008), 'Shadow Places and the Politics of Dwelling', *Australian Humanities Review*, 44.

Povinelli, E. A. (2014), 'Geontologies of the Otherwise', *Theorizing the Contemporary, Cultural Anthropology*, 13 January 2014. Available online: http://www.culanth.org/fieldsights/465-geontologies-of-the-otherwise (accessed 10 February 2016).

Povinelli, E. A. (2015), 'Transgender Creeks and the Three Figures of Power in Late Liberalism', *differences*, 26(1): 168–187.

Probyn, E. (2013), 'Women Following Fish in a More-Than-Human World', *Gender, Place and Culture*, 21(5): 589–603.

Probyn, E. (2000), *Carnal Appetites; Foodsexidentities*, London; New York: Routledge.

Protevi, J. (2001), *Political Physics: Derrida, Deleuze and the Body Politic*, New York: Continuum.

Protevi, J. (2005), 'Organism', in A. Parr (ed.), *The Deleuze Dictionary*, New York: Columbia University Press.

Protevi, J. (2007), 'Water', *Rhizomes*, 15. Available online: http://www.rhizomes.net/issue15/protevi.html (accessed 5 May 2008).

Puar, J. (2012), 'I Would Rather Be a Cyborg than a Goddess', *philoSOPHIA*, 2(1): 49–66.

Raeworth, K. (2014), 'Must the Anthropocene Be a Manthropocene?', *The Guardian*, 20 October 2014. Available online: http://www.theguardian.com/

commentisfree/2014/oct/20/anthropocene-working-group-science-gender-bias (accessed 21 April 2015).

Rajan, K. S., ed. (2012), *Lively Capital: Biotechnologies, Ethics and Governance in Global Markets*, Durham: Duke.

Rich, A. (1986), 'Notes towards a Politics of Location', in *Blood, Bread and Poetry*, New York: Norton.

Roburn, S. (2013), 'Sounding a Sea Change: Acoustic Ecology and Arctic Ocean Governance', in C. Chen, J. MacLeod, and A. Neimanis (eds), *Thinking with Water*, 106–128, Montreal and Kingston: McGill-Queen's University Press.

Rockstrom, J., et al. (2009), 'A Safe Operating Space for Humanity', *Nature: International Weekly Journal of Science*, 461: 472–475.

Roughgarden, J. (2004), *Evolution's Rainbow: Diversity, Gender, and Sexuality in Nature and People*, Berkeley: University of California Press.

Sandilands, Catriona (2001), 'From Unnatural Passions to Queer Nature', *Alternatives*, 27(3), Summer: 30–35.

Sawchuk, K. (2000), 'Biotourism, Fantastic Voyage and Sublime Inner Space', in J. Marchessault and K. Sawchuk (eds), *Wild Science: Reading Feminism, Medicine and the Media*, 9–23, London: Routledge.

Scott, J. W. (1997), *Only Paradoxes to Offer*, Harvard: Harvard University Press.

Serres, M. (2007), *The Parasite*, trans. L. Schehr, Minneapolis and London: University of Minnesota Press.

Seymour, N. (2013), *Strange Natures: Futurity, Empathy, and the Queer Ecological Imagination*, Chicago: University of Illinois Press.

Sheets-Johnstone, M. (2007), 'Finding Common Ground Between Evolutionary Biology and Continental Philosophy', *Phenomenology and Cognitive Science*, 6: 327–348.

Sheldon, R. (2013), 'Somatic Capitalism: Reproduction, Futurity, and Feminist Science Fiction', *Ada: A Journal of Gender, New Media, and Technology*, 3: Available online: http://adanewmedia.org/2013/11/issue3-sheldon/ (accessed 10 February 2016).

Sheldon, R. (2015), 'Form / Matter / Chora: Object-Oriented Ontology and Feminist New Materialism', in R. Grusin (ed.), *The Nonhuman Turn*, 193–222, Minneapolis and London: University of Minnesota Press.

Shildrick, M. (1997), *Leaky Bodies and Boundaries: Feminism, Postmodernism and (Bio)ethics*, New York: Routledge.

Shiva, V. (2002), *Water Wars*, Toronto: Between the Lines.

Showalter, E. (1981), 'Feminist Criticism in the Wilderness', *Critical Inquiry*, 8(2): 181–187.

Simms, E. (2009), 'Eating One's Mother: Female Embodiment in a Toxic World', *Environmental Ethics*, 31: 263–277.

Smith, A. (1997), 'Ecofeminism through an Anticolonial Framework', in K. Warren, *Ecofeminism: Women Nature Culture*, Indianapolis: University of Indiana Press.

Smith, D. (1997), 'Introduction "A Life of Pure Immanence": Deleuze's "Critique et Clinique" Project', in G. Deleuze, *Essays Critical and Clinical*, xi–vi, trans. D. Smith and M.A. Greco, Minneapolis: University of Minnesota Press.

Smith, J. L. (2014), 'Fluid', in J. Cohen (ed.), *Inhuman Nature*, 115–132, New York: Punctum Books.

Smith, L.T. (2012), *Decolonizing Methodologies: Research and Indigenous People*, London: Zed Books.

Somers-Hall, H. (2006), 'Deleuze and Merleau-Ponty: An Aesthetics of Difference', *Symposium*, 10(1): 213–221.

Somerville, M. (2013), *Water in a Dry Land: Place-Learning Through Art and Story*, London: Routledge.

Somerville, M. (2014), 'Developing Relational Understandings of Water through Collaboration with Indigenous Knowledges', *Wiley Interdisciplinary Reviews: Water*, 1(4): 401–411.

Spiegelberg, H. (1965), *The Phenomenological Movement*, The Hague: Matinus Nijhoff.

Spivak, G. (1988), 'Can the Subaltern Speak?', in C. Nelson and L. Grossberg (eds), *Marxism and the Interpretation of Culture*, 271–313, Chicago: University of Illinois Press.

Spivak, G. (2003), *Death of a Discipline*, New York: Columbia University Press.

Steffen, W., A. Persson, L. Deutsch, J. Zalasiewicz, M. Williams, K. Richardson, C. Crumley, P. Crutzen, C. Folke, L. Gordon, M. Molina, V. Ramanathan, J. Rockstrom, M. Scheffer, H. Schelinhuber, and U. Svedin (2011), 'The Anthropocene: From Global Change to Planetary Stewardship', *Ambio*, 40: 719–738.

Stephens, E. (2014), 'Feminism and New Materialism: The Matter of Fluidity', *InterAlia: A Journal of Queer Studies*, 9: 186–202.

Stone, A. (2003), 'The Sex of Nature: A Reinterpretation of Irigaray's Metaphysics and Political Thought', *Hypatia*, 18(3): 60–84.

Stone, A. (2006), *Luce Irigaray and the Philosophy of Sexual Difference*, Cambridge: Cambridge University Press.

Stone, A. (2015), 'Irigaray's Ecological Phenomenology: Towards An Elemental Materialism', *Journal of the British Society for Phenomenology*, 46(2): 117–131.

Strang, V. (2013), 'Conceptual Relations: Water, Ideology and Theoretical Subversions', in C. Chen, J. MacLeod, and A. Neimanis (eds), *Thinking with Water*, 185-211, Montreal and Kingston: McGill-Queen's University Press.

Sullivan, N. (2012), 'The Somatechnics of Perception and the Matter of the Non/ Human: A Critical Response to the New Materialism', *European Journal of Women's Studies*, 19(3): 299–313.

SymbioticA. (2012), *Adaptation* (exhibition catalogue). Available online: http://www.symbiotica.uwa.edu.au/activities/exhibitions/adaptation (accessed 29 February 2015).

Toadvine, T. (2004), 'Singing the World in a New Key: Merleau-Ponty and the Ontology of Sense', *Janus Head*, 7(2): 273–283.

Toadvine, T. (2007), 'How Not to Be a Jellyfish', in C. Painter and C. Lotz (eds), *Phenomenology and the Non-Human Animal*, 39–55, The Netherlands: Springer.

Toadvine, T. (2014), 'The Elemental Past', *Research in Phenomenology*, 44: 262–279.

Trainor, S., et al. (2010), 'Environmental Injustice in the Canadian Far North: Persistent Organic Pollutants and Arctic Climate Impacts', in J. Agyeman, et al. (eds), *Speaking for Ourselves: Environmental Justice in Canada*, 144-162, Vancouver: UBC Press.

Trinh, T. M. (1989), *Woman, Native, Other: Writing Postcoloniality and Feminism*, Bloomington: Indiana University Press.

Tuana, N. (2004), 'Coming to Understand: Orgasm and the Epistemology of Ignorance', *Hypatia*, 19(1): 194–232.

United Nations Conference on Sustainable Development (2012), *Drop by Drop Campaign*. Available online: http://www.dropbydrop.eu/en (accessed 10 February 2016).

Van der Tuin, I. and R. Dolphijn (2010), 'The Transversality of New Materialism', *Women: A Cultural Review*, 21(2): 153–171.

Vandermassen, G. (2004), 'Sexual Selection: A Tale of Male Bias and Feminist Denial', *European Journal of Women's Studies*, 11(1): 9–26.

Verhaegen, Marc, Pierre-Francois Puech, and Stephen Munro (2002), 'Aquaboreal Ancestors?' *Trends in Ecology and Evolution*, 3(5): 212–217.

Vizenor, G. (1999), *Manifest Manners: Narratives on Postindian Survivance*, Lincoln: Nebraska University Press.

Waldby, C. (2002), 'Biomedicine, Tissue Transfer and Intercorporeality', *Feminist Theory*, 3(3): 235–250.

Warren, K., ed. (1997), *Ecofeminism: Women, Culture Nature*, Bloomington: Indiana University Press.

Water in the Anthropocene (2013), [film], Welcome to the Anthropocene online project. Available online: https://vimeo.com/66087863 (accessed 10 February 2016).

Weiss, G. (1999), *Body Images: Embodiment as Intercorporeality*, New York: Routledge.

Wekker, G. (2007), 'The Arena of Disciplines: Gloria Anzaldua and Interdisciplinarity', in R. Buikema and I. Van Der Tuin (eds), *Doing Gender in Media, Art and Culture*, 54–69, London: Routledge.

Whitehouse, D. (2002), 'Ice Reservoirs Found on Mars', *BBC News*, 28 May 2002. Available online: http://news.bbc.co.uk/1/hi/sci/tech/2009318.stm (accessed 10 May 2008).

Whitford, M. (1991), *Luce Irigaray: Philosophy in the Feminine*, London: Routledge.

Wiegman, R. (2012), *Object Lessons*, Durham: Duke University Press.

Williams, F. (2012), *Breasts: A Natural and Unnatural History*, Melbourne: The Text Publishing Company.

Wilson, E. A. (2002), 'Biologically Inspired Feminism: Response to Helen Keane and Marsha Rosengarten, "On the Biology of Sexed Subjects"', *Australian Feminist Studies*, 17(39): 283–285.

Wilson, E. A. (2008), 'Organic Empathy: Feminism, Psychopharmaceuticals, and the Embodiment of Depression', in Stacy Alaimo and Susan Hekman (eds), *Material Feminisms*, 373–399, Bloomington: Indiana University Press.

Wilson, E. A. (2015), *Gut Feminism*, Durham: Duke University Press.

Woolf, V. (2000), *Mrs. Dalloway*, New York: Penguin Classic.

Wooster, M. (2009), *Living Waters*, Albany, GA: SUNY Press.

Yusoff, K. (2015), 'Anthropogenesis: Origins and Endings in the Anthropocene', *Theory, Culture & Society*, 29: 1–26.

Zimmer, C. (1998), *At the Water's Edge: Macroevolution and the Transformation of Life*, Toronto: The Free Press.

Index

Note: Page references with letter 'n' followed by locators denote note numbers.

aboriginal 52, 117, 133, 172, 206. *See also* Akwesasne; Anishinabe; indigenous; Inuit; Six Nations; Syilx Okanagan
accountability 49, 64
acequias 187, 211
adaptations 32, 123. *See also* evolution
agency 17, 42, 166, 185, 199
Ahmed, Sara 8, 12, 42, 43, 62, 188 n.1, 194 n.9, 201 n.11
Akwesasne 35–8. *See also* aboriginal; indigenous; Katsi Cook
Alaimo, Stacy. *See also* transcorporeality
posthuman feminism 6, 43
transcorporeality 33–4, 37–8, 56, 77, 95
uncertainty 17, 49
Alberta Tar Sands 21, 104, 146
alter-imaginary/ies 116, 148, 168, 175–7, 182–3, 185
Amazon river 146
amniotics 98–9, 107, 111, 113. *See also* membrane
as onto-logic 68, 96, 111, 199 n.37
amphimixis 34, 41, 147
Anishinabe 171–4, 205 n.6. *See also* aboriginal; indigenous
Ansell Pearson, Keith 201 n.7, 201 n.8
Anthropocene
alter-imaginaries of 169, 171, 172, 175, 182, 183
and colonialism 163–4, 166
definition 160
feminist critiques of 9–15, 168
imaginary 156, 160, 161–3, 167, 168, 169, 170, 183
water 18, 20, 26, 156, 160, 161–2, 168, 170, 172, 177, 184–5
anti-abortion imagery 180
anticolonial 8–9, 11, 35, 39, 62, 156, 168–74. *See also* decolonial

Anzaldua, Gloria 8
Aquatic Ape Theory 135–6. *See also* Morgan, Elaine
aquifers
as body of water 27
and the hydrological cycle 20, 58, 66, 104, 117, 146
Arctic. *See also* breast milk
and biomagnification 35–8, 64, 104, 164, 188
and climate change 17
and coloniality 165
Armstrong, Jeanette 14, 187 n.7
art
as phenomenological amplifier 55–6, 153
and water imaginary 155, 172–3
Åsberg, Cecilia 10, 11, 62
aspiration 147–51. *See also* breath
Athabasca watershed 146, 159
Australia 23, 52, 117, 140, 146, 149, 205 nn.7–8 , 206 n.9

Barad, Karen 6, 34, 40, 43, 147, 183, 191 n.18. *See also* intra-actionism
barnacle 129
Baryonyx Walkeri 125
Bauman, Zygmunt 22
becoming-milieu. *See* milieu
Belmore, Rebecca
as artist 174, 204 n.1, 205 n.6
Fountain (2002) 55, 153–4, 171
and Idle no More 206 n.10
Temple (1996) 154, 171, 177
Bennett, Jane 17, 73
benthic zones 57, 116, 146. *See also* hydrothermal vents
Bergson, Henri 114, 198 n.32, 200 n.4, 201 n.8
bioaccumulation 33. *See also* Arctic

biological life 110
biological unconscious 133. *See also*
    Ferenczi, Sandor
biological water 66
black feminism 8, 165, 187 n.5
Bodies without Organs (BwO) 46–7, 193
    n.6. *See also* Deleuze
bottled water 154–5, 178, 182, 199 n.41
Braidotti, Rosi
    figurations 5
    and Irigaray 72, 193 n.4, 193 n.5, 193
        n.6, 197 n.28
    evolution 114, 200 n.7
    embodiment 1, 191 n.19
    posthumanism 6, 10, 11, 16
    sexual difference 91, 93
breast milk
    breastfeeding 32
    colonialism 32, 34
    Inuit 35–6, 164
    multispecies 35, 37–40, 48, 56, 58, 164
    racism 32
    toxins 33–4, 46, 164, 166
breath. *See also* aspiration; free diving;
        mammalian diving reflex
    fish 131, 133
    in Irigaray 70, 73, 76–7, 82, 194 n.12
    whales 134, 140, 141

Calvino, Italo 109, 131, 149, 150
Canada 20, 23, 38, 55, 153, 159, 171, 175,
        204 n.1, 205 n.8
capitalism 15, 40, 112, 149, 150, 157, 167,
        204 n.25
Capitalocene 166, 169
carrier bag
    bodies of water as 123, 125–6, 129, 132,
        138, 147–8
    plastic 149
    story 121–2, 136, 139
Census of Marine Life 146
Cesaire, Aime 166, 186 n.1
cetaceans
    dolphins 130
    encephalization quotient (EQ) 203 n.22
    evolution of 133–4, 136–7, 142, 150
    genitalia 128–9
    whales 35, 50, 140–1, 149–50
Chandler, Mielle 102, 193 n.2, 193 n.3, 199
        n.39

Chen, Cecilia 144
Chen, Mel Y. 6, 8, 39, 43
Christian, Dorothy 23, 205 n.8
Chthulucene 169
Cixous, Hélène 7, 43, 137, 195 n.15
climate change 11, 27, 42, 117, 164
Coelacanthus 131
Colebrook, Claire 114, 167, 186 n.3, 193 n.6
colonialism 36, 91, 166–7
coloniality 15, 144, 154, 165, 172, 179
communal water tanks, Rajasthan 187 n.7
Connolly, William 24, 190 n.7
consumerism 40, 104, 172, 178
Cook, Katsi 35, 38
Cousteau, Jacques 140, 142
creation stories 117. *See also* evolution
Crutzen, Paul 11

dams 20, 63, 64, 82, 85, 103, 160, 161, 184,
        184
Darwin, Charles 109, 115, 116, 119, 120,
        126, 127, 129, 133, 134
Darwinism 115, 199 n.2, 200 n.5, 200 n.7,
        202 n.16
de Beauvoir, Simone 43, 62
decolonial 156. *See also* anticolonial
dehydration 50, 54, 179
Deleuze, Gilles
    actual and virtual 47, 53, 71, 190 n.10
    Bodies without Organs (BwO) 46, 102,
        190 n.9, 192 n.24
    Borders of the liveable, threshold 141, 170
    concepts 5, 41
    difference and repetition 87–9, 92–3,
        111, 196 n.24, 204 n.2
    embodiment 44, 45, 190 n.8, 192 n.23
    embryology and the egg 93, 97, 109,
        120, 126, 130, 198 n.34, 200 n.6, 201
        n.12
    evolution 114, 121–2, 130, 200 n.6, 201
        n.9
    and feminism 44
    and Irigaray 193 n.6, 196 n.25, 198 n.31,
        198 n.32
    molar and molecular 47–8
    and phenomenology 44, 189 n.6,
        190 n.7
    and posthumanism 23, 53
    rhizomatics 6
Diprose, Rosalind 43

dimorphism, sexual 93, 126–7, 192 n.1, 202 n.16, 202 n.17
dolphin. *See* cetaceans
Drop by Drop campaign 179, 181–2

E.coli 171, 172
echolocation 139, 41
ecofeminism 8, 9, 186–7 n.4
Econocene 166
écriture féminine 6–8
ectogenesis 197 n.26
Edelman, Lee 180
egg as embryo. *See* Deleluze
embryology 92, 120, 200 n.6. *See also* Deleuze
Emoto, Masaru 52
epistemology of ignorance 146
essentialism 7, 22, 174, 187 n.4, 189 n.5. *See also* Irigaray
ethics
    and bodies of water as figuration 175–6
    ecological 7, 75, 104, 197 n.26
    embodied 7, 33, 67
    flat 188 n.2
    and politics 34, 176
    posthuman 17, 38, 64, 91, 105, 107
    of sexual difference 75, 94, 105
evolution. *See also* Aquatic Ape Theory; cetaceans; Deleuze; gestationality; Grosz; Haraway; Irigaray; Merleau-Ponty; tree of life
    feminist interventions 136, 200 n.7
    and Hypersea 123–5
    multivalent 115
    ontogeny and phylogeny 120, 133, 137
    and phenomenology 114, 200 n.3
    and sexual difference 127–31
    stories of 111, 114–16, 121–2, 132, 142, 147–8

Fanon, Frantz 62, 166
feminine seas, imaginary of 81, 117
feminist objectivity 61, 136. *See also* situated knowledge
Ferenczi, Sandor 34, 132–3, 137, 203 n.19, 203 n.20
Fielding, Helen 72, 189 n.5
figuration. *See also* Braidotti; Haraway
    bodies of water as 9, 12, 18, 21, 41, 63, 111–12, 156, 170–1, 176, 182–3, 185
    definition of 5–6, 22, 168–9

First Nations. *See* aboriginal; Akwesasne; Anishinabe; indigenous; Inuit; Kashechewan; Six Nations; Syilx Okanagan
fish 129
    food chain 35
    gestational milieu 122
    and human origin stories 10, 131–3, 137–8
    and sexual difference 129–30
Fisher, Elizabeth 121–2, 136. *See also* carrier bag; evolution
fluid
    bodily 28, 37, 55, 59, 66, 84, 95 (*see also* Hypersea)
    and Irigaray 70, 77, 78–9, 90, 193 n.5
    male/masculine 80, 195 n.17
    vs. water 22–3, 80
Foucault, Michel
    'dense transfer point' 164
    heterotopia 144
free divers 202 n.18
Fukuyama, Francis 10

Gaard, Greta 8, 9, 32
Gatens, Moira 9
genderqueer 107, 130
genealogy of 'water' 19–20, 155–60. *See also* global water; Linton; modern water
gestationality
    as difference and repetition 86–7, 94, 99, 103
    and evolution 124–6 (*see also* Hypersea)
    in Irigaray 70, 113–14, 193 n.3
    posthuman 3–4, 39, 68–9, 106, 111, 118
    and sexual reproduction 91–2
Giggs, Rebecca 35, 140, 149, 150
glacier 26, 46, 55, 104
'global water' 4, 19–20, 155, 158–9, 161–2, 167–8. *See also* genealogy of 'water'
Global Water Systems Project 162
'God trick'. *See* Haraway
golden spike 160, 166, 204 n.4. *See also* Anthropocene
Great Barrier Reef 104, 146
Great Lakes 23, 173, 204 n.1

Grosz, Elizabeth
  concepts 4–5, 41, 156, 168–9
  evolution 114–15, 118–20, 200 n.7
  feminist theory 18–19
  feminist phenomenology 43
  and Irigaray 72, 193 n.5, 193 n.6, 198
    n.32, 201 n.10
  posthumanism 6, 186 n.3
  sexual difference 126–7, 202 n.16, 202
    n.17
Guenther, Lisa 43
Gulf of Mexico 104

H₂O 19, 157–8
Haeckel, Ernst 120, 132, 133, 137
Haiven, Max 175–6
Haraway, Donna. *See also* situated
    knowledge; feminist objectivity
  Anthropocene, Plantationcene,
    Chthulucene 167, 169, 205 n.5
  embodiment 2, 34
  evolution 114–15, 201 n.7
  figurations 5–6, 183
  future 15, 176
  'God Trick' 60, 142, 159, 162
  posthumanism 6, 10–11, 18
  stories 114–15, 170
Hardy, Sir Alister 135
Hawkins, Gay 154, 182
Hayward, Eva 129, 130, 131
Head, Lesley 12, 13, 163, 166, 167, 168. *See
    also* species-error; Anthropocene
Helmreich, Stefan 115, 116, 117, 118, 121,
    125, 143, 188 n.9
hermaphrodism 109, 129–30, 202 n.17
heteronormativity
  vs. posthuman gestationality 4, 106, 118
  and water imaginary 181
heterotopia. *See* Foucault, Michel
Hird, Myra 6, 128
hooks, bell 8
human rights 2, 159
Husserl, Edmund 23, 41
hydrocommons
  difference in 143
  embodied 2, 64, 80, 86, 95, 99, 104, 111,
    169
hydrological cycle 3, 19, 59, 65–7, 88, 106,
    142, 157

hydrology, science of 157, 158, 162
hydrothermal vents 57, 121, 143
Hypersea 121–5, 131, 202 n.14
hyperthermophiles. *See* hydrothermal
    vents

ice thaw 164
Idle No More 155, 175, 177, 179, 181, 206
    n.10. *See also* indigenous
Illich, Ivan 157
indigenous. *See also* aboriginal; Inuit;
    Kashechewan; Sylix Okenagan
  'ecological Indian' 174
  embodiment 153
  environmental justice 171
  and posthuman feminism 39, 187 n.5
  and scientific knowledge 60, 189 n.3
  water imaginaries 171, 172–5, 206 n.9
Indohyus 134
interval. *See* membrane
intra-actionism 183
Inuit 36, 164, 188 n.3. *See also* aboriginal;
    Arctic; indigenous
Irigaray. *See also* ecriture feminine;
    gestationality; membrane
  critiques of 7, 71, 72, 193 n.4
  and Deleuze 71, 103, 193 n.6
  elementality 76–7, 138, 149
  evolution 113–14
  fluids 22, 78–80, 82 (*see also* fluid)
  Marine Lover of Friedrich Nietzsche 68,
    80–5, 113–14
  ontology 94–100
  origin 101, 114
  phenomenology 68, 69, 74–7
  posthumanism 43, 68, 73–4, 77,
    104–7
  'sensible transcendental' 72
  sexuate difference 70, 82–5, 89–96, 99,
    126, 192 n.1
  'strategic essentialism' 71

Jackson, Zakikyyah 10–11, 18, 186 n.1,
    187 n.6
Jones, Rachel 72, 192 n.1, 193 n.4, 197 n.28,
    198 n.35

Kashechewan 171. *See also* aboriginal;
    indigenous

Khasnabish, Alex 175–6
Kingsolver, Barbara 117
kinship
    biogenetic 117–18, 121
    human-cetacean 112, 141
    imaginary 116, 142, 150
    water as 154, 206 n.9
Kirby, Vicki 9, 72, 73, 115, 190 n.13, 198
    n.34, 201 n.11
Kwe 171, 173, 174, 185, 204 n.1, 205 n.6

LaDuke, Winona 8
Lake Ontario 154, 158
larvae. *See* Deleuze; embryology
latency 36–7, 47, 49, 89, 120. *See also*
    Michelle Murphy
Leder, Drew 54, 191 n.20
Lee, Rona 57
LeGuin, Ursula 121–2, 125, 126, 149
Lingis, Alphonso 137, 138, 139–40, 195 n.17
Linton, Jamie 1, 19–21, 155–63, 167–9,
    180, 184, 187 n.7. *See also* genealogy
    of water
Lorde, Audre 8, 28, 36, 43, 165, 170
Lorraine, Tamsin 93, 190 n.7, 193 n.5, 193
    n.6, 194 n.14, 198 n.33

MacLeod, Janine 23
Mallin, Samuel 25, 54, 190 n.11, 191 n.16
mammalian diving reflex 59, 137, 203 n.18
Mandamin, Josephine. *See* water walks
Manthropocene 12–13
Maracle, Lee 185
mastery
    and humanism 10
    and knowledge 22, 30, 38, 42, 112, 143,
        145
maternal body 4, 32, 39, 58
    in Irigaray 70–1, 80–6, 90–2, 113–14
    in posthuman gestationality 102, 106,
        118–19, 125
McGregor, Deborah 172–3, 175
McMenamin, Mark and Dianna. *See*
    Hypersea
membrane 29, 38, 50, 95–6, 98–9, 100, 101.
    See also amniotics
    water's edge or surface as 131, 141
Merleau-Ponty, Maurice. *See also*
    phenomenology

ablism 190 n.12
    and Deleuze 189 n.6, 190 n.7
    embodiment 48–9, 59, 190 n.13,
        190 n.14
    and evolution 114, 132, 200 n.5
    gestationality 198 n.34
    and Irigaray 75, 195 n.20
    phenomenological method 6, 41–5,
        189 n.5
    and posthumanism 24, 189 n.6
    proximal distance 51
    and science 56–7, 60
    and time 191 n.15
Mesonychid 134
metaphor
    material 49, 77, 84, 138, 139, 192 n.23,
        193 n.5
    whale as 150
Midgley, Mary 10
milieu 3, 39, 68, 77, 97
    becoming-milieu 102–3
Mitchell, Audra 166
modern water 4, 19–20, 21, 155–9, 162,
    168, 180, 187 n.7. *See also* genealogy
    of 'water'
Mohawk. *See* Akwesasne
molecularity 46–7, 49, 50–1, 52, 54, 62, 191
    n.20. *See also* Deleuze
Morgan, Elaine 135–7
Mother Sea imaginary 117–18
Muecke, Stephen 171, 174, 205 n.8
Murphy, Michelle 36, 40, 47

Nambian desert beetle 123
new materialism
    and genealogies of feminism 7, 30, 194
        n.9, 194 n.10
    and Irigaray 7, 70, 73, 104
    and Object-oriented ontology 186 n.2
Nietzsche, Friedrich 80, 84, 87, 89, 113,
    114, 194 n.14, 196 n.23
Niger Delta 104, 146

Object-oriented ontology 13, 186 n.2, 191
    n.15
ocean. *See* Pacific Ocean; benthos;
    evolution
ocean acidification 5, 42, 117
oceanic Orientalism 143

oil spills 144
Oliver, Kelly 194 n.14
onto-logic 96, 199 n.37. *See also* amniotics; ontology
ontology. *See also* Object-oriented ontology; onto-logic
  collaborative 11, 14, 16
  and epistemology, onto-epistemology 143, 147
  flat 34, 188 n.2
  geontology 160, 170
  multiple or expanded 97, 99–100, 166
  sexual difference 126
  of water 184
  Western 51, 70, 96, 102, 105, 111
Orbis hypothesis. *See* golden spike
origin stories. *See* Darwin; Darwinism; evolution; gestationality; Mother Sea imaginary; Ursula LeGuin
oysters 129

Pacific Ocean 83
Parker, Emily 193 n.7, 197 n.27
pentasome 124–5
phallogocentrism 3, 5, 7, 9, 11, 12, 43, 70, 79, 90, 96, 105
pharmacokinetics 59
phenomenology. *See also* Merleau-Ponty; Irigaray
  and attunement 53–4
  and Deleuze 6, 44
  and feminism 42, 43
  and intuition 54
  politics of location and situated knowledge 61–2, 139
  posthuman 23–6, 31, 51–3, 62, 64
  problem of scale 55
  and science 56–7, 60, 111
Phillips, Anne 16–17
placenta 9, 29, 70, 73, 74, 78, 193 n.3, 203 n.18
planetarity 145, 147, 174.
  See also Spivak
Plantationocene 167, 169
plastic 5, 50, 64, 104, 149. *See also* bottled water; carrier bags; Rebecca Belmore, *Temple*
Plumwood, Val 13, 105
politics
  and ethics 26, 78, 144
  and radical imaginary 176

politics of citation
  bodies of water as 119, 127, 201 n.11
  feminist 9, 11, 30, 201 n.11
politics of location. *See also* Rich, Adrienne
  and the Anthropocene 165
  and bodies of water as figuration 170
  and coloniality 36–8
  and phenomenology 61–2
  posthuman 4, 14, 25, 30, 33, 36, 41, 63
  watery 49, 55
posthuman. *See also* gestationality; phenomenology; politics of location
  critical race critique 186 n.1, 187 n.5
  feminisms 6–9, 10–12, 18–19, 30, 34, 36–40, 62, 73, 77, 99
  feminist critiques of 10, 15–17, 186 n.4
Potter, Emily 154, 182
Povinelli, Elizabeth 52, 160, 206 n.9
primates
  genealogy of 134–5
  and humans 61, 135, 203 n.22
Probyn, Elspeth 9, 144
prosthetic vision. *See* feminist objectivity
psychopharmaceuticals 25, 58
Puar, Jasbir 6, 170, 188 n.1

queer
  genealogies 8, 11
  humans 39, 60, 62, 103, 188 n.1
  Irigaray 69, 85
  non-humans 39, 129–30, 133, 151, 170
  queering 37, 42, 128, 182
  temporality 4, 37, 62, 128
  water as 86, 102

Race, Kane 154, 182
radical imagination 175–6
Raeworth, Kate. *See* Manthropocene
reproductive futurism 180–1, 198 n.29
reprosexuality
  vs. gestationality 4, 39, 69, 106, 197 n.26
  heteronormative 181
  womb 3, 16, 84, 94, 102–3 (*see also* placenta)
rhizomatics. *See* Deleuze
Rich, Adrienne 13, 14, 25–36, 38, 43, 62.
  See also politics of location
rising sea levels 26, 50, 117, 123, 160
Roughgarden, Joan 127–31

Sandilands, Catriona 8, 170
Savannah Theory 135–6
science. *See also* hydrological sciences
 as amplifier 56
 and Deleuze 192 n.23
 dominant imaginaries of 10, 60, 65, 111
 and feminism 8, 60, 61–2, 200 n.3
 and humanities 62, 114, 200 n.7
 and phenomenology 56–7, 200 n.3
 and stories 4, 25, 56
 and water 19, 57, 65, 157
sea squirts 129, 132
sexual reproduction
 and essentialism 173
 and Grosz 127–30, 202 n.16, 202 n.17
 non-human 125–30, 198 n.32
 and sexual difference 92–3, 127–30
sexuate difference. *See also* Irigaray, sexuate
  difference
 and Deleuze 89, 92–3
 essentialism critiques 93–4, 127, 197 n.29
 and Irigaray 68, 70, 72, 79, 82, 89–94,
  198 n.36
 posthumanism 99
 vs. sexual difference 92, 192–3 n.1
 and watery bodies 69, 76, 86
Seymour, Nicole 8, 180, 181
Sheets-Johnstone, Maxine 114, 200 n.3,
 200 n.7
Shildrick, Margrit 9, 43, 62, 72, 193 n.4,
 196 n.22
Shiva, Vandana 187 n.7
Simms, Eva-Marie 33, 188 n.3
situated knowledge 24, 62, 112, 131,
 136, 139, 141. *See also* feminist
 objectivity
Six Nations 171. *See also* aboriginal;
 indigenous
Smith, Andrea 8, 147
Smith, Stevie 165
Somerville, Margaret 27, 171
sovereign subject 69, 102, 146
species-error 12, 14, 18, 25, 163
speciesism 32
Spiegelberg, Herbert 53
Spivak, Gayatri
 Death of a Discipline 144
 globalization 144–5
 planetarity 145, 147, 174
 postcolonial theory 112, 144

starfish 129
Steingraber, Sandra 84, 188
Stephens, Elizabeth 71, 79, 194 n.8
Stoermer, Eugene 11
Stone, Alison 72, 75, 197 n.28
Strang, Veronica 23
Suzuki, David 109, 138
Syilx Okanagan 2, 187 n.7. *See also*
 aboriginal; indigenous
symbiogenesis. *See* symbiosis
symbiosis 29, 44, 114–15, 121–5, 139, 148,
 202 n.14

terraforming 161
terrestrial invasion 110, 133, 148
tetrapods 110, 132, 147
Torres, Felix Gonzalez 55, 191 n.17
trans* 52, 129
transcorporeality. *See also* Stacy Alaimo
 definition of 33, 77
 and embodied hydrocommons 93, 95, 113
 and ethics 38, 78, 166
 and evolution 114, 138
tree of life 115, 121
Trinh T Minh-ha 62
Tuana, Nancy 38, 43, 146
Turtle Island. *See* Canada

unknowability
 as colonial epistemology 143–4
 and Deleuze 47, 53, 120, 126
 Irigaray 74, 83, 85, 87, 113, 193 n.5
 as onto-epistemology 112, 146
 planetarity as 139–46, 145
 virtuality as 47, 53 (*see also* virtuality)
 of water 69, 84, 88, 102, 112, 118, 130,
  143, 147, 170, 185

virtuality. *See* Deleuze

Walkerton 172
'Water in the Anthropocene' video 161–2,
 174
Water is life imaginary 155–6, 174–5,
 177–84, 199 n.41
water walks 173
Waterbirth 203
WATERisLIFE.org project 178–9
'we' as feminist problematic 15, 27–30, 38,
 63, 165

Weiss, Gail 43, 72, 190 n.7
Wekker, Gloria 9, 201 n.11
wetlands 13, 161, 184
whale. *See* cetaceans
Wiegman, Robyn 14, 186 n.3, 187 n.4
Williams, Florence 32–4, 188 n.3
Wilson, Elizabeth A. 6, 25, 33–4, 37, 43, 60, 73, 129, 200 n.3
Wong, Rita 23, 205 n.8

woodlice 123
Woolf, Virginia 2
Wooster, Margaret 23

Yusoff, Kathryn 6, 160, 163, 170

Zimmer, Carl 110–12, 121, 123, 128, 130, 131, 134, 139, 141, 203 n.24

aug
55/5 mass
@
45 n

CPSIA information can be obtained
at www.ICGtesting.com
Printed in the USA
LVHW081839120422
715998LV00004B/76

9 781350 112551